The Rights
of Animals

Other Books in the Current Controversies Series:

The Rights of Animals

Tamara L. Roleff, *Book Editor*
Jennifer A. Hurley, *Assistant Editor*

David Bender, *Publisher*
Bruno Leone, *Executive Editor*

Bonnie Szumski, *Editorial Director*
David M. Haugen, *Managing Editor*

CURRENT CONTROVERSIES

Cover photo: D. Vo Trung/Eurelios/Science Photo Library

Library of Congress Cataloging-in-Publication Data

The rights of animals / Tamara L. Roleff, book editor, Jennifer A. Hurley, assistant editor.
    p. cm. — (Current controversies)
    Includes bibliographical references and index.
    ISBN 0-7377-0069-6 (lib. : alk. paper). — ISBN 0-7377-0068-8 (pbk. : alk. paper)
    1. Animal rights. 2. Animal welfare—Moral and ethical aspects.
I. Roleff, Tamara L., 1959–   . II. Hurley, Jennifer A., 1973–   .
III. Series.
HV4708.R54   1999
179'.3—dc21   98-45934
                                                CIP

Contents

comparing the moral status of animals to that of humans, the philosophy of animal rights renders the concept of rights meaningless.

Chapter 2: Is Animal Experimentation Justified?

Chapter 3: Is Hunting Ethical?

Yes: Hunting Is Ethical

hoods. If these peoples are allowed to sell ivory from the elephants or permits to hunt the animals, the people will have an incentive to put up with the animals' depredations and to protect the animals and their habitat from poachers.

No: Hunting Is Not Ethical

Chapter 4: Should Animals Be Bred for Human Consumption?

Yes: Animals Should Be Raised for Human Consumption

No: Animals Should Not Be Raised for Human Consumption

Chapter 5: Are Animals in the Entertainment Industry Abused?

No: Animals Are Not Abused

Yes: Animals Are Abused

Foreword

By definition, controversies are "discussions of questions in which opposing opinions clash" (Webster's Twentieth Century Dictionary Unabridged). Few would deny that controversies are a pervasive part of the human condition and exist on virtually every level of human enterprise. Controversies transpire between individuals and among groups, within nations and between nations. Controversies supply the grist necessary for progress by providing challenges and challengers to the status quo. They also create atmospheres where strife and warfare can flourish. A world without controversies would be a peaceful world; but it also would be, by and large, static and prosaic.

The Series' Purpose

The purpose of the Current Controversies series is to explore many of the social, political, and economic controversies dominating the national and international scenes today. Titles selected for inclusion in the series are highly focused and specific. For example, from the larger category of criminal justice, Current Controversies deals with specific topics such as police brutality, gun control, white collar crime, and others. The debates in Current Controversies also are presented in a useful, timeless fashion. Articles and book excerpts included in each title are selected if they contribute valuable, long-range ideas to the overall debate. And wherever possible, current information is enhanced with historical documents and other relevant materials. Thus, while individual titles are current in focus, every effort is made to ensure that they will not become quickly outdated. Books in the Current Controversies series will remain important resources for librarians, teachers, and students for many years.

In addition to keeping the titles focused and specific, great care is taken in the editorial format of each book in the series. Book introductions and chapter prefaces are offered to provide background material for readers. Chapters are organized around several key questions that are answered with diverse opinions representing all points on the political spectrum. Materials in each chapter include opinions in which authors clearly disagree as well as alternative opinions in which authors may agree on a broader issue but disagree on the possible solutions. In this way, the content of each volume in Current Controversies mirrors the mosaic of opinions encountered in society. Readers will quickly realize that there are many viable answers to these complex issues. By questioning each author's conclusions, students and casual readers can begin to develop the critical thinking skills so important to evaluating opinionated material.

Current Controversies is also ideal for controlled research. Each anthology in the series is composed of primary sources taken from a wide gamut of informational categories including periodicals, newspapers, books, United States and foreign government documents, and the publications of private and public organizations. Readers will find factual support for reports, debates, and research papers covering all areas of important issues. In addition, an annotated table of contents, an index, a book and periodical bibliography, and a list of organizations to contact are included in each book to expedite further research.

Perhaps more than ever before in history, people are confronted with diverse and contradictory information. During the Persian Gulf War, for example, the public was not only treated to minute-to-minute coverage of the war, it was also inundated with critiques of the coverage and countless analyses of the factors motivating U.S. involvement. Being able to sort through the plethora of opinions accompanying today's major issues, and to draw one's own conclusions, can be a complicated and frustrating struggle. It is the editors' hope that Current Controversies will help readers with this struggle.

"During the past two centuries, the status of animals has changed from one of no rights, in which animals could be treated in whatever way the owner saw fit, to one in which animal rights activists and their opponents debate whether animals have the same moral rights as humans."

Introduction

In China, consumers ensure that the food they buy is fresh by buying live animals—chickens, ducks, fish, frogs, and turtles, among others—and having the animals butchered either in front of them in the market or at home. In the United States, many Chinese immigrants continue this practice, sometimes to the consternation of a segment of the American population that considers the housing of these animals and their subsequent slaughter to be inhumane. In San Francisco's Chinatown, the Chinese desire for fresh meat led to a lawsuit in 1998 by animal rights activists against Chinatown's market owners.

The animal advocates sought a ban on the selling of live frogs and turtles in Chinese markets, and contended that the butchering of the animals violated health codes and anticruelty statues. According to the advocates' charges, the animals were kept in cramped, unsanitary containers and were inhumanely butchered. Eric Mills, an animal rights activist with Action for Animals, argued that even animals destined to be killed for food have the right to be housed and killed in humane conditions. He maintains that he has seen frogs and turtles stacked so high atop one another that the ones on the bottom are crushed to death. Mills also claims the animals were routinely denied food and water, and he says frogs were skinned alive and the shells ripped off turtles that were also still alive, all practices that he asserts are cruel and inhumane.

The lawsuit brought by the animal rights activists was dismissed in July 1998 by Superior Court judge Carlos T. Bea, who ruled that people have the right to kill animals for food. He quoted verses from the Bible that said man has dominion over "every living thing that moveth upon the earth" to support his decision. Moreover, Bea doubted whether animals even feel pain. "Absent such evidence of [a pain-sensing constitution], to find pain in the animal would be to indulge in anthropomorphic speculation, which is hardly a sufficient basis for the application of criminal statutes," he wrote. Following the dismissal of their lawsuit, animal rights activists reached a compromise with the Chinese markets. The Chinese market owners agreed to house the animals humanely; to kill the animals before they leave the market and before removing their feathers, skin, or shells.

Introduction

The controversy over the killing of animals in the Chinese markets of San Francisco's Chinatown illustrates how most Americans' views toward animals have changed in the last two centuries. Until the early 1800s, animals were viewed mostly as unfeeling property whose sole purpose in life was to benefit humans by providing needed food, labor, and clothing. At the end of the twentieth century, many Americans have come to believe that animals are capable of experiencing pain and suffering and that humans should do all they can to protect them, whether that means not eating or hunting them, wearing their fur, using them in experiments, or exploiting them for their labor or companionship.

This change in thinking was a very gradual process that began in the eighteenth century when a few noted philosophers began writing treatises on the rights of animals. Jeremy Bentham (1748–1832) considered the question of animal rights and concluded, "The question is not, Can they reason? nor Can they talk? but Can they suffer?" Bentham and others believed the answer was "yes," and therefore, animals had the right to be treated humanely and to be free from pain and suffering. The idea of treating animals humanely spread until New York passed the first anticruelty statute in the United States in 1829. The law—which prohibited the malicious injuring or killing of farm animals such as horses, oxen, cattle, or sheep—followed an 1822 English law known as Martin's Act that was the first law to prohibit cruelty toward animals. By 1907 every state had passed anticruelty legislation, and by 1923 the laws also prohibited animal neglect and abandonment, cockfighting, and certain hunting traps, among other restrictions.

In 1958, Congress passed the first federal law concerning the humane treatment of farm animals, the Humane Methods of Slaughter Act. The act required slaughterhouses to stun animals prior to killing them if their meat was to be sold to the federal government. This law eventually became the standard for all animals sent to slaughter for their meat. In 1966, Congress passed the Laboratory Animal Welfare Act, which regulated the care and treatment of animals other than rodents used in research experiments. Zoo and circus animals were added to the act's provisions in 1970 and 1976. New rules concerning the treatment of research animals were passed in 1985 after an activist from the animal rights group People for the Ethical Treatment of Animals (PETA), who was working undercover at a research lab, released a videotape of monkeys being mistreated.

PETA soon became an important force in the animal rights movement. By going undercover and videotaping animal treatment at research facilities and by recruiting celebrities to promote its point of view, PETA was able to attract much media attention to its cause. PETA and its followers believe that animals are not put on the earth for humans "to eat, wear, perform experiments on, or use for entertainment." This view has gained wider acceptance as more people make a conscious choice to demonstrate against the use of animals in circus acts, to forgo the wearing of fur, and to eat less meat or become vegetarian.

Not all Americans share the point of view of PETA and its supporters, however. As Bea makes clear in his decision supporting the Chinese markets, many people continue to view animals as creatures whose purpose is to provide food, clothing, labor, and companionship for humans. Furthermore, those who support the use of animals in medical research point out the hypocrisy of animal rights advocates who push scientists to find a cure for breast cancer, AIDS, or other diseases. Performing experiments on animals is vital to determine how cancerous cells are formed, the researchers argue, or discover how a drug will affect the disease or the body. Researchers and scientists have come to accept, along with most other people, that all animals, whether used in experiments or not, should be treated humanely. What they do not accept, however, are the views of animal rights activists who claim that animals have the same moral rights as humans, and therefore, denounce medical cures if they have been achieved through animal experimentation.

Furthermore, some contemporary philosophers support the argument against endowing animals with an intrinsic worth equal to that of humans. R.G. Frey, a professor of philosophy at Bowling Green University in Ohio and the author of several books and articles on animal rights, asserts, "One can perfectly consistently oppose cruelty to all sentient creatures without having to suppose that the lives of all such creatures are equally valuable." Human life is more valuable than animal life, he argues, because it is richer and full of choices that add a dimension that animals are unable to experience.

During the past two centuries, the status of animals has changed from one of no rights, in which animals could be treated in whatever way the owner saw fit, to one in which animal rights activists and their opponents debate whether animals have the same moral rights as humans. The moral equivalency of animals and humans is at the heart of the issues considered in *The Rights of Animals: Current Controversies*. Throughout this anthology, the authors examine the rights of animals and whether humans have the right to experiment on them and use them for food, clothing, and entertainment.

Chapter 1

Do Animals Have Rights?

Chapter Preface

Primatologist Jane Goodall, in her studies of the wild chimpanzees of Tanzania, found that chimpanzees demonstrate the abilities to use tools, convey abstract concepts, express a broad range of emotions, and make decisions based on reason—all characteristics that were previously thought to be uniquely human. If Goodall's conclusions are accurate, the distinction between animals and humans is no longer easy to define. This notion that the differences between humans and chimpanzees are merely differences of degree has inspired a proposal to grant chimpanzees, gorillas, and orangutans the same legal rights as children and mentally retarded adults. The Great Ape Project, developed in 1993 by a group of anthropologists, ethicists, and scientists, aims to give apes the right to life, liberty, and freedom from torture—which means that they could no longer be used in medical experiments or kept in zoos.

Advocates of the Great Ape Project maintain that since apes match or even exceed the intellectual and social capabilities of children and mentally retarded adults, there is no logical justification for denying apes basic rights. According to Peter Singer, cofounder of the project, "We now have sufficient information about the capacities of great apes to make it clear that the moral boundary we draw between us and them is indefensible."

Opponents, in contrast, challenge the assertion that the cognitive abilities of apes are comparable to those of humans. Ronald Nadler of the Yerkes Regional Primate Research Center in Atlanta, Georgia, claims that Jane Goodall has "exaggerated the intellectual nature of the animal." Moreover, claim some researchers, the genetic similarities between apes and humans make the use of chimpanzees in medical experiments invaluable. Critics warn that the Great Ape Project would constrain the potential for medical progress, thereby risking human lives.

Underlying the controversy over animal rights is the question of whether animals deserve the same moral status as humans. In the chapter that follows, authors provide contrasting opinions on this challenging issue.

Animals Have the Right to Live Free of Suffering

by Peter Wilson

About the author: *Peter Wilson is a graduate student at Cornell University. He writes for* AnimaLife, *a publication of the Cornell Students for the Ethical Treatment of Animals. The following viewpoint is excerpted from a speech given to the Cortland Rotary Club on April 8, 1997.*

Despite the negative hype in the media portraying the animal rights movement as the lunatic fringe, and efforts by some to discredit the movement by claiming it is composed of fanatical terrorists, most Americans support the basic idea behind animal rights. According to a 1995 survey commissioned by the Associated Press, two-thirds of Americans agree with the statement, "An animal's *right* to live free of suffering should be *just as important* as a person's." This overwhelming public support shouldn't come as a big surprise. No one likes to see an animal suffer. Indeed, kindness towards animals is a praised virtue in our society. Animal rights is really little more than an effort to live up to this ideal.

Most activists, including myself, have followed similar paths to the animal rights movement. We all started off with the same sympathy for animals that everyone feels, and blindly accepted our society's tradition of using animals for food, clothing, and entertainment. Then we gradually learned about how poorly most animals are treated in this society. Rather than rationalize and dismiss the suffering of animals as unimportant, we decided to make the necessary changes in our lives to end our own contribution to animal suffering. We stopped buying clothing containing fur; we bought only cruelty-free cosmetics; and we stopped eating meat, eggs, and dairy products.

A Philosophy of Compassion

Compassion, rather than a fanatical adherence to some radical philosophy, is ultimately the driving force behind the animal rights movement. We see animals

Excerpted from Peter Wilson, "Animal Rights: A Revolution of Compassion," a speech given at the Rotary Club of Cortland, N.Y., April 8, 1997. Reprinted by permission of the author.

suffering and we want to stop it. However, compassion alone cannot be the final arbiter in deciding right and wrong. Compassion, though innate in every human being, can be twisted to uncompassionate ends. One need only look at Nazi Germany to see how easy it is to convince people to turn a blind eye to immense cruelties inflicted on others and to even believe such cruelties are a good thing. Our actions need a better justification than merely our feelings.

"Compassion . . . is ultimately the driving force behind the animal rights movement."

In searching for a just foundation for ethical behavior, we must reject all the irrational and emotional influences that can lead us astray. This includes our feelings of compassion, our intuitions, and even our most deeply held beliefs. To weed out our hidden prejudices we must be willing to question everything we believe to be true and accept only those beliefs which survive critical scrutiny. Only through the use of logic and reasoned argument can we hope to reliably distinguish fact from folly. Only through philosophy and scientific inquiry will we know whether our natural instincts for compassion towards others is rationally justified or simply foolish sentimentalism.

Philosophers have been arguing for millenia over exactly where rights come from. There have been nearly as many theories put forward as there have been philosophers. They range from divine commandment to majority rule to pure self-interest. Some philosophers even deny that there are such things as rights. In the interest of time, let's take the pragmatic approach and just assume rights exist and that humans possess them. Animal rights must then stand or fall on the ability to show that it is inconsistent or irrational to grant rights to humans but to deny them to animals.

Look at the people around you. Unless you have an identical twin, you are absolutely unique. Everyone else is different from you: different sizes, shapes, colors, etc. You, of course, can think and feel, but can they? Perhaps only you were born with the right combination of genes to create consciousness. It may be far-fetched, but it is certainly possible that they are all merely complex biological machines only simulating the appearance of thought and feeling. How do you know what goes on inside other people's minds if you can't get inside their heads and experience exactly what they experience? The best you can do is infer it from what you can observe: their behavior and biology.

Thoughts and feelings come about by complex processes in the brain. Do the people around you have complex brains? Do they have nerves? If you injure them do they react in ways similar to how you would react under similar circumstances? Yes, on all counts. The people around you have biologies and behaviors which are nearly identical to your own. The few differences, such as shoe size, height, age, gender, and skin color, are irrelevant to the issue of consciousness. It would be illogical of you to believe only you were conscious given the absence of significant and relevant differences between yourself and others. One must follow the same argument when looking at the differences between humans and animals.

Several years ago, a group of scientists and philosophers considered the issue of animal pain. They came up with a list of 7 possible criteria by which the ability to feel pain might be judged. These criteria include biological similarities in nerve and brain structure, and behavioral responses to possibly noxious stimuli. While these tests do not provide an absolute basis for identifying animal pain, they do serve as a useful tool for determining the likelihood that living beings other than ourselves feel pain.

Mammals pass the tests with flying colors. There is no reason to doubt that all mammals can suffer pain. Birds also score very high. Fish score lower, but still satisfy many of the criteria, so it is still probable that fish can suffer. Insects fail most of the tests, so there is reason to doubt the existence of pain in insects. Plants weren't considered, but they certainly would do even worse than insects. This does not prove that plants can't feel pain, but there is no reason to believe that they do.

The same argument can be made for all the other sensations and mental abilities we experience. It is just a matter of identifying the relevant similarities and differences between humans and animals. Who can deny that a cat playing with a ball of yarn isn't getting some pleasure from it; or that a dog begging at the dinner table isn't anticipating the food about to be given to him? Some call this anthropomorphic, but if there aren't significant differences in either behavior or biology between humans and animals, it seems extremely arrogant of us to believe these feelings exist only in humans.

> *"The differences between humans and animals amount to differences of degree, not of kind."*

No Fundamental Difference

Despite numerous efforts, scientists have not been able to find any fundamental difference between humans and animals. By all measures, the differences between humans and animals amount to differences of degree, not of kind. It seems quite illogical, then, to believe in a morality that treats humans and animals in fundamentally different ways.

This does not mean we must now grant every animal every human right simply because we cannot draw an absolute line between humans and animals. We don't even grant every *human* every human right. Among other rights, children are denied the right to vote and criminals are denied their right to freedom. There are relevant differences between normal adult humans and both children and criminals which justify this discrimination. Children lack the maturity and civic knowledge to exercise a right to vote. Criminals have violated another person's rights, so their right to freedom is removed as punishment. Both children and criminals, though, are still within our sphere of ethical concern. They have some rights, just not all of them.

The question, then, is whether there are relevant differences between humans and nonhumans to justify denying nonhumans each of the rights we claim for ourselves. It goes without saying that the rights dealing with living in our society—constitutional type protections—are not applicable to animals. The rights we really need to consider are the rights to life, liberty, and freedom from torture.

Intelligence and Rights

The most common difference put forth to justify denying animals these basic rights is our intelligence. . . . There are two major problems with this.

First, all humans are not smarter than all nonhumans. Koko, a gorilla which has been taught sign language, has taken several IQ tests. She scores around an IQ of 80. The average IQ of humans is 100, a mere 20 points higher. In order to exclude Koko, are people willing to also exclude mildly retarded or even severely retarded humans, allowing them to be used for food and medical experiments? Certainly not.

The second problem is that intelligence is not even relevant to the rights in question. Consider the right not to be tortured. Torture is the intentional infliction of pain and suffering. Do smart people suffer from pain differently than dumb people? If not, why would we believe the suffering of a dog is any different or less important than our own, simply because he can't understand algebra? Intelligence might be relevant to the right to life, but only to a very limited degree. People value their lives because they know they have a life that will continue into the future. Anyone who has had a pet can probably identify behaviors that indicate the animal expects something to happen in the near future, be it feeding time or a walk in the park.

The use of high intelligence as a requirement for possessing rights such as life, liberty, and freedom from torture is both inadequate and irrelevant. The same goes for all the other characteristics usually put forward: language ability, tool use, tool creation, complex emotions, altruism, etc. Besides being irrelevant, they have all been seen in some animals and are lacking in some humans.

> *"The use of high intelligence as a requirement for possessing rights . . . is both inadequate and irrelevant."*

Is it perhaps enough to just say that we are human, so we should only care about and respect the rights of our fellow humans? That seems to be a very common view. From a historical perspective, though, using species membership as the basis for ethical concern is just the latest of a long line of unjustified prejudices. For most of human history we have excluded fellow humans from our sphere of ethical concern on the grounds that they belonged to the wrong group.

For a long time in this country, rights were reserved for white men. Blacks and Native Americans were subhuman, and it was thought that women lacked the mental capacity to control their own lives. Today this bigotry is readily apparent, but back then it was common sense. Even people dedicated to rational thought could point to the racial and sexual differences that obviously meant white men were superior. Efforts of oppressed groups to gain their rights were met with ridicule and insult.

In the 18th century, Mary Wollstonecraft, an early feminist, published *Vindication of the Rights of Woman*. Shortly thereafter she was satired with an anonymously published work, *Vindication of the Rights of Brutes*. The author of this work argued that following the logic that Mary Wollstonecraft used to defend women's rights, animals should also be granted rights, but that was clearly absurd!

> *"Using species membership as the basis for ethical concern is just the latest of a long line of unjustified prejudices."*

In 1858 a Virginia judge stated in a court ruling,

> So far as civil rights and relations are concerned, the slave is not a person but a thing. The investiture of chattel with civil rights or legal capacity is indeed a legal absurdity. The attribution of legal personality to a chattel-slave implies a palpable contradiction in terms.

It has only been in the recent past that most people have realized that regardless of whether someone is black or white, male or female, gay or straight, Protestant or Catholic, Christian or Jew, rich or poor, Democrat or Republican, they all have fundamental rights that cannot be violated even if doing so would provide some benefit to ourselves. Being a member of some group does not, by itself, provide a valid justification for giving, or denying, rights to that individual. Instead, one must be able to identify a relevant difference in the characteristics of the individual which justifies different treatment. Just as racism, sexism, and all the others, have been recognized as unjust prejudices, so we must now recognize speciesism.

Animal Suffering Is Avoidable

The argument thus comes down to this. Animals can suffer, therefore we should not cause them to suffer unnecessarily. One may think this is just a common sense concern for animal welfare without any need to invoke the presence of rights. The distinction between animal welfare and animal rights comes down to the meaning of "unnecessary." Currently, our society takes it for granted that animals will be used for clothing, food, entertainment, and scientific research. Animal welfarists consider "unnecessary suffering" as any suffering beyond that which is required to use the animal for any given purpose.

Take trapping. Several million wild animals are killed every year to make fur coats. The animal is typically caught in a leg-hold trap which almost never instantly kills the animal. Instead, the animal's leg is caught, perhaps broken, and the animal may spend several days struggling to free himself. Besides the sheer terror, the animal is likely to be in constant pain. To escape, he may even chew his own leg off only to bleed to death or die from an infection. If still alive when the trapper returns, the trapper will kill the animal by stepping on his neck and chest, crushing his lungs.

To the animal welfarist, all of this suffering is unavoidable. There is no simple and cheap method of trapping large numbers of animals without inflicting some suffering. *Unnecessary* suffering would take place if the trapper were to skin the animal alive. It isn't an inconvenience on the trapper to kill the animal first, and it does not lower the quality of the final fur coat, so the welfarist will decry skinning animals alive but tolerate the suffering inherent in trapping.

Animal rightists look at the bigger picture and ask whether trapping itself is necessary. Obviously it is not, so trapping is deemed unethical. In addition, believing that killing animals is just another form of cruelty, animal rightists further claim that the fur industry would be unethical even if there were no physical suffering caused to the animals. The mere fact that animals are unnecessarily killed is sufficient reason to have an ethical objection to fur. A person's right to choose what they wear is not a more important right than an animal's right to life, so the animal's right takes precedence.

Discrimination on the Basis of Species Is Unjust

by Richard Ryder

About the author: *Richard Ryder is a psychologist and the author of* Victims of Science *and* Animal Revolution. *He has served in the Royal Society for the Prevention of Cruelty to Animals since 1972, and is a political consultant with the Political Animal Lobby.*

Speciesism means hurting others because they are members of another species. In 1970 I invented the word partly in order to draw the parallel with racism and sexism. All of these forms of discrimination, based as they are upon physical appearances, are irrational. They overlook the one great similarity between all races, sexes and species: our capacity to suffer pain and distress. For me, pain (in its broadest sense) is the only evil and therefore forms the foundation for all morality.

I believe that morality is, by definition, about how we behave toward others. By "others" I mean all those who can suffer pain or distress, that is, all those who are "painient." I used to use the word "sentient" but this is, strictly speaking, too wide in its meaning as I am only concerned with that part of sentience which involves unpleasant feelings. Aliens from another planet might be sentient without having any sense of pain at all!

Painism—the concern for pain and distress of others—is extended, therefore, to any painient thing regardless of sex, class, race, nationality, or species. Indeed, if aliens from outer space do turn out to be painient, or if we ever manufacture machines that are painient, then we must widen the moral circle to include them.

The Only Basis for Rights

Painience is the only convincing basis for attributing rights or, indeed, interests to others. Many other qualities, such as inherent value, have been suggested. But value cannot exist in the absence of consciousness or potential consciousness. Thus, rocks and rivers and houses have no interests and no rights of

Reprinted from Richard Ryder, "Speciesism and 'Painism,'" *The Animals' Agenda*, January/February 1997. Reprinted with permission from *The Animals' Agenda*, P.O. Box 25881, Baltimore, MD 21224, USA.

their own. This does not mean, of course, that they are not of value to us, and to many other painients, including those who need them as habitats and who, without them, would suffer.

Many moral principles and ideals have been proposed over the centuries, including justice, freedom, equality, and brotherhood. But I regard these as mere stepping-stones to the ultimate good, which is happiness, and happiness is made easier by freedom from all forms of pain or suffering. (As nouns I will use the words "pain" and "suffering" interchangeably.) Indeed, if you think about it carefully you can see that the reason why these other ideals are considered important is that people have believed that they are essential to the banishing of suffering. In fact they do sometimes have this result, but not always.

The One True Evil

Why am I emphasizing pain and other forms of suffering rather than pleasure and happiness? One answer is that I consider pain to be much more powerful than pleasure. (Would you not rather avoid an hour's torture than gain an hour's bliss?) Pain is the one and only true evil.

One of the important tenets of painism is that we should concentrate upon the individual because it is the individual, not the race, nation, or species, who does the actual suffering. I believe, for this reason, that pains and pleasures cannot be aggregated between individuals as occurs in Utilitarianism. But consciousness, surely, is bounded by the boundaries of the individual. My pain and the pain of others are thus in separate categories; you cannot add or subtract them from each other. They are worlds apart. Without directly experiencing pains and pleasures they are not really there—we are counting merely their husks. For example, inflicting 100 units of pain on one individual is, in my opinion, far worse than inflicting a single unit of pain on a thousand or a million individuals, even though the total of

> *"We can treat different species differently, but always we should treat equal suffering equally."*

pain in the latter case is far greater. In any situation we should thus concern ourselves primarily with the pain of the individual who is the maximum sufferer. It does not matter, morally speaking, who or what the maximum sufferer is—whether human, nonhuman or machine. Pain is pain regardless of its host.

Treating Equal Suffering Equally

Of course, each species is different in its needs and in its reactions. What is painful for some is not necessarily so for others. So we can treat different species differently, but always we should treat equal suffering equally. In the case of nonhumans, we see them mercilessly exploited in factory farms, in laboratories, and in the wild. A whale may take 20 minutes to die after being harpooned. A lynx may suffer for a week with her broken leg held in a steel-toothed trap. A battery hen lives all her life unable even to stretch her wings. An animal in a toxicity test, poisoned with a household product, may linger in agony for hours or days before dying. These are major abuses causing great suffering, yet they are still justified on the grounds that these painients are not of the same species as ourselves. It is almost as if some people had not heard of Charles Darwin!

> *"If we are going to care about the suffering of other humans, then logically we should care about the suffering of nonhumans too."*

According to Darwin we are related through evolution to the other animals. We are all animals. Yet we treat the others not as relatives but as unfeeling things! We would not dream, I hope, of treating our babies, or mentally handicapped adults, in these ways—yet these humans are sometimes less intelligent and less able to communicate with us than are some exploited nonhumans.

There is, of course, very good scientific evidence that other animals can suffer like we do. They scream and writhe like us, their nervous systems are similar and contain the same biochemicals that we know are associated with the experience of pain in ourselves.

The Abuse of Human Power

The simple truth is that we exploit the other animals and cause them suffering because we are more powerful than they are. Does that mean that if those aforementioned aliens landed on Earth and turned out to be far more powerful than us that we would let them—without argument—chase and kill us for sport, experiment on us, or breed us in factory farms and turn us into tasty humanburgers? Would we accept their explanation that it was perfectly moral for them to do all these things because we were not of their species?

Basically, it boils down to cold logic. If we are going to care about the suffering of other humans, then logically we should care about the suffering of nonhumans too. It is the heartless exploiter of animals, not the animal protectionist, who is being irrational, showing a sentimental tendency to put his or her own species on a pedestal. We all, thank goodness, feel a natural spark of sympathy for the sufferings of others. We need to catch that spark and fan it into a fire of rational and universal compassion.

Humans Are Not Superior to Animals

by Gary L. Francione

About the author: *Gary L. Francione is Professor of Law and Katzenbach Scholar of Law and Philosophy at Rutgers University Law School in New Jersey, and is codirector of the Rutgers Animal Rights Law Center. He is the author of* Animals, Property, and the Law; Rain Without Thunder: The Ideology of the Animal Rights Movement; *and the forthcoming* Introduction to Animal Rights: Your Child or the Dog? *all published by Temple University Press.*

In 1996, I had the opportunity to address students at Hahnemann Medical College in Philadelphia. The occasion was a debate between me and a professor from the University of Pennsylvania Veterinary School, Adrian Morrison. Morrison has used cats in rather grisly experiments and, over the years, he has been the object of numerous protests by animal rights advocates. I was arguing against experiments using animals; Morrison was obviously defending their use.

The debate began with a question from the moderator: Can we justify the use of animals in experiments? Morrison responded that such use was surely justified in light of the benefits that animal use had produced for human health.

Now, we have to be careful about assessing the benefits of animal research. An increasing number of health care professionals have expressed considerable skepticism about the *scientific* validity of animal experiments. But even if we do get benefits from animal experiments, benefit alone cannot justify morally the exploitation of animals. If getting benefits from exploiting animals was alone sufficient to justify their exploitation, then why does that argument work when humans are concerned? After all, no one would dispute that we would get even greater benefits if we used unconsenting humans in experiments. So why not use unconsenting humans if there would be great benefits for all the rest of us? The answer is, of course, simple: We do not use unconsenting humans because, as a society, we believe that humans have certain interests that must be protected. Humans have certain rights. And their most fundamental right is not

Reprinted from Gary L. Francione, "Animal Rights Commentary: Human Superiority," *Rutgers Animal Law Center*, February 15, 1996, by permission of the author.

to be treated as property, or as means to the ends of owners. That is why almost all nations agree that slavery, or the legally-sanctioned and legally-mandated treatment of humans as things, is a true universal moral taboo to be condemned.

Justifying Animal Exploitation

But can the slavery of animals be justified? We are not talking about how to resolve issues such as whether it is morally right to kill an animal who is attacking us, or whether animals have some "right to life" in the abstract. We are, instead, asking a more simple question: Is there *any* moral justification for our slaughter of over 8 billion animals in this country alone every year for food? Is there *any* moral justification for using over 100 million animals annually in this country alone for experiments, most of which have little direct impact on human health anyway? Is there *any* moral justification for using millions of animals for entertainment, as in rodeos, circuses, zoos, and movies?

Morrison's answer—that animal exploitation can be justified by benefit for humans—is illogical because it assumes the very point at issue: Whether animals, like humans, have a fundamental right not to be enslaved for the benefit of their human masters.

If we are to justify this exploitation, it is necessary that we somehow distinguish animals from humans, and that is much easier said than done. After all, precisely what characteristic or "defect" is it that animals have that justifies our treatment of them as our slaves, as our things, as property that exists only for the sake of us, the human masters?

Some people say that animals are different because they cannot think. But that is simply not true. We know that mammals and birds, for example, have very complex mental faculties. And besides, there are human beings who cannot think. Some people were born without parts of their brain, and they have less cognitive functioning than a healthy rat. Some people say that animals are different because they cannot talk. But animals communicate in their own ways, and besides, some people are unable to talk.

> *"Precisely what characteristic . . . is it that animals have that justifies our treatment of them as our slaves?"*

The list goes on and on but the bottom line remains the same: There is no "defect" that is possessed by animals that is not possessed by some group of humans, and yet we would never think of using that group of humans in experiments, or of eating those people.

Animals, like humans, have certain interests in their own lives that transcend what their so-called "sacrifice" might do for us. And it is precisely those interests that preclude us as a matter of simple morality from treating them merely as "things."

Back to the debate at the medical school: At this point, Dr. Morrison offered a criterion that he triumphantly proclaimed did separate humans from animals—Humans are "superior."

Now this is a curious response for a scientist to make. After all, where in the natural world does one find "superiority"? Sorry, Dr. Morrison, "superiority" of species is, like superiority of race or sex, a social construction, and not a scientific one. It is a concept that is formulated and used to sustain hierarchical power relationships. Superiority is not an argument for anything; it is a conclusion that assumes the very point it starts out to prove. It begs the question, as it were.

> *"There is no 'defect' that is possessed by animals that is not possessed by some group of humans."*

Morrison pointed out that dogs do not write symphonies and humans do. I replied that I had never written a symphony and, as far as I knew, neither had Morrison. Did that mean that it was ok for people to eat us, or use us in experiments?

A Value, Not a Fact

And besides, his example proved my point: Writing symphonies is only a "superior" act if you happen to be a human that values that activity. Some dogs can jump six feet in the air from a sitting position. Now that's what I call "superiority." But "superiority," like many of the buzz words of modern life, such as "merit" and "beauty" is a matter of value, not of fact.

To say that we can exploit animals because we are "superior" is nothing more than to say that we are more powerful than they. And nothing more. And, with the exception of the Republican party, most of us reject the view that might makes right. So why, do tell, is that principle so blindly embraced when it comes to our treatment of animals?

We progressives like to think that we have eschewed all vestiges of slavery from our lives, but the reality is that we are all slave owners, the plantation is the earth, sown with the seeds of greed, and the slaves are our nonhuman sisters and brothers.

Animal Life Is Less Valuable than Human Life

by R.G. Frey

About the author: *R.G. Frey is a professor of philosophy at Bowling Green State University in Ohio.*

From teaching to research, the use we make of animals in human health care is vast. Although it is always possible that the animals themselves may benefit from this use (in fact, they rarely do), the search for health-care benefits for ourselves motivates it. This raises an ethical problem: What justifies this systematic use of animals for human gain? . . .

First, however, a word on why some obvious ploys to avoid our question carry little conviction. Animals use each other, so why should we not use them? Because we are reflective creatures capable of moral thought and moral assessment of our actions; nothing follows about the rightness of killing creatures who are not thus capable (babies, the severely mentally subnormal, animals). If your child were dying, would you not want any and all animal experimentation done, if the child could be saved? Yes, I would, but that is precisely why we do not do our reflective moral thinking in the heat of the moment, when we might want every penny in the land spent on our child.

Does not the law permit us, given approved protocols and project licenses, to experiment on animals? Yes, it does, but it also permits us to stand on shore and watch a man drown. In certain cases, we expect more of ourselves than merely what the law permits; morality can apply even when the law does not. This is particularly true when what we do is deliberately, intentionally done. We are morally responsible for what we deliberately, intentionally do, whatever the state of the law, and everyone involved in and supportive of medical research knows this.

A last ploy leads us to the heart of the matter. This ploy consists in the claim that animals do not count morally. This claim looks odd, however, in the light of the way medical researchers themselves behave today. For it is their standard practice, as ethics review committees, journal and peer review procedures, and

Reprinted from R.G. Frey, "Medicine and the Ethics of Animal Experimentation." This article appeared in the April 1995 issue and is reprinted with permission from *The World & I*, a publication of The Washington Times Corporation, copyright ©1995.

the like all insist, to seek to ensure that animal pain and suffering are controlled, that they are limited so far as possible, that they are mitigated with drugs where feasible, and that they be justified in the course and by the nature of the experiment proposed. Oversight committees, including governmental ones, can now shut down research where these matters are ignored.

Animal Life Has Value

If, however, one thinks animal suffering counts, then it seems very odd to think that animal lives do not; the worry about pain and suffering in part is simply the worry about the very negative drawbacks to a life that they impose, whether in humans or animals. Unless we thought that those lives had *some* value, it is hard to see why we would care about ruining them or severely lowering their quality or why we would go to such great lengths to cite the actual or potential benefits that justify their sacrifice. But if animal life has even *some* value, then its deliberate destruction or the drastic lowering of its quality is something morally serious people must address.

But surely, someone will insist, our morality cannot prevent us from preserving our own lives. No, of course, it cannot; the issue is how *far* we can go in preserving our lives. What are the limits? We ask *this* question even in the human case, when we ponder what, in order to save our own lives

> *"Normal adult human life is more valuable than animal life."*

or enhance the quality of our lives, we may do to others. So one cannot look the question of limits away.

Having come this far, we can see why what animal liberationists call "speciesism" cannot be part of these limits. In the play *Equus*, a man goes around blinding horses; it seems extraordinary to claim that his doing this to children is wrong, whereas his doing it to horses is not. Pain is pain, whatever the creature that experiences it. Nor do I expect many people today at bottom think differently: Even if it were true, legally, that a horse could be whipped to death with impunity at one time in our country, I doubt that such an act was ever thought morally above reproach.

The situation, then, seems to me to be this: Where pain and suffering are concerned, I can see no difference between the human and animal cases; where the destruction of valuable lives is concerned, those who destroy these valuable things owe us an explanation of how it can possibly be that species membership suffices to distinguish morally between two relevantly similar acts of killing. Although not an animal liberationist, then, I can see their point here.

Human Life Is More Valuable than Animal Life

Suppose we focus on killing: The boundaries to our discussion are clear. Animals count, morally; their lives have some value; and the destruction of these valuable things requires justification. This concern with the value of animal lives in turn raises the question of the comparative value of human and animal life, and one of the great virtues of my position on this issue is that it coheres nicely with recent discussions of the value of life in medical ethics and allied areas. That is, what matters is not life but quality of life. The value of a life is a function of its quality, its quality of its richness, and its richness of its capacities and scope for enrichment; it matters, then, what a creature's capacities for a rich life are.

> *"The fullest chicken life there has ever been . . . does not approach the full life of a human."*

Here, the human and animal cases differ. The question is not, say, whether a chicken's life has value; I agree that it does. The chicken has an unfolding series of experiences and can suffer, and it is perfectly capable of living out a life appropriate to its species. The question is whether the chicken's life approaches normal adult human life in quality (and so value), given its capacities and the life that is appropriate to its species, and this is a matter of the comparative value of such lives. It is in this context that the claim that normal adult human life is more valuable than animal life occurs, and I defend it on the ground of the greater richness and potentialities for enrichment in the human case.

One must be careful here not to resort to a kind of extreme skepticism, namely, that we can know nothing of the richness of animal lives. A good deal of recent work by ethologists and animal behaviorists, including those very sympathetic to the "animal rights" case, such as Marian Dawkins and Donald Griffin, would seem to show that we can know something of the richness and quality of life of "higher" animals. That we cannot know everything in no way implies that we cannot know a good deal.

Determining the Value of a Life

Quality-of-life views of the sort described turn upon richness, and if we are to answer the question of the comparative value of human and animal life we must inquire after the richness of their respective lives. *Intraspecies* comparisons are sometimes difficult, as we learn in medical ethics, when we try to judge the respective quality of life of each of two human lives; but such comparisons are not completely beyond us. They are made every day in our hospitals in allocating resources. *Interspecies* comparisons of richness and quality of life are likely to be even more difficult, though again not impossible.

I agree that, as we descend from the "higher" animals, we are likely to lose all behavioral correlates that we use to gain access to the interior lives of animals. Yet, scientific work increasingly appears that gives us a glimpse into animal lives, though it is hard as yet to make out much of a claim of extensive richness on the strength of this work. On this count, ethologists are usually cautious.

In trying to judge the richness and quality of an animal's life, we must exercise care in two further directions. First, we must not use in some unreflective manner criteria appropriate for assessing the richness of human lives as if they applied straightforwardly to the animal case. Rather, we must use all that we know about animals, especially those closest to us, to try to gauge the quality of their lives in terms appropriate to their species. Then, we must try to gauge the differences we allude to when we say, first of a chicken, then of a fellow human, that each has led a rich, full life. The fullest chicken life there has ever been, so science suggests, does not approach the full life of a human; the differences in capacities are just too great.

Second, if one nevertheless wants to maintain, as some animal liberationists would seem to want to do, that the chicken's life is equally as valuable as the life of a normal adult human, then it must be true that, whatever the capacities of the chicken and however limited those capacities may be, they confer a richness upon the chicken's life that approximates the richness of the human's life, despite all the different and additional capacities present in the typical human case. Evidence is needed to support this claim, because by its behavior alone we will not ordinarily think this of a chicken.

The Richness of Human Life

Of course, we share many activities with chickens; we eat, sleep, and reproduce. But such activities do not exhaust the richness of lives with music, art, literature, culture generally, love, science, and all the many products and joys of reflection. Indeed, even this list does not take account of how we fashion our lives into and so live out lives of striving to exemplify excellences of various sorts, whether as painters, ball players, or plumbers. These are ways of living that are themselves sources of value to us. No chicken has ever lived thus.

One might try to retain a quality-of-life view of the value of a life but drop the provision that quality be determined by richness; in this way, one might seek to block my judgment of reduced richness in the animal case. But if quality of life is not to be determined by richness—that is, by the extent, variety, and quality of experiences—I do not know what else is to determine it. Certainly, there is nothing else cited in those quality-of-life views with which I am familiar.

Why not opt, it might be asked, for a much simpler view: The chicken and the man have different capacities

> *"I have . . . no reason to believe that the dog's life possesses anything like the variety and depth . . . that my life possesses."*

and lives; judged by their respective capacities, each leads a full, though different, life. The problem here has a deeper aspect: One seems to be saying that these lives, and so the ingredients that make up these lives, are in some sense incommensurable, when, in fact, the central ingredients, experiences and the unfolding of experiences in a life, appear remarkably alike.

Can I know what it's like to be a dog? More or less. And this is why I believe playing fetch with it enriches its life. Can I know exactly the degree to which fetch enriches its life? No, just as I sometimes cannot know the degree of enrichment in the case of humans. But I have absolutely no reason to believe that the dog's life possesses anything like the variety and depth of ways of enrichment that my life possesses, and I especially need evidence to make me believe that the enrichment of the dog's life through any one of its capacities can make up for this extensive variety and depth in my case.

> *"The man's life is more valuable than the chicken's because of its higher quality, greater enrichment, and greater scope for enrichment."*

The eagle can see farther and deeper than I can, but how does this fact transform the richness of its life to approximate the richness that the variety and depth of my capacities confer upon me? I need evidence to believe that it does.

Killing and the Value of Life

Why all this matters should be obvious: If killing is related to the value of a life, then I can explain why we think that killing a man is worse than killing a chicken and in a way that does not rely upon species membership to account for the wrongness of killing. Whatever the full account of this matter, a part of it seems clearly bound up with our view that the man's life is more valuable than the chicken's life. And I can explain this issue of value also in a nonspeciesist way: The man's life is more valuable than the chicken's because of its higher quality, greater enrichment, and greater scope for enrichment.

This explanation allows that the chicken's life has some value; what it denies is that the chicken's life has the same value as the man's. Here, then, is how we might approach the killing of animals, and it is an account that coheres nicely with quality-of-life views that we encounter regularly in many areas and aspects of medical ethics and life.

Only Humans Can Possess Rights

by Edwin Locke

About the author: *Edwin Locke is senior writer at the Ayn Rand Institute, a center for the advancement of rational thought, individualism, and capitalism.*

Recently a sixth grade student threatened to bomb the headquarters of a prominent corporation, the Gillette Company. Gillette's "crime"? The use of animals to test the safety of their products. This student's role models have not been so hesitant. In the name of so-called "animal rights," terrorists have committed hundreds of violent crimes. They have vandalized or fire-bombed meat companies, fur stores, fast-food restaurants, leather shops and medical research laboratories across North America. The animal "rights" movement, however, is not about the humane treatment of animals. Its goal is the animalistic treatment of human beings.

According to these terrorists, it is immoral to eat meat, to wear fur coats or leather shoes, and to use animals in research—even if it would lead to cures for deadly diseases. The terrorists are unmoved by the indisputable fact that animal research saves human lives. PETA (People for the Ethical Treatment of Animals) makes this frighteningly clear: "Even if animal tests produced a cure for AIDS, we'd be against it."

Rights Depend upon Reason

How do the animal "rights" advocates try to justify their position? As someone who has debated them for years on college campuses and in the media, I know firsthand that the whole movement is based on a single—invalid—syllogism, namely: men feel pain and have rights; animals feel pain; therefore, animals have rights. This argument is entirely specious, because man's rights do not depend on his ability to feel pain; they depend on his ability to think.

Rights are ethical principles applicable only to beings capable of reason and choice. There is only one fundamental right: a man's right to his own life. To live successfully, man must use his rational faculty—which is exercised by

Reprinted from Edwin Locke, "Animal 'Rights' and the New Man Haters," 1997, at www.aynrand.org/objectivism/animals.html, by permission of the Ayn Rand Institute.

choice. The choice to think can be negated only by the use of physical force. To survive and prosper, men must be free from the initiation of force by other men—free to use their own minds to guide their choices and actions. Rights protect men against the use of force by other men.

Animals Have No Morals

None of this is relevant to animals. Animals do not survive by rational thought (nor by sign languages allegedly taught to them by psychologists). They survive through inborn reflexes and sensory-perceptual association. They cannot reason. They cannot learn a code of ethics. A lion is not immoral for eating a zebra (or even for attacking a man). Predation is their natural and only means of survival; they do not have the capacity to learn any other.

Only man has the power to deal with other members of his own species by voluntary means: rational persuasion and a code of morality rather than physical force. To claim that man's use of animals is immoral is to claim that we have no right to our own lives and that we must sacrifice our welfare for the sake of creatures who cannot think or grasp the concept of morality. It is to elevate amoral animals to a moral level higher than ourselves—a flagrant contradiction. Of course, it is proper not to cause animals gratuitous suffering. But this is not the same as inventing a bill of rights for them—at our expense.

> *"Rights are ethical principles applicable only to beings capable of reason and choice."*

Haters of Humankind

The granting of fictional rights to animals is not an innocent error. We do not have to speculate about the motive, because the animal "rights" advocates have revealed it quite openly. Again from PETA: "Mankind is the biggest blight on the face of the earth"; "I do not believe that a human being has a right to life"; "I would rather have medical experiments done on our children than on animals." These self-styled lovers of life do not love animals; rather, they hate men.

The animal "rights" terrorists are like the Unabomber and Oklahoma City bombers. They are not idealists seeking justice, but nihilists seeking destruction for the sake of destruction. They do not want to uplift mankind, to help him progress from the swamp to the stars. They want mankind's destruction; they want him not just to stay in the swamp but to disappear into its muck.

There is only one proper answer to such people: to declare proudly and defiantly, in the name of morality, a man's right to his life, his liberty, and the pursuit of his own happiness.

Animals Are the Property of Humans

by L. Neil Smith

About the author: *L. Neil Smith is the publisher of the* Libertarian Enterprise, *an on-line magazine that advocates free-market enterprise and a limited role for government.*

Recently I watched an episode of *X-Files* in which innocent zoo animals were being abducted—apparently by benign, superior UFOsies (the ones who mutilate cattle and stick needles in women's bellies)—to save them from a despicable mankind responsible for the erasure of thousands of species every year.

Or every week, I forget which.

I was reminded of a debate I'd found myself involved in about sea turtles; I'd suggested that laws prohibiting international trade in certain animal products be repealed so the turtles might be privately farmed and thereby kept from extinction. After all, who ever heard of chickens being an endangered species? From the hysteria I provoked—by breathing the sacred phrase "animal rights" and the vile epithet "profit" in one sentence—you'd have thought I'd demanded that the Virgin be depicted henceforth in mesh stockings and a merry widow like Frank N. Furter in *The Rocky Horror Picture Show*.

The Religion of Animal Rights

That debate convinced me of two things. First: I wasn't dealing with politics, here, or even philosophy, but with a religion, one that would irrationally sacrifice its highest value—the survival of a species—if the only way to assure it was to let the moneylenders back into the temple. Its adherents abominate free enterprise more than they adore sea turtles.

Second (on evidence indirect but undeniable): those who cynically constructed this religion have no interest in the true believers at its gullible grassroots, but see it simply as a new way to pursue the same old sinister objective. A friend of mine used to refer to "watermelons"—green on the outside, red on the inside—who use environmental advocacy to abuse individualism and capi-

Reprinted from L. Neil Smith, "Animals Are Property," *The Libertarian Enterprise*, March 1996, by permission of the author.

talism. Even the impenetrable Rush Limbaugh understands that animal rights and related issues are just another way socialism pursues its obsolete, discredited agenda.

In my experience, those who profess to believe in animal rights usually don't believe in human rights. That's the point, after all. It's also proof that the Left comprehends the mechanism of inflation perfectly. Inflation is a process in which the value behind a currency (gold, silver, whatever) is systematically diluted by creation of additional, *unbacked* currency. If it were anyone but government, we'd call it *counterfeiting*, and that's *exactly* what it is, no matter who's responsible.

Destroying the Concept of Rights

Likewise, human liberty is being diluted by a process of *moral* inflation (similar to that by which emotion, in our culture, replaces reason), in which absurd, unsupportable assertions about "rights"—to state education, to government healthcare, to a clean litterbox—are used to render valueless the rights that really do exist. Where does it stop and on what principle? Is vegetarianism enough or must we all wear masks, as some do in India, to avoid inhaling insects and killing them? Are we morally obliged to keep those frozen lab vials that are all that remains of the once deadly scourge of smallpox? Or even to let it out again?

If you take nothing else from this viewpoint, take this: the sillier the situation created by the other side's claims, the better they like it. Their goal is not to uphold the rights of animals (animals *have* no rights, nobody knows it better than the Left) but to render absurd—and destroy—the very *concept* of rights.

What are rights? Lions have teeth, giraffes have long necks, birds have wings, we have rights. They are our primary—if not only—means of survival. They arise from a quality unique to human beings (although it's politically incorrect to say so), a difference between people and animals so profound that the ramparts of the Himalayas are no more than a ripple in the linoleum by comparison. That difference—the wellspring of human rights—is *sapience*.

Note that I don't follow *Star Trek*'s lexicon by saying "sentience." Sentience is awareness, which all animals possess to some degree. Sapience is *awareness of that awareness*. Some animals (cats and dogs) clearly think. Only humans think about *thinking*.

I'm not saying anything new here. Pretending you can't see a difference between people and animals (a difference any three-year-old can easily discern) is not just an outworn, phony tactic—comparable to psychologists who pretend the human mind doesn't exist—it's a confession that you're stupid.

> *"Those who profess to believe in animal rights usually don't believe in human rights."*

Animals are genetically programmed like computers. Although a few near the pinnacle of the evolutionary pyramid (I said it, and I'm glad) are capable of learning, they make no choices about what to do with their lives. Human beings, by contrast, employ their sapience to assess what they see, hear, smell, taste, and feel, then act on that assessment, not just to insure survival, but to enhance its quality. The freedom to see, hear, smell, taste, feel, assess, and act— without any impediment other than those imposed by the nature of reality—is what we refer to when we say "rights."

The Purpose of Animals

More to the point in this context, *purpose*, another product of sapience, is a phenomenon as unique to humanity as rights. People are the only thing in the universe with purpose. And purpose—regarding themselves or anything else they lay their hands on in the environment they dominate—is whatever people say it is.

Robert LeFevre observed that, in moral terms, there are just two kinds of entity in the universe, people and property. Animals are not people. Some—wild animals—are unclaimed property that would be better off with owners. (My plain-spoken brother says, "America's wildlife—kill it, eat it, wear it!") Animals are groceries. They're leather and fur coats. They're for medical experiments and galloping to hounds. That's their *purpose*. I, a human being, declare it.

> *"Animals are groceries. They're leather and fur coats. ... That's their purpose."*

Do what you like with *your* animals.

If species are going extinct by the thousands—a claim which, judging by the Left's historic disregard for the truth, we've no reason to believe—it's for the same reason the Soviets collapsed and there's never a cop around when you need one. Socialism has been in charge of them, and it doesn't work.

Not in any venue.

Chapter 2

Is Animal Experimentation Justified?

Animal Experimentation: An Overview

by Joy Mench

About the author: *Joy Mench is a professor of animal science at the University of California at Davis.*

> After four months' experience [working as an assistant in a physiology laboratory conducting experiments on dogs and rabbits], I am of the opinion that not one of those experiments on animals was justified or necessary. The idea of the good of humanity was simply out of the question . . . the great aim being to keep up with, or get ahead of, one's contemporaries in science, even at the price of an incalculable amount of torture needlessly and iniquitously inflicted on the poor animals.
>
> —Letter from English physician George Hoggan, *The Morning Post, 1875*

> Every year in Britain alone millions of animals suffer and die in laboratory experiments. . . . In the past, people had to rely on bland assurances that animal experiments were strictly controlled, of enormous benefit, and, in any case, the scientists had the welfare of the animals at heart . . . [however] animal experiments are not only unnecessary but dangerously misleading . . . adding to the burden of disease.
>
> —Robert Sharpe, *The Cruel Deception, 1988*

Old wine, new bottles? Yes. And no.

Few issues have generated such sustained and passionate controversy as the use of animals in scientific research. Yet, at least on the surface, little seems to have changed in the debate over the last century.

Opponents of animal research claim that most research is cruel and unnecessary and that animals are poor models for human diseases. Defenders of animal research counter that most experiments do not involve pain or suffering and that, according to the National Association for Biomedical Research, "virtually every major medical advance of the last century has depended upon research with animals."

Excerpted from Joy Mench, "Animal Research Arouses Passion, Sparks Debate," *Forum for Applied Research and Public Policy*, Spring 1996. Reprinted by permission of the author.

In between these views lies the "troubled middle," an ill-defined ethical landscape likely occupied by most people, including many research scientists and those who belong to animal protection organizations. It is a middle that holds complex and sometimes contradictory attitudes toward both animals and science, making the development of coherent public policy a difficult, if not impossible, task.

The Beginning of Animal Rights

In the United States, animal experimentation emerged as a public-policy issue in the 19th century, largely through the efforts of Henry Bergh, founder of the American Society for the Prevention of Cruelty to Animals (ASPCA). One of Bergh's first efforts as head of the ASPCA was to draft a statute prohibiting cruelty to animals in New York state.

Bergh later lobbied unsuccessfully for vivisection to be incorporated into this act and then, in 1880, introduced legislation to make vivisection a misdemeanor in New York. The legislation failed, as did two bills introduced in the District of Columbia in 1896 and 1890 that would have placed controls on animal experimentation.

Although these latter bills generated a national discussion about animal experimentation, popular support for the anti-vivisection movement ebbed. The movement had failed to marshall a convincing argument against animal research. Medical researchers, on the other hand, were able to demonstrate the human health benefits derived from animal research.

The animal research community, in fact, began to mount an organized defense against the anti-vivisection movement. In 1907, the American Medical Association founded the Council for the Defense of Medical Research under the leadership of the eminent Harvard physiologist Walter Cannon. The council disseminated information about the benefits of research and developed regulations for the treatment of animals used in medical schools.

Meanwhile, the need for experimental animals burgeoned due to the accelerated pace of scientific discovery and the greatly increased public funding for health research. The research community, in turn, took steps to guarantee that a sufficient supply of animals would be available by championing legislation that would allow researchers to obtain dogs and cats from municipal pounds.

> *"The use of dogs in research has always elicited strong emotion."*

This last practice, so-called "pound seizure," and more generally the increasing use of dogs in research, eventually led to a resurgence of the research animal protection movement in the United States and ultimately to the regulation of animal experimentation through the Animal Welfare Act of 1966.

The use of dogs in research has always elicited strong emotion. Impetus for passage of the Animal Welfare Act was not a reasoned debate about the merits and conduct of research but public outrage over a *Life* magazine article that exposed deplorable conditions in the facilities of several dealers who supplied dogs to research institutions.

The article also recounted an incident in which a pet dog was stolen and sold to a research facility. As a result of such reports, the Animal Welfare Act initially did not provide broad regulation of animal research but focused primarily on the use and acquisition of dogs and cats.

Two other widely publicized incidents also sparked changes in public views and policies. The first incident, in 1981, involved Edward Taub, a neuroscientist working at the Institute for Behavioral Research in Silver Spring, Maryland. Taub invited a young volunteer, Alex Pacheco, who had expressed an interest in Taub's research on monkeys, to work in his laboratory.

Taub did not know that Pacheco had recently founded a small local animal rights organization, People for the Ethical Treatment of Animals (PETA). While Taub was on vacation, Pacheco assembled documentation and solicited affidavits attesting to unsanitary conditions in the laboratory and lack of adequate treatment for the monkeys' injuries.

> *"The number of animals used in research in the United States is small . . . compared to the number kept as pets . . . or used for the production of food or fiber."*

Pacheco presented his documentation to the local police, who raided Taub's laboratory and removed the monkeys from his care in the first such action ever taken against a research institution in the United States. Taub, who was charged with 17 counts of cruelty, was initially found guilty of six misdemeanors for failing to provide proper veterinary care. He was eventually acquitted of all charges after a series of appeals.

Nevertheless, the National Institutes of Health (NIH) terminated Taub's grant, citing a lack of veterinary care, inappropriate institutional oversight, and unsanitary and inadequate physical facilities. Although bitter controversy still smolders over the Taub case, at the time it sparked an animated—indeed sometimes agitated—discussion about the oversight of laboratory research by both local institutions and federal agencies.

The Taub case also launched PETA as a major force in the battle over animal research. Accordingly, PETA was involved in the next incident, involving University of Pennsylvania scientist Thomas Gennarelli. Gennarelli had inflicted head injuries on baboons for 15 years in an effort to develop and study laboratory models that might shed light on serious head injury in humans.

In 1984, The Animal Liberation Front raided Gennarelli's laboratory and stole videotapes that he had made of his research. PETA edited the tapes to produce a film, *Unnecessary Fuss,* excerpts from which were aired on national television.

The film is shocking, showing head injuries being inflicted on improperly anesthetized monkeys, unsterile surgical conditions, and a callous attitude toward the monkeys by those conducting the research.

NIH, which investigated the conditions in Gennarelli's laboratory, likely would have renewed his grant because of the importance of his work. Sixty members of Congress, however, successfully petitioned the NIH to have funding suspended, and the University of Pennsylvania was eventually fined $4,000 for violations of the Animal Welfare Act.

Congress Speaks

The next year, Congress strengthened the act by passing an amendment requiring institutions to establish committees to review proposed research involving animals at their facilities. Each facility committee was given the lengthy but descriptive name, Institutional Animal Care and Use Committee. The amendment also required research facilities to exercise dogs and offer an environment that promoted the "psychological well-being" of non-human primates.

Orchestrated media events such as those that animal rights groups executed against Taub and Gennarelli have tended to overshadow the efforts of more moderate animal protection organizations to educate the public about responsible treatment of animals and to strengthen legislation affecting animal care and use. Such events also have often overshadowed continuing efforts within the scientific community to improve animal care through self-regulation.

As early as 1963, NIH published voluntary guidelines for laboratory animal husbandry. These guidelines have been revised and expanded several times and now include a requirement for an institutional oversight committee similar to that required under the Animal Welfare Act.

With passage of the Health Research Extension Act of 1985, these guidelines became mandatory for all institutions receiving funding from the Public Health Service. The guidelines, in fact, are more encompassing than the Animal Welfare Act because they include all vertebrate animals.

A voluntary certification organization, the American Association for the Accreditation of Laboratory Animal Care, was founded in 1965. The association conducts periodic site visits to institutions to ensure that they comply with government guidelines and regulations, maintain high standards of animal care, and pursue thorough reviews of animal research and teaching.

The American Association for the Accreditation of Laboratory Animal Care has certified nearly 600 research facilities. Other less formal mechanisms for oversight also exist. Many scientific and professional societies, for example, have developed animal care policies or guidelines for use by their members. Some societies—for instance, the Animal Behavior Society—also review manuscripts submitted to the society's journal to ensure that the research has been conducted in accordance with the society's guidelines. Despite the many controls on animal research, however, concerns persist.

Chapter 2

Sympathy and Empathy

Of all the aspects of animal use in society—in food production and consumption, zoos, circuses, and theme parks—why has animal research generated so much controversy?

After all, the number of animals used in research in the United States is small (approximately 20 million per year) compared to the number kept as pets (500 million) or used for the production of food or fiber (8 billion per year), as well as compared to the millions of animals exterminated each year as predators or pests. Yet, of all of these activities, only animal research is so extensively regulated.

Factors influencing the growth of the anti-vivisection movement in the 19th century and the current animal rights movement have been the subject of several recent books, as well as numerous newspaper stories and television broadcasts. When it comes to public attitudes toward animal research, however, two factors seem to be particularly important: the public's increasing empathy towards animals and its heightened sensitivity toward pain and suffering in both animals and humans.

> *"People, and particularly children, have expressed less and less willingness to accept human use and domination of animals."*

Yale University wildlife biologist Steven Kellert, who has conducted several surveys of public attitudes toward animals, has found that people, and particularly children, have expressed less and less willingness to accept human use and domination of animals. The rise in pet ownership and the emotional bond this creates between people and pets is primarily responsible for these changing attitudes.

Increased empathy, however, is not restricted to dogs and cats. Wild animals, which once posed a direct threat to human survival as predators and competitors, now can be viewed through a more distant lens by a largely urban population. Studies of both wild and captive animals—and more importantly, nature films—have demonstrated the complexity of animal behavior and emphasized the similarities between animals and humans.

Observations that animals can make and use tools, apply reason to solve problems, and display human-like social behavior and language-like communication skills have had a particularly strong impact. People (or at least psychology students, the perennial subjects of attitude surveys) are inclined to believe that animals, and particularly dogs, cats, dolphins, and primates, experience emotions and thoughts similar to those of humans.

Pain and Suffering

People may be especially concerned about animal research because they perceive it to involve significant pain and suffering. An opinion poll conducted by the Animal Industry Foundation, a group supported by agribusinesses, found

45

that only 33 percent of respondents thought that laboratory animals were treated humanely, as compared to nearly 80 percent who believed that farm animals used in production agriculture were treated humanely.

Effective pain relief for humans was not available until the discovery of morphine and aspirin in the latter part of the 19th century. Such medical breakthroughs, which dramatically changed peoples' attitudes toward human suffering, led philosopher William James to assert:

> We no longer think that we are called upon to face physical pain with equanimity. It is not expected of a man that he should either endure it or inflict much of it, and to listen to the recitals of cases of it makes our flesh creep morally as well as physically.

This revulsion against pain, coupled with the fact that, for most people, science is an enterprise that is abstract and remote from daily life in ways that eating meat or keeping pets is not, has likely led people to focus on animal use in research.

Nevertheless, surveys conducted in the United States show that the public broadly supports—in fact, 70 to 80 percent of all Americans—favor the use of animals in research. However, certain types of research generate more negative feelings than others.

For example, more people oppose the use of animals for product testing than for biomedical research. And when asked in a recent survey sponsored by the National Science Foundation whether "scientists should be allowed to do research that causes pain and injury to animals like dogs and chimpanzees if it produces new information about human health problems," more than 40 percent say no. Disagreement with this statement is even higher in many European countries, sometimes exceeding 65 percent.

> *"People perceive the benefits of some research (for example, cosmetic testing) as less significant for humans than the costs to the animal."*

These surveys illustrate two points. First, people perceive the benefits of some research (for example, cosmetic testing) as less significant for humans than the costs to the animal. Second, the infliction of pain on the "like-us" species of animals is an issue of concern even when the human benefits of the research are potentially high.

Finally, it is important to note that the National Science Foundation survey found no clear relationship between attitudes toward animal research and levels of scientific literacy. This finding contradicts an often-repeated claim that public opposition to animal research is due to a lack of understanding of scientific methods and a disregard for the accomplishments of science.

Looking Ahead

Science no longer occupies the privileged and unassailable position that it once did. People increasingly question the benefits of "progress" in extending life, engineering the human and animal genome, and developing new reproductive and biomedical technologies. Science, moreover, is largely a publicly funded activity. Appropriately, accountability is the new watchword, and public education and consensus-building are the new goals.

The ethical issues surrounding animal research will likely be difficult to resolve, at least in the near future, for several reasons. First, there is a lack of adequate information to allow competing claims about animal experimentation in the United States to be fairly evaluated.

> *"The ethical issues concerning animal research will likely be difficult to resolve, at least in the near future."*

Estimates of the numbers of animals used annually in research, for example, range from 17 to 150 million, with most calculations suggesting a figure of about 20 million. Since statistics compiled by the U.S. Department of Agriculture (USDA) do not include all vertebrates, even these estimates are suspect. And because reporting practices have changed since the USDA began compiling statistics, it is also difficult to determine if animal use is increasing, decreasing, or remaining the same. Nevertheless, a recent report prepared by Tufts University estimates that animal use has declined by as much as 40 percent in the last 25 years.

Although the proportion of animals used in different types of research also is not known, the largest drops in animal use are likely in toxicity and product testing, where many alternative tests have been developed. For example, both Johnson & Johnson and Proctor and Gamble have decreased their use of animals for safety testing by about 90 percent.

Similar confusion surrounds statistics on animal pain. According to USDA, between 1982 and 1986 only 6 to 8 percent of animals were exposed to unalleviated pain, while 58 to 62 percent were used in procedures that were not considered painful or distressing at all. For the remaining animals, pain and distress were alleviated by analgesics, anesthetics, or tranquilizers. Again, these statistics cover only a limited number of species.

In addition, USDA requires researchers to specify whether they use analgesics or anesthetics but does not require them to provide information about the severity of pain associated with a particular procedure. Reporting procedures for both animal numbers and pain are more extensive, and thus more reliable, in Canada and most European countries than they are in the United States.

Feelings Count

The primary difficulty encountered in resolving the animal research debate, however, is not a lack of statistical information, but a lack of agreement about the moral and legal status of animals. Attitudes toward animals are shaped by a complex mixture of notions about animals' symbolic and aesthetic value, their usefulness, and their similarity to us.

Although philosophers in the last 20 years have begun to seriously address the basis, nature, and scope of our moral obligations to animals, they have yet to reach a consensus. The legal status of animals is equally perplexing and contradictory.

Not only does the definition of an animal vary from one state to another, but the same animal can have a different legal status (and also be treated differently) depending on the use to which it is put. Pigs used in biomedical research, for example, are closely regulated under the Animal Welfare Act and NIH standards, while pigs used in agricultural research fall under different (and nonmandatory, although widely endorsed) guidelines developed by the nongovernmental body, the Consortium for Developing a Guide for the Care and Use of Agricultural Research and Teaching.

At the same time, pigs kept as pets fall under the jurisdiction of most state anti-cruelty laws (although aside from prohibiting overt cruelty, their treatment is not regulated), while pigs kept on farms are usually exempt from those laws provided they are used in "normal" agricultural enterprises.

As a result, long-term close confinement of a sow, which would be acceptable (and normal) in many agricultural enterprises and in agricultural research, might or might not be acceptable for a pet owner, depending on the state, and would not be acceptable for a sow used in biomedical research unless there was a strong scientific reason for such confinement.

Given this lack of consensus, the primary overseers of animal research ethics, members of the federally mandated Institutional Animal Care and Use Committees, have been forced to negotiate a difficult and largely uncharted path. Unlike committees that review proposed research involving humans, animal-care committees receive little guidance from existing laws and regulations. While this situation allows institutions a great deal of flexibility, it also creates dilemmas.

> *"The primary difficulty encountered in resolving the animal research debate . . . is . . . a lack of agreement about the moral and legal status of animals."*

The "Three R's"

Although the committees generally follow the principles known as the "Three R's"—that experimental procedures should be *refined* to minimize pain and suffering, the number of animals used should be *reduced,* and animals should be *replaced* with animals lower on the phylogenetic scale or with nonanimal models whenever possible—complex questions remain.

How should the costs and benefits of a research project be weighed? Should the merits of the research be taken into account, or does the incremental nature of scientific discovery make assessments of merit too difficult and thus serve as an obstacle to scientific progress? Does a chimpanzee or a dog deserve more moral consideration than a rat or a frog, and if so how much more?

How can degrees of pain, suffering, and harm in different species of animals be determined? Should the potential stress associated with keeping animals confined in an "unnatural" laboratory enclosure be part of the ethical considera-tion, and if so how could the animals' responses to the environment be real-istically assessed? Are there some types of research that cause so much pain or distress that they should not be permitted, even if the potential benefits are great?

> *"Does a chimpanzee or a dog deserve more moral consideration than a rat or a frog, and if so how much more?"*

The Institutional Animal Care and Use Committees, which are composed mainly of animal researchers, are some-times accused of being the "foxes guarding the henhouses." My own experi-ence, however, is that the members approach these problems thoughtfully and make an earnest attempt to minimize the costs of the proposed research to the animal. Moreover, the committees have had an enormous influence in changing attitudes and improving animal-care programs at many institutions. At my for-mer institution, the University of Maryland, for example, animal facilities have been modernized and training programs have been established for researchers and animal-care technicians under the guidance of committee members.

Admittedly, animal researchers are likely to view animal research as impor-tant and necessary, and thus may give more weight to research needs when they evaluate a proposed project than would a non-researcher. Whether this attitude creates a bias that may be balanced by the requirement that Institutional Animal Care and Use Committees contain a "nonscientist" and a person not affiliated with the institution who represents "general community interests" in the treat-ment of animals, is a matter of debate.

Animal Medical Experimentation Is Justified

by American Association for Laboratory Animal Science

About the author: *The American Association for Laboratory Animal Science is an association of individuals, businesses, and organizations that disseminates scientific information about the procurement, study, and care of laboratory animals.*

Over the years, scientists have solved many medical problems, cured diseases, and developed vaccines—all by using animals in biomedical research. An important issue, use of animals in biomedical research has come under attack by people who seek to portray the research as inhumane. Knowing the facts surrounding the use of animals in research can help determine the outcome of the debate as well as decide how soon cures will be found for deadly diseases such as cancer, heart disease, and AIDS—all of which affect millions of people around the world. . . .

Why Do We Need Biomedical Research?

Understanding causes and treatment of diseases, developing new drugs or vaccines and testing the safety of chemicals are just a few of the goals of biomedical researchers today. Still other projects attempt to discover more about how the body and its systems work. While not all biomedical research involves the use of animals, animal-based research remains essential in many areas. All scientists recognize that the animals used in research must be healthy, well cared for, and adequately housed to produce accurate research results.

Each year more than 20 million animals are used in biomedical research projects, and more than 90 percent of them are mice, rats, and other rodents. Rats are valuable research subjects because their body systems are similar to humans and other animals in many respects. The animals are also susceptible to many of the diseases that affect humans. However, rodents are not good subjects for certain types of experimental techniques, such as surgery. In these cases, other

Reprinted, by permission, from the American Association for Laboratory Animal Science publication "Use of Animals in Biomedical Research: Understanding the Issues," March 1998.

animals such as dogs, cats, rabbits, sheep, cattle, fish, frogs, birds, and nonhuman primates may be used. Whenever surgery is performed, anesthesia is used.

Why Are Animals Used in Biomedical Research?

Every person in the United States has benefited from the results of research involving animals.

In the early 1900's, Dr. Simon Brimhall became the first laboratory animal veterinarian. When he started his research, the average lifespan of adults in the United States was just over 47 years. In the years since, that lifespan has increased to over 75 years—mostly due to medical advances that have been based on animal research. Understanding the effect research efforts have on our lives will clarify the importance of animal research.

Years ago, for example, polio was one of the most feared diseases. Between 1948 and 1952, more than 11,000 people in the United States died from the disease. In addition, almost 200,000 Americans were partially or completely paralyzed by polio. Today, children routinely receive a vaccine that provides a lifetime of protection from the disease. Children are also immunized against typhus, diphtheria, whooping cough, smallpox, and tetanus. Untold millions of people around the world are healthy because of these vaccines made possible through animal research.

Diabetes is another example of the importance of biomedical research. One out of every 20 Americans (more than 15 million people) has diabetes. Almost 600,000 additional people develop the disease each year. More than 1 million diabetic people in the United States require daily doses of insulin to regulate their blood sugar levels or they will die. Dogs were crucial to the research that identified the cause of diabetes, which led to the development of insulin. Recently, researchers have developed insulin pumps to replace injections, and current transplant research offers the hope that diabetes can be cured.

The importance of animal research to those suffering from heart and circulatory diseases cannot be overlooked. More than 50 million Americans have high blood pressure, which can cause strokes, heart attacks, and heart disease. Research involving animals has helped identify the causes of high blood pressure and develop more effective drugs to control the problems. Other research has resulted in treatments for strokes and heart attacks that save thousands of lives and reduce recovery time.

> *"Every person in the United States has benefited from the results of research involving animals."*

Dogs have been especially important to researchers who developed open-heart surgery, pacemakers, and heart transplants. These techniques have revolutionized the therapy for people who have severe heart disease.

In spite of the remarkable medical progress during the last century, there is still much work to be done. As the average life span increases, more people will develop diseases that primarily affect the elderly—Alzheimer's, Parkinson's, and certain types of cancers.

There is much to be learned about new diseases such as AIDS. And millions of people around the world suffer from other incurable diseases such as cystic fibrosis, multiple sclerosis, muscular dystrophy, and genetic birth defects. Researchers are trying to learn the causes and the cures of these diseases.

Animals Benefit as Well

Animals benefit from biomedical research as well. Feline leukemia virus is a highly contagious disease, which is a major cause of illness in cats. It can be a particularly difficult disease to treat because it may take months for symptoms to appear. A vaccine is available to prevent the disease, but much additional work is necessary to fully understand both its cause and treatment.

Sometimes research can have unexpected benefits. In 1978 there was a sudden, worldwide outbreak of a virus among dogs, which caused vomiting, diarrhea, dehydration and, frequently, death. Researchers soon discovered that this disease, called canine parvovirus, was similar to the feline panleukopenia virus. Since a vaccine was already available for the feline panleukopenia virus, a vaccine for parvovirus was developed, tested, and made available for distribution within a year.

Now recognized as one of the most significant success stories of modern veterinary science, the parvovirus vaccine checked the spread of the disease among adult dogs in the United States almost immediately. However, puppies between 6 and 16 weeks of age are still at significant risk of being infected by the virus, and further research is needed to protect pets of all ages.

> *"Most research projects either do not involve pain or the pain is alleviated with analgesic or anesthetic drugs."*

Putting It in Perspective

Some people argue that animal research should be stopped because of the pain inflicted on the animals. But most research projects either do not involve pain or the pain is alleviated with analgesic or anesthetic drugs. Researchers understand that pain causes stress for the animal, and this stress can seriously affect the result of the project. This argument also ignores the fact that both humans and animals suffer from diseases that cause years or even a lifetime of pain.

Other people argue that medical scientists already know enough; we need to use what we already know. But do we know enough about diseases such as cancer, heart disease, AIDS and Sudden Infant Death Syndrome? If enough is known about these diseases, why are thousands of people dying from them each year?

Currently, an earnest struggle is being waged between those who are seeking to reduce pain and suffering through the judicious use of animal research, and those who wish to eliminate all human use of animals—not only for research, but for food and even as pets. In recent years, some groups have resorted to threats and even violence to try to disrupt important research. Laboratories have been broken into, animals stolen and scientific equipment and important research data destroyed.

Distorting the Facts

These groups have attempted to distort the facts about animal research. They refuse to acknowledge the important contribution of this research and argue that no research using animals is justified. They claim that the medical community no longer supports the use of animals in research. Nothing could be farther from the truth. A recent survey of members of the American Medical Association shows that the majority of the physicians recognize the importance of animal research and support continued research.

The Nobel Prize provides a measure of the importance of animal research to the advancement of medical knowledge. Since its inception in 1901, over 70 percent of the Nobel Prizes for physiology or medicine have been awarded for research involving animals. According to Dr. Joseph Murray, winner of the 1990 Nobel Prize for Medicine, "There would not be a single person alive today as a result of organ transplant or bone-marrow transplant without animal experimentation."

These same groups also grossly exaggerate the number of animals in research. They claim the majority of such animals are primates and stolen pets. As previously stated, 90 percent of the 20 million animals used each year in research are mice, rats and other rodents. Only 1 percent are primates.

They also attempt to portray researchers as "mad scientists" who work with no supervision or control. But stringent controls are in place by the Federal government through the Animal Welfare Act and its amendments, now in place for more than 25 years.

Research laboratories where animals are used must meet strict federal, state and local requirements. Federal regulators routinely inspect laboratories to ensure that animals are adequately housed and cared for. In addition, many laboratories also submit to additional inspection for accreditation through the Association for the Assessment and Accreditation of Laboratory Animal Care, International (AAALAC).

Some people also argue that animal research is no longer necessary because modern technology can replace the use of animals. Researchers frequently use modern technology, such as computer models and tissue cultures in their research. However,

> *"The use of research animals has been and will continue to be essential to finding the causes and cures for many diseases."*

many factors affecting both human and animal lives can only be studied using research animals. The use of research animals has been and will continue to be essential to finding the causes and cures for many diseases.

It is essential that more people become involved in this debate because the health of the entire nation will be affected by its outcome. We also hope that you will encourage others to become informed about the vital issue of using animals in biomedical research. As you begin to understand the facts more fully, you will agree that the judicious use of animals in research offers the greatest hope of improving the lives of both humans and animals.

Animal Research Is Vital to Medicine

by Jack H. Botting and Adrian R. Morrison

About the authors: *Jack H. Botting is a retired university lecturer and the former scientific adviser to the Research Defense Society in London. Adrian R. Morrison is the director of the Laboratory for the Study of the Brain in Sleep at the University of Pennsylvania School of Veterinary Medicine.*

Experiments using animals have played a crucial role in the development of modern medical treatments, and they will continue to be necessary as researchers seek to alleviate existing ailments and respond to the emergence of new disease. As any medical scientist will readily state, research with animals is but one of several complementary approaches. Some questions, however, can be answered only by animal research. We intend to show exactly where we regard animal research to have been essential in the past and to point to where we think it will be vital in the future. To detail all the progress that relied on animal experimentation would require many times the amount of space allotted to us. Indeed, we cannot think of an area of medical research that does not owe many of its most important advances to animal experiments.

In the mid–19th century, most debilitating diseases resulted from bacterial or viral infections, but at the time, most physicians considered these ailments to be caused by internal derangements of the body. The proof that such diseases did in fact derive from external microorganisms originated with work done by the French chemist Louis Pasteur and his contemporaries, who studied infectious diseases in domestic animals. Because of his knowledge of how contaminants caused wine and beer to spoil, Pasteur became convinced that microorganisms were also responsible for diseases such as chicken cholera and anthrax.

To test his hypothesis, Pasteur examined the contents of the guts of chickens suffering from cholera; he isolated a possible causative microbe and then grew the organism in culture. Samples of the culture given to healthy chickens and rabbits produced cholera, thus proving that Pasteur had correctly identified the offending organism. By chance, he noticed that after a time, cultures of the microorganisms lost their ability to infect. But birds given the ineffective cultures became resistant to fresh batches that were otherwise lethal to untreated birds. Physicians had previously observed that among people who survived a severe attack of certain diseases, recurrence of the disease was rare; Pasteur had found a means of producing this resistance without risk of disease. This experience suggested to him that with the administration of a weakened culture of the disease-causing bacteria, doctors might be able to induce in their patients immunity to infectious diseases.

In similar studies on rabbits and guinea pigs, Pasteur isolated the microbe that causes anthrax and then developed a vaccine against the deadly disease. With the information from animal experiments—obviously of an extent that could never have been carried out on humans—he proved not only that infectious diseases could be produced by microorganisms but also that immunization could protect against these diseases.

Pasteur's findings had a widespread effect. For example, they influenced the views of the prominent British surgeon Joseph Lister, who pioneered the use of carbolic acid to sterilize surgical instruments, sutures and wound dressings, thereby preventing infection of wounds. In 1875 Queen Victoria asked Lister to address the Royal Commission inquiry into vivisection—as the queen put it, "to make some statement in condemnation of these horrible practices." As a Quaker, Lister had spoken publicly against many cruelties of Victorian society, but despite the

> *"To restrict research with animals would prevent discoveries that would benefit humankind."*

request of his sovereign, he was unable to condemn vivisection. His testimony to the Royal Commission stated that animal experiments had been essential to his own work on asepsis and that to restrict research with animals would prevent discoveries that would benefit humankind.

Dozens of Vaccines and Antibiotics

Following the work of Pasteur and others, scientists have established causes of and vaccines for dozens of infectious diseases, including diphtheria, tetanus, rabies, whooping cough, tuberculosis, poliomyelitis, measles, mumps and rubella. The investigation of these ailments indisputably relied heavily on animal experimentation: in most cases, researchers identified candidate microorganisms and then administered the microbes to animals to see if they contracted the illness in question.

Similar work continues to this day. Just recently, scientists developed a vaccine against *Hemophilus influenzae* type B (Hib), a major cause of meningitis, which before 1993 resulted in death or severe brain damage in more than 800 children each year in the U.S. Early versions of a vaccine produced only poor, short-lived immunity. But a new vaccine, prepared and tested in rabbits and mice, proved to be powerfully immunogenic and is now in routine use. Within two months of the vaccine's introduction in the U.S. and the U.K., Hib infections fell by 70 percent.

Animal research not only produced new vaccines for the treatment of infectious disease, it also led to the development of antibacterial and antibiotic drugs. In 1935, despite aseptic precautions, trivial wounds could lead to serious infections that resulted in

> *"A lack of proper animal experimentation unfortunately delayed for a decade the use of the remarkable antibiotic penicillin."*

amputation or death. At the same time, in both Europe and the U.S., death from puerperal sepsis (a disease that mothers can contract after childbirth, usually as a result of infection by hemolytic streptococci) occurred in 200 of every 100,000 births. In addition, 60 of every 100,000 men aged 45 to 64 died from lobar pneumonia. When sulfonamide drugs became available, these figures fell dramatically: by 1960 only five out of every 100,000 mothers contracted puerperal sepsis, and only six of every 100,000 middle-aged men succumbed to lobar pneumonia. A range of other infections could also be treated with these drugs.

The story behind the introduction of sulfonamide drugs is instructive. The team investigating these compounds—Gerhard Domagk's group at Bayer Laboratories in Wuppertal-Elberfeld, Germany—insisted that all candidate compounds be screened in infected mice (using the so-called mouse protection test) rather than against bacteria grown on agar plates. Domagk's perspicacity was fortunate: the compound prontosil, for instance, proved to be extremely potent in mice, but it had no effect on bacteria in vitro—the active antibacterial substance, sulfanilamide, was formed from prontosil within the body. Scientists synthesized other, even more powerful sulfonamide drugs and used them successfully against many infections. For his work on antibacterial drugs, Domagk won the Nobel Prize in 1939.

A lack of proper animal experimentation unfortunately delayed for a decade the use of the remarkable antibiotic penicillin: Alexander Fleming, working in 1929, did not use mice to examine the efficacy of his cultures containing crude penicillin (although he did show the cultures had no toxic effects on mice and rabbits). In 1940, however, Howard W. Florey, Ernst B. Chain and others at the University of Oxford finally showed penicillin to be dramatically effective as an antibiotic via the mouse protection test.

Despite the success of vaccines and antibacterial therapy, infectious disease remains the greatest threat to human life worldwide. There is no effective vaccine against malaria or AIDS; physicians increasingly face strains of bacteria resistant to current antibacterial drugs; new infectious diseases continue to emerge. It is hard to envisage how new and better vaccines and medicines against infectious disease can be developed without experiments involving animals.

Research on animals has been vital to numerous other areas in medicine. Open-heart surgery—which saves the lives of an estimated 440,000 people every year in the U.S. alone—is now routine, thanks to 20 years of animal research by scientists such as John Gibbon of Jefferson Medical College in Philadelphia. Replacement heart valves also emerged from years of animal experimentation.

The development of treatments for kidney failure has relied on step-by-step improvement of techniques through animal experiments. Today kidney dialysis and even kidney transplants can save the lives of patients suffering from renal failure as a result of a variety of ailments, including poisoning, severe hemorrhage, hypertension or diabetes. Roughly 200,000 people require dialysis every year in the U.S.; some 11,000 receive a new kidney. Notably, a drug essential for dialysis—heparin—must be extracted from animal tissues and tested for safety on anesthetized animals.

Transplantation of a kidney or any major organ presents a host of complications; animal research has been instrumental in generating solutions to these problems. Experiments on cats helped develop techniques for suturing blood vessels from the host to the donor organ so that the vessels would be strong enough to withstand arterial pressure. Investigators working with rabbits, rodents, dogs and monkeys have also determined ways to suppress the immune system to avoid rejection of the donor organ.

"It is hard to envisage how new and better vaccines and medicines against infectious disease can be developed without experiments involving animals."

The list continues. Before the introduction of insulin, patients with diabetes typically died from the disease. For more than 50 years, the lifesaving hormone had to be extracted from the pancreas of cattle or pigs; these batches of insulin also had to be tested for safety and efficacy on rabbits or mice.

When we started our scientific careers, the diagnosis of malignant hypertension carried with it a prognosis of death within a year, often preceded by devastating headaches and blindness. Research on anesthetized cats in the 1950s heralded an array of progressively improved antihypertensive medicines, so that today treatment of hypertension is effective and relatively benign. Similarly, gastric ulcers often necessitated surgery with a marked risk of morbidity afterward. Now antiulcer drugs, developed from tests in rats and dogs, can control the condition and may effect a cure if administered with antibiotics to eliminate *Helicobacter pylori* infection.

Common Misconceptions

Much is made in animal-rights propaganda of alleged differences between species in their physiology or responses to drugs that supposedly render animal experiments redundant or misleading. These claims can usually be refuted by proper examination of the literature. For instance, opponents of animal research frequently cite the drug thalidomide as an example of a medicine that was thoroughly tested on animals and showed its teratogenic effect only in humans. But this is not so. Scientists never tested thalidomide in pregnant animals until after fetal deformities were observed in humans. Once they ran these tests, researchers recognized that the drug did in fact cause fetal abnormalities in rabbits, mice, rats, hamsters and several species of monkey. Similarly, some people have claimed that peni-

> *"Transplantation of a kidney or any major organ presents a host of complications; animal research has been instrumental in generating solutions to these problems."*

cillin would not have been used in patients had it first been administered to guinea pigs, because it is inordinately toxic to this species. Guinea pigs, however, respond to penicillin in exactly the same way as do the many patients who contract antibiotic-induced colitis when placed on long-term penicillin therapy. In both guinea pigs and humans, the cause of the colitis is infection with the bacterium *Clostridium difficile*.

In truth, there are no basic differences between the physiology of laboratory animals and humans. Both control their internal biochemistry by releasing endocrine hormones that are all essentially the same; both humans and laboratory animals send out similar chemical transmitters from nerve cells in the central and peripheral nervous systems, and both react in the same way to infection or tissue injury.

Animal models of disease are unjustly criticized by assertions that they are not identical to the conditions studied in humans. But they are not designed to be so; instead such models provide a means to study a particular procedure. Thus, cystic fibrosis in mice may not exactly mimic the human condition (which varies considerably among patients anyway), but it does provide a way to establish the optimal method of administering gene therapy to cure the disease. Opponents of animal experiments also allege that most illness can be avoided by a change of lifestyle; for example, adoption of a vegan diet that avoids all animal products. Whereas we support the promulgation of healthy practices, we do not consider that our examples could be prevented by such measures.

A Black Hole

Our opponents in this debate claim that even if animal experiments have played a part in the development of medical advances, this does not mean that they were essential. Had such techniques been outlawed, the argument goes, researchers would have been forced to be more creative and thus would have invented superior technologies. Others have suggested that there would not be a gaping black hole in place of animal research but instead more careful and respected clinical and cellular research.

In fact, there was a gaping black hole. No outstanding progress in the treatment of disease occurred until biomedical science was placed on a sound, empirical basis through experiments on animals. Early researchers, such as Pasteur and the 17th-century scientist William Harvey, who studied blood circulation in animals, were not drawn to animal experiments as an easy option. Indeed, they drew on all the techniques available at the time to answer their questions: sometimes dissection of a cadaver, sometimes observations of a patient, sometimes examination of bacteria in culture. At other times, though, they considered experimentation on animals to be necessary.

We would like to suggest an interesting exercise for those who hold the view that animal experiments, because of their irrelevance, have retarded progress: take an example of an advance dependent on animal experiments and detail how an alternative procedure could have provided the same material benefit. A suitable example would be treatment of the cardiac condition known as mitral valve insufficiency, caused by a defect in the heart's mitral valve. The production of prosthetic heart valves stemmed from years of development and testing for efficacy in dogs and calves. The artificial valve can be inserted only into a quiescent heart that has been bypassed by a heart-lung machine—an instrument that itself has been perfected after 20 years' experimentation in dogs. If, despite the benefit of

"There are no basic differences between the physiology of laboratory animals and humans."

35 years of hindsight, critics of animal research cannot present a convincing scenario to show how effective treatment of mitral valve insufficiency could have developed any other way, their credibility is suspect.

Will animal experiments continue to be necessary to resolve extant medical problems? Transgenic animals with a single mutant gene have already provided a wealth of new information on the functions of proteins and their roles in disease; no doubt they will continue to do so. We also anticipate major progress in the treatment of traumatic injury to the central nervous system. The dogma that it is impossible to restore function to damaged nerve cells in the mammalian spinal cord has to be reassessed in the light of recent animal research indicating that nerve regeneration is indeed possible. It is only a matter of time before treatments begin to work. We find it difficult to envision how progress in this field—and so many others in biological and medical science—can be achieved in the future without animal experiments.

Animal-to-Human Organ Transplants Could Benefit Humans

by Rebecca D. Williams

About the author: *Rebecca D. Williams is a freelance writer in Oak Ridge, Tennessee.*

"You'll need a liver transplant," Dr. Zeno says. She scribbles quickly on her prescription pad and dates it: April 17, 2025. "Take this to the hospital pharmacy and we'll schedule the surgery for Friday morning."

The patient sighs—he's visibly relieved that his body will be rid of hepatitis forever.

"What kind of liver will it be?" he asks.

"Well, it's from a pig," Zeno replies. "But it will be genetically altered with your DNA. Your body won't even know the difference."

Obviously, this is science fiction. But according to some scientists, it could be a reality someday. An animal organ, probably from a pig, could be genetically altered with human genes to trick a patient's immune system into accepting it as its own flesh and blood.

Called "xenotransplants," such animal-to-human procedures would be lifesaving for the thousands of people waiting for organ donations. There have been about 30 experimental xenotransplants since the turn of the century.

Rebuilding Bodies

Xenotransplants are on the cutting edge of medical science, and some scientists think they hold the key not only to replacing organs, but to curing other deadly diseases as well.

In December 1995, for example, after getting permission from the Food and Drug Administration (FDA), researchers at the University of California, San Francisco, injected an AIDS patient with baboon marrow. The hope was that the

Reprinted from Rebecca D. Williams, "Organ Transplants from Animals," *FDA Consumer*, June 1996.

baboon marrow, which is resistant to HIV and a source of immune cells, could provide a replacement for the patient's damaged immune system.

In April 1995, also with FDA permission, doctors at Lahey Hitchcock Medical Center in Burlington, Mass., injected fetal pig brain cells into the brains of patients with advanced Parkinson's disease. The hope was that the fetal tissue would produce dopamine, which the patients' brains lack. Both experiments were primarily to test the safety of such procedures, not whether they are effective.

> *"Animal-to-human [transplant] procedures would be lifesaving for the thousands of people waiting for organ donations."*

Other xenotransplant experiments have involved implanting animal hearts, livers and kidneys into humans.

According to Scott McCartney's book on transplantation, *Defying the Gods: Inside the New Frontiers of Organ Transplants*, the first organ transplant was performed in the early twentieth century by Alexis Carrel, a French physician practicing in Chicago. He had developed a technique to sew blood vessels together, and in 1906 he transplanted a new heart into a dog and a new kidney into a cat.

The first animal-to-human transplant was in the same year, when the French surgeon Mathieu Jaboulay implanted a pig's kidney into one woman and a goat's liver into another. Neither survived.

Today, human organ transplants are commonplace. For example, more than 10,000 Americans received kidney transplants in 1995, with a three-year life expectancy of more than 85 percent, according to the United Network for Organ Sharing (UNOS), an organization of transplant programs and laboratories in the United States. Under contract to the U.S. Department of Health and Human Services, UNOS administers a national organ network, and its members set policies for equitable organ allocation.

Surgeons have made great strides in perfecting transplant techniques, but two problems endure. First, there are never enough organs to go around. Second, once patients receive organs, it is a constant battle to keep their immune systems from rejecting them. Both problems may be eventually solved by xenotransplants and the genetic engineering techniques developed from such experiments.

Baboons and Pigs

Of all animals, baboons and pigs are the favored xenotransplant donors. Baboons are genetically close to humans, so they're most often used for initial experiments. Six baboon kidneys were transplanted into humans in 1964, a baboon heart into a baby in 1984, and two baboon livers into patients in 1992.

Although all the patients died within weeks after their operations, they did not die of organ rejection. Rather, they died of infections common to patients on immunosuppressive drugs.

One drawback to using baboons is that they harbor many viruses. They also reproduce slowly, carrying only one off-spring at a time. Some people have raised ethical objections, especially since baboons are so similar to humans. They have human-like faces and hands and a highly developed social structure. Although it's conceivable that baboons could donate bone marrow without being killed, recent experiments have required extensive tissue studies, and the animals have been sacrificed.

For long-term use, pigs may be a better choice. Pigs have anatomies strikingly similar to that of humans. Pigs are generally healthier than most primates and they're extremely easy to breed, producing a whole litter of piglets at a time. Moral objections to killing pigs are fewer since they're slaughtered for food.

Pig organs have been transplanted to humans several times in the last few years. In 1992, two women received pig liver transplants as "bridges" to hold them over until human transplants were found. In one patient, the liver was kept outside the body in a plastic bag and hooked up to her main liver arteries. She survived long enough to receive a human liver. In the other patient, the pig liver was implanted alongside the old diseased liver, to spare the patient the rigors of removing it. Although that patient died before a human transplant could be found, there was some evidence that the pig liver had functioned for her.

"Xenotransplantation could be very good news for patients with end-stage organ diseases. There would be no more anxious months of waiting for an organ donor."

By genetically altering pig livers, some scientists believe they can make a pig liver bridge more successful. In July 1995, FDA permitted the Duke University Medical Center to test genetically altered pig livers in a small number of patients with end-stage liver disease. The pig livers contained three human genes that will produce human proteins to counter the rejection process.

Safe or Disastrous?

Xenotransplantation could be very good news for patients with end-stage organ diseases. There would be no more anxious months of waiting for an organ donor. Disease-free pigs would provide most of the organs. Raised in sterile environments, they would be genetically altered with human DNA so that the chance of rejection is greatly reduced.

Transplant surgery would be scheduled at the patient's convenience, as opposed to emergency surgery performed whenever a human donor is found. Patients wouldn't have to wait until their diseases were at a critical stage, so they would be stronger for recovery.

Today, however, xenotransplantation is still experimental, and there are serious risks to the procedures.

Although many researchers believe it is slight, one legitimate concern is that animal diseases will be transmitted into the human population. Baboons and swine both carry myriad transmittable agents that we know about—and perhaps many more we cannot yet detect. These bacteria, viruses and fungi may be fairly harmless in their natural host, a baboon or pig, yet extremely toxic—even deadly—in humans.

The two types of animal viruses that are especially troublesome are herpes viruses and retroviruses. Both types have already been proven to be rather harmless in monkeys, but fatal to humans. HIV, for example, is a retrovirus that many researchers believe was transmitted to humans from monkeys. The problem occurs in reverse as well. Measles, for example, a serious but manageable disease in humans, can destroy a whole colony of monkeys quickly.

By regulating xenotransplants, FDA will provide a framework for collecting safety data and tracking patients' health. The process should involve open and public discussion by scientists about their experiments, allowing their peers to evaluate and critique them, and their patients to understand the risks and make informed decisions.

"Will [xenotransplants] cause an outbreak of a new infectious disease? We don't know," says Phil Nogouchi, M.D., a pathologist and director of FDA's division of cellular and gene therapies. "But we want all these procedures discussed in public. We need to make people aware of the hazards."

Nogouchi emphasizes the importance of monitoring and tracking all recipients of xenotransplants so that if any new diseases do develop, they will be detected quickly and the threat to public health will be minimized.

"We cannot say that's not a possibility," says Nogouchi. "But we do feel the potential benefits are great and that efforts can be made to make everyone responsible. There are ways to deal with problems should they arise."

As of June 1996, FDA, the national Centers for Disease Control and Prevention, and the National Institutes of Health were working on recommendations for researchers doing xenotransplant experiments.

Although the new recommendations will be for researchers, patients will likely also recognize their importance.

"Our biggest allies are the patients," says Nogouchi. "They should be asking, 'Where'd you get that pig?'" Xenotransplants cannot be "fresh off the farm." They should be bred and raised in a biomedical animal facility under strict conditions.

Battling Rejection

The other formidable obstacle to xenotransplants is that posed by the human body's own immune system. Even before a person is born, his or her immune system learns to detect and resist foreign substances in the body called antigens. These could be from anything that's not supposed to be there: viruses, bacteria, bacterial toxins, any animal organs, or even artificial parts.

Antigens trigger the body's white blood cells, called lymphocytes, to produce antibodies. Different lymphocytes recognize and produce antibodies against particular antigens. B cell lymphocytes produce antibodies in the blood that remove antigens by causing them to clump or by making them more susceptible to other immune cells. T cell lymphocytes activate other cells that cause direct destruction of antigens or assist the B cells.

Transplant physicians try to suppress the immune system with powerful drugs. While these drugs are often successful, they leave the patient vulnerable to many infections. FDA-approved immunosuppressive drugs include Sandimmune (cyclosporine), Imuran (azathioprine), Atgam (lymphocyte immune globulin), Prograf (tarolimus), and Orthoclone (muromonab-CD3). New drugs are also being researched, including some "designer" immune suppressants. These drugs may enable doctors to suppress the immune system from rejecting a particular organ, but leave the rest of the body's immune system intact.

> *"Researchers have begun experimenting with ways to insert human genes into animal organs, so that the organs will produce proteins the body will recognize as 'human.'"*

Drugs designed to help transplant patients may end up also aiding those who are stricken with diseases such as arthritis, multiple sclerosis and diabetes, because these involve problems with the human immune system. For example, Imuran is approved to treat severe rheumatoid arthritis, and Prograf has already shown some promise to MS patients. A large study is under way to determine if it is effective.

Genetic Engineering Is the Next Step

Genetic engineering is the next step in battling organ rejection. Researchers have begun experimenting with ways to insert human genes into animal organs, so that the organs will produce proteins the body will recognize as "human." FDA is active in basic research that may lead to better gene therapies and ways of manipulating animal organs.

For example, Judy Kassis, Ph.D., an FDA biochemist, has been studying a fruit fly gene that is important to the insects' early development. Using some DNA and a harmless virus, she has developed a way to insert this gene precisely into its natural position on the fly's chromosomes. Carolyn Wilson, Ph.D., an FDA virologist, has been researching pig viruses and whether they could infect humans in a transplant setting.

FDA scientists are also studying ways that individual genes "turn on" as they develop, how viruses activate each other, and how viruses can be used safely to deliver genes for new therapies.

"Gene therapy is really in its infancy," says Kassis. "That's the thing about basic research—you can't really predict how useful this will be in the future. Hopefully, it will have direct relevance someday."

Gene therapies and their role in xenotransplantations are still in the early stages of development. For now, it's only in science fiction that doctors can order a custom-designed pig liver from the hospital pharmacy. Whether or not that ever becomes reality, FDA's goal in regulating xenotransplant experiments is to make sure these procedures are openly discussed, that data are carefully collected, that patients give their fully informed consent, and that safety precautions are taken with every effort.

Animal Cloning Experiments Will Benefit Humans

by Ian Wilmut, interviewed by Andrew Ross

About the author: Ian Wilmut is an embryologist and researcher at the Roslin Institute in Edinburgh, Scotland. He and his colleagues are credited with cloning a lamb named Dolly, the first creature cloned from the cells of a mature animal. Andrew Ross is managing editor of Salon, *a monthly on-line magazine.*

"Researchers Astounded . . . Fiction Becomes True and Dreaded Possibilities Are Raised." So went the headlines in Sunday's [February 23, 1997] *New York Times* about Dr. Ian Wilmut, the embryologist in Edinburgh who has made history by creating a lamb from the DNA of an adult sheep. The research, performed at the Roslin Institute in Edinburgh, was sponsored by a drug company, PPL Therapeutics.

Mixed Reactions

Dr. Wilmut says the primary purpose of the cloning is to advance the development of drug therapies to combat certain life-threatening human diseases. Other scientists, especially in the United States, appear to have adopted a more apocalyptic view of the news. "It basically means there are no limits," Dr. Lee Silver, a biologist at Princeton University, told the *New York Times*. "It means all of science fiction is true." Dr. Ronald Munson, a medical ethicist at the University of Missouri, said, "This technology is not, in principle, policeable." Munson even speculated about the possibility of cloning the dead.

Are such scenarios remotely possible? And if drug treatment is the main priority, how soon will we see animal clone-based drugs on the market? *Salon* spoke with Wilmut by telephone from his home in Edinburgh.

Andrew Ross: *Science fiction. Cloning the dead. A technology out of control. What do you make of such reactions to your work?*

Reprinted from Ian Wilmut, interviewed by Andrew Ross, "Dr. Frankenstein, I Presume?" *Salon*, February 24, 1997. This article first appeared in *Salon*, an online magazine, at http://www.salonmagazine.com. An online version remains in the *Salon* archives. Reprinted with permission.

Ian Wilmut: I think they're over the top. The point is that what we thought happens in all life is that you have a single fertilized egg and as it divides, it progressively differentiates and you get brain and muscle and all of the different kinds of cells that we have. People assumed until now that this was an irreversible process. And what we have shown is that it's not. Now people will have to think in slightly different ways about the mechanisms that control these changes—for example, about what happens when things go

> *"The primary purpose of the cloning is to advance the development of drug therapies to combat certain life-threatening human diseases."*

wrong and you get a cancer instead of a normal development. So it is going to open people's eyes a lot in terms of biology.

And does it mean that cloning humans is possible?

We don't know. It is quite likely that it is possible, yes. But what we've said all along—speaking for both the (Roslin) Institute and the PPL staff—is that we would find it ethically unacceptable to think of doing that. We can't think of a reason to do it. If there was a reason to copy a human being, we would do it, but there isn't.

Is the idea of cloning the dead totally fanciful?

Yep.

Still, even if you can't clone the dead and you see no reason to clone the living, the genie is out of the bottle, so to speak. Others might find reasons for human cloning, and they may not have the same standard of ethics as you.

That does worry me, both in principle and in detail. It worries me in detail because the successes we have at present are of such low efficiency that it would really be quite appalling to think of doing that with people. I would feel desperately sorry for the women and the children that were involved.

Why? Because the clone could turn out to be some kind of monster?

It's possible. Perhaps you don't know that in the first experiment that we reported, five lambs were born alive and three of them died quickly. There was nothing monstrous, they just simply died. That in itself is very distressing if you think of a mother who carries a child and it dies within a few days of birth.

The Benefits for Humans

Your main goal, you have said, is to develop health-related products from animal clones. In what areas, specifically?

Hemophilia. With animals, you could make the clotting factors which are missing. It could also be beneficial for cystic fibrosis.

What's the difference between using animal clones and other kinds of biotechnology techniques?

Speed and efficiency. You could take cells from an animal, grow them in the laboratory and make very precise genetic changes—it's called gene targeting—

which you insert in the cloned offspring. So, for example, you put into the cells of the offspring DNA sequences which would say, "Don't make this particular milk protein, but instead make clotting factor 8," which is needed for hemophilia. You can do that now, but by using a much more primitive technique. Cloning and gene targeting requires fewer animals. It will be quicker, which means new health products will come on line more quickly.

There's another major advantage. Presuming this technique with sheep will successfully extend to cattle and then to pigs, it will speed xeno-transplantation—using organs from pigs to treat human patients. That can be done now, but what happens now is that you put a human protein into the pig organ which kind of damps down the immune response in the transplant patient. Now with gene targeting, we can do that, but we can also change the *surface* of the cells, so that they would be less antigenic when the pig organ is put into a human patient—which makes it more likely that organ transplantation will work.

So, instead of waiting for a human donor, we'll be seeing many more animal organ-to-human transplants.

Yes, with pig organs in particular.

And who would be helped the most?

Well, there is a need for more hearts and more kidneys. At present people die before human hearts can be made available to them.

There have been attempts to use baboon transplants in AIDS patients.

Yes, but people feel it's more acceptable to think of using pigs because baboons seem so much more—

—human?

That's right. Aware of their environment.

With animal cloning research, will it be possible to go in and fix genetic defects in humans? For example, there are already tests for a predisposition to breast cancer.

I think that is so far away that it's not really credible. I mean you're quite right theoretically. But the efficiencies we have at the present time and our understanding are so naive and primitive that you wouldn't contemplate doing it. I think we could contribute in a smaller way to certain genetic diseases—breast cancer is not one that I've thought of—but, for example, with cystic fibrosis. It has been suggested that we study the role of

> *"Cloning and gene targeting requires fewer animals. It will be quicker, which means new health products will come on line more quickly."*

the gene which is defective in people who suffer from cystic fibrosis with the hope that better therapies can be developed. We could also provide model test animals in which methods of gene therapy can be developed.

Which is being done with mice.

Yes, but mice are so different and so small that experimentation is very difficult. Sheep would be much more appropriate.

Do you see a therapy for cystic fibrosis based on animal clones in your lifetime?

Yes. I'm 52, I reckon I've got 20 years. I'm fairly comfortable predicting we'll see something in that time period.

The Benefits for Animals

In addition to drug therapy for humans, your research has major implications for animals.

Yes, it may open a whole range of things we can't imagine at the present time. Remember, we only know about what, 5 or 10 percent of the animal genes? But there is a particular project which is of immediate relevance in Britain concerning the disease scrapie.

Mad Cow Disease?

That's right. What people believe is that the agent which causes scrapie in sheep causes BSE (Bovine Spongiform Encephalitis) in cows and some of the CJD (Creuzfeld-Jacob Disease) in humans. It is believed to start with a particular gene in sheep. Now what if we could modify that gene; could we make sheep that are resistant to scrapie? That's very important for sheep, but also for BSE and CJD in humans.

When?

Twenty years or so.

There is also talk of "supercows" producing enormous quantities of milk. Could it be made cholesterol-free, by the way?

> *"There are real potential benefits, and it's important that the concern to prevent misuse doesn't also prevent the really useful benefits that can be gained from this research."*

There are all sorts of questions like that. The answer to them is, we don't know. One thing I would say is that history shows that people are very bad at predicting the way that technology will be used.

Any implications for world hunger?

Not immediately. But if we can maybe make animals resistant to some diseases—to the tsetse fly, for example—it is quite possible that we can contribute to a whole range of things.

You've been working on this project for 10 years. Did you ever ask yourself, "Am I Dr. Frankenstein here? I know what I want to achieve but am I contributing to something I don't want to see happen?"

Of course. And we've tried to have this information released responsibly to journalists like yourself, to ethicists, to people concerned with legislation, because what we want is to stimulate an informed public discussion of the way in which the techniques might be misused as well as used and to ensure legislation was put in place to prevent misuse. But what we're also concerned with as well is that we don't throw the baby out with the bathwater. There are real potential benefits, and it's important that the concern to prevent misuse doesn't also prevent the really useful benefits that can be gained from this research.

What misuse are you most concerned with?

Any kind of manipulation with human embryos should be prohibited.

Are you concerned that your work will be stopped?

I have some concerns about it. I totally understand that people find this sort of research offensive, and I respect their views. It's also possible for a minority to have very large influence. Now, if society says it doesn't want us to do this kind of research, well, that's fine. But I think it has to be an overall view made by an informed population.

Assuming it goes forward, when will we see the first concrete applications?

I think there will be animals on the ground with interesting new products in three years. I think we'll come up with clotting factors, possibly in cattle as well as in sheep. Of course there will be a long time for testing the products before they go into commercial use. But there will be animals that are able to secrete new proteins, different proteins, in three years.

Animal Medical Experimentation Is Unjustified

by Peggy Carlson

About the author: *Peggy Carlson is a physician in the Washington, D.C., area and a research scientist for the Humane Society of the United States.*

As an emergency room physician I often see the suffering of patients ill and dying from diseases that could have been avoided if more resources were devoted to prevention, if healthier dietary guidelines were advocated, and if more research applicable to humans was conducted. I also know that behind this human suffering is another level of suffering, more hidden from view: the suffering of animals used in costly and needless experiments that benefit no one.

The practice of using nonhuman animals to mimic or study human disease is often unreliable, and occasionally misleads scientific investigation. It also squanders precious financial resources that are urgently needed for crucial clinical and epidemiological studies, preventive medicine, public health programs, and *in vitro* (test tube and cell culture) studies.

Real Advances

Claims that people are living longer today primarily because of animal experimentation have been shown to be false. Researchers at Boston and Harvard Universities found that medical measures (drugs and vaccines) accounted for at most between 1 and 3.5 percent of the total decline in mortality in the United States since 1900. The researchers noted that the increase in life expectancy is primarily attributable to the decline in such killer epidemics as tuberculosis, scarlet fever, smallpox, and diphtheria, among others, and that deaths from virtually all of these infectious diseases were declining before (and in most cases long before) specific therapies became available. The decline in mortality from these diseases was most likely due to such factors as improvements in sanitation, hygiene, diet, and standard of living.

Excerpted from Peggy Carlson, "Whose Health Is It, Anyway?" *The Animals' Agenda*, November/ December 1996. Reprinted with permission from *The Animals' Agenda*, P.O. Box 25881, Baltimore, MD 21224, USA.

Certainly, however, medical research has played an important role in improving people's lives. The list of those advances made without the use of animals is extensive, and includes the isolation of the AIDS virus, the discovery of penicillin and anesthetics, the identification of human blood types, the need for certain vitamins, and the development of x-rays. The identification of risk factors for heart disease—probably the most important discovery for decreasing deaths from heart attacks—was made through human population studies. John Marley and

> *"The practice of using nonhuman animals to mimic or study human disease is often unreliable, and occasionally misleads scientific investigation."*

Anthony Michael wrote in the *Medical Journal of Australia* in 1991, "Our formal knowledge about the factors that 'cause' disease comes primarily from epidemiological research, in which systematic comparisons are made between selected groups of representative individuals."

Reliable or Risky?

A major problem with animal experiments is that the results frequently do not apply to humans. For example, Irwin Bross, Ph.D., former director of biostatistics at the Roswell Institute for Cancer Research, testified before Congress in 1981 that "[w]hile conflicting animal results have often delayed and hampered advances in the war on cancer, they have never produced a single substantial advance either in the prevention or treatment of human cancer."

A 1980 editorial in *Clinical Oncology* asks why so much attention is devoted to the study of animal tumors when "it is . . . hard to find a single common solid human neoplasm [cancer] where management and expectation of cure have been markedly influenced by the results of laboratory research." The writer D.F.N. Harrison explains that "most cancers behave differently from the artificially produced animal models," and concluded that "it is in the study of human patients where the relevant answers will be found."

Animal tests that attempt to predict which substances cause human cancers have also been shown to be unreliable. A 1981 U.S. Congress Office of Technology Assessment Report on the causes of cancer placed more weight on epidemiological data than on animal experiments because its authors argued that animal tests "cannot provide reliable risk assessments." According to a 1977 *Nature* article, of all the agents known to cause cancer in humans, the vast majority were first identified by observation of human populations.

Neurological diseases are another major cause of death and disability in the United States. Again, animal experiments in this area have not correlated well with human disease. A 1990 editorial in the journal *Stroke* noted that of 25 compounds "proven" effective for treating strokes in animal models over the last 10 years, none have proven effective for use in humans.

Stephen Kaufman, M.D., reviewed animal models of such degenerative neurological diseases as Alzheimer's and Parkinson's and concluded that "animal models designed to improve our understanding and treatment of these conditions have had little impact, and their future value is highly dubious." Dennis Maiman, M.D., Ph.D., of the Department of Neurosurgery at the Medical College of Wisconsin noted in the *Journal of the American Paraplegia Society* in 1988, "In the last two decades at least 22 agents have been found to be therapeutic in experimental [laboratory] spinal cord injury. . . . Unfortunately, to date none of these has been proven effective in clinical spinal cord injury."

Two other areas where animal experimentation has been both consumptive of health care dollars and unproductive are psychology and addiction. A review of two clinical psychology journals, *Behavior Therapy* and the *Journal of Consulting and Clinical Psychology,* showed that only 0.75 percent of the references were to animal research studies. Yet in 1986 alone the National Institute of Mental Health funded 350 animal experiments in psychology at a cost of more than $30 million. The Alcohol Studies Center in Scotland stated in 1985 that "[n]othing of clinical relevance has been achieved to date for the vast range of experiments in alcoholism" and that "animal models of addiction are not relevant to human addiction."

> *"A major problem with animal experiments is that the results frequently do not apply to humans."*

However, in 1995 the National Institute on Alcohol Abuse and Alcoholism spent $50 million on nearly 300 animal experiments dealing with alcohol abuse. In 1995 the National Institute on Drug Abuse spent $90 million on animal experiments involving drug abuse. Yet alcohol and drug abuse treatment centers for human sufferers remain underfunded.

Using animals to test therapeutic drugs has also proven unreliable. There are scores of examples of differing reactions of drugs between animals and humans. Penicillin kills guinea pigs and hamsters, but is very beneficial for humans. Thalidomide, a tranquilizer formerly prescribed for pregnant women with morning sickness, caused serious birth defects in more than 10,000 children but does not cause birth defects in numerous species of nonhuman animals. Acetaminophen (Tylenol), a common human pain reliever, is deadly to cats. The antibiotic chloramphenicol was thoroughly tested on animals before being released for clinical use, but was found to cause an often-fatal blood disease in humans.

Of the 198 drugs that were tested on animals in accordance with Food and Drug Administration guidelines between 1976 and 1985, 51.5 percent caused reactions serious enough to result in withdrawal from the market or, more commonly, substantial labeling changes. These reactions included heart failure, respiratory problems, convulsions, kidney and liver failure, and death. A consequence of using inaccurate animal tests is that drugs that pass animal trials can be approved for human use and later prove harmful to people; conversely, drugs that fail animal tests but might actually be beneficial to humans can be wrongly discarded.

Unreliable animal experiments have led science astray in other ways, as well. For example, unsuccessful attempts to induce lung cancer in lab animals by forcing them to inhale tobacco smoke cast doubt on human clinical findings, delaying health warnings and possibly costing thousands of lives. Although not opposed to vivisection, Albert Sabin, M.D., who discovered one of the major polio vaccines, testified before Congress that "the work on the prevention [of polio] was long delayed because of an erroneous conception of the nature of the human disease based on misleading experimental models of the disease in monkeys."

Using animals in health care research also presents another problem of unknown magnitude: the risk of animal viruses infecting the human population. Some primate viruses, when transmitted to humans, can cause disease and even death. Most scientists now believe that the virus that causes AIDS is a descendent of a virus found in nonhuman primates. In the case of xenotransplantation (transplants of animal organs or tissues into humans), the risk of animal viruses entering the human population could have devastating consequences.

Research Budgets

Despite the problems inherent in using animals in research, billions of U.S. health care dollars are spent on animal experimentation each year. U.S. health care expenditures totaled $884 billion in 1993 and are expected to have reached $1 trillion in 1995. Included are medical costs for hospitalizations, medicines, physicians, and public health and preventive medicine programs. Also included are expenditures for health (biomedical) research, which in 1993 totaled $14.4 billion. This excludes industry (i.e., drug companies, etc.) spending for research and development, which totaled about $16 billion in 1993. Health care research money is divided among such diverse areas as animal experimentation, human studies, computer studies, and *in vitro* studies.

The vast majority of federal health care research funds are channeled through the National Institutes of Health (NIH), whose 1995 budget was $11.3 billion. Eighty percent of the NIH budget goes to actual research projects. According to the NIH, at least 40 percent of its grants currently have an animal component.

> *"Animal tests that attempt to predict which substances cause human cancers have also been shown to be unreliable."*

While enormous sums of money are being consumed by animal experimentation, greater emphasis on other areas could lead to huge improvements in the health of this nation. These include human clinical and epidemiological studies, prevention initiatives, public health programs, and *in vitro* tests.

Emphasize Prevention

We can learn how to improve public health by looking first at what threatens it. The three leading causes of death in this country today are heart disease, cancer, and stroke—diseases that can very often be prevented. Heart disease and stroke have similar risk factors, including high-fat, meat-based diets; cigarette smoking; high blood pressure; obesity; and sedentary lifestyles. A study presented at the 1975 meeting of the American Public Health Association found the heart disease mortality for lacto-ovo-vegetarians to be only one third that of meat-eaters. Pure vegetarians (vegans) had only one tenth the heart disease rate of meat-eaters.

> *"There are scores of examples of differing reactions of drugs between animals and humans."*

Cancer may also have a significant preventable component. In 1985 the International Agency for Research on Cancer estimated that as much as 80–90 percent of human cancer is determined by such things as diet, lifestyle (including smoking), and environmental carcinogens. John Bailer and Elaine Smith from the Harvard School of Public Health and the University of Iowa Medical Center wrote in the *New England Journal of Medicine* that "thirty-five years of intense effort focused largely on improving treatment [of cancer] must be judged a qualified failure." They further stated that despite progress against some rare forms of cancer (particularly among patients under 30, accounting for 1–2 percent of total cancer deaths), the overall cancer-related death rate has increased since 1950. They recommended a shift in emphasis from treatment research to prevention research if substantial progress against cancer is to be forthcoming.

The fourth leading cause of death (bronchitis, emphysema, and asthma) also has a very large component that is caused by a preventable factor: cigarette smoking. In addition, other of the ten leading causes of death—injuries, suicide, AIDS, and homicide—could be reduced through prevention. Clearly, prevention should be a priority for health care funding. . . .

The health of this country could be substantially improved if health care dollars were more appropriately distributed. Animal experimentation is currently being inappropriately overfunded at the expense of crucial clinical and epidemiological studies, preventive medicine, public health programs, and *in vitro* studies.

Product Testing on Animals Is Unjustified

by Animal Alliance of Canada

About the author: *Animal Alliance of Canada is an animal rights advocacy and education group that focuses on local, regional, national, and international issues concerning the respectful treatment of animals by humans.*

Every day in North America animals are poisoned, blinded and burned in consumer product tests. Products ranging from mascara, shampoo and nail polish to oven cleaner, ink and children's toys are tested on animals. These tests, which are conducted in the name of protecting consumers, are crude and outdated: They result in pain and suffering for the animals involved, and provide little protection to the consumer.

Eye and Skin Irritancy Tests

The Draize Test is one method used to measure the harmfulness of ingredients contained in household products and cosmetics. The Draize involves dripping the test substance into a rabbit's eye and recording the damage over three to twenty-one days. Scientists use rabbits for these tests because rabbits' eyes have no tear ducts to wash away the irritant, and their eyes are large enough for any inflammation to be clearly visible. Reactions can vary from slight irritation to ulceration and complete blindness. The rabbits are confined in restraining devices to prevent them from clawing at the injured eye. All of the animals are usually killed at the end of the test period, or "recycled" into toxicity tests.

Problems with Irritancy Tests

The Draize Test has been criticized on several grounds. Ophthalmologist Dr. Stephen Kaufman of the Medical Research Modernization Committee points out that a rabbit's eye has a thinner cornea and is more sensitive than a human eye. Consequently, results of tests conducted on rabbits' eyes cannot be legitimately extrapolated to humans.

Dr. Neal Barnard of the Physicians' Committee for Responsible Medicine has

Excerpted from Animal Alliance of Canada, "Cosmetic and Product Testing on Animals," *Non-line Pro-Con*, May 17, 1997. Reprinted by permission.

condemned the Draize for being highly subjective and inconsistent. Indeed, the inconsistency of the Draize was demonstrated by a Carnegie University of Pittsburgh study in which substances were distributed to twenty-four laboratories for testing. The laboratory results showed substantial variations in the methods different laboratories used to evaluate a rabbit's reactions. Furthermore, some laboratories reported unusually severe reactions to a substance, while other laboratories concluded that the same substance was non-irritating. If different scientists using the Draize cannot agree on the effects of a substance, how useful can the test be?

The Lethal Dose "X" Percent test, or LD-X, is the classic method used to measure the acute toxicity of certain ingredients. The test is used to determine the dosage of a given substance that is required to kill a percentage of the test animals within a specified time period. Animals are force fed, injected with or forced to inhale toxic substances such as body lotion or drain cleaner. As the dosage of the test substance increases, the animals' internal organs may become blocked or ruptured, causing symptoms such as convulsions, chronic diarrhea and massive bleeding. The animals eventually die as a result of the tests or are killed. The percentage of animals subjected to the lethal dose can be up to 50%.

Problems with Toxicity Tests

Toxicity tests have been widely criticized as inhumane, inconsistent and irrelevant to humans. Results from specific tests indicate the amount of a given substance necessary to kill a certain species, such as dogs, rabbits or mice, not humans. However, the test animals may actually die as a consequence of the sheer volume of the dosage, not because the substance itself is poisonous. Other animals may die from the severe burns they receive to their throats and stomachs after they are force fed caustic substances such as laundry bleach or liquid drain cleaner.

> *"There are safe, economical, fast and humane alternatives which accurately predict the effect of a substance on humans without using live animals."*

Furthermore, the Lethal Dose test does not take into consideration numerous factors, such as species, age, diet or gender of the test animals, which can affect test results. Ultimately, the Lethal Dose test does not even provide useful information on such crucial subjects as the exact poisonous dose of a substance to humans; the prevention or treatment of an overdose; the long-term effects of a specific substance on the human body; or determining which human organs are affected by a given dose of a specific substance.

Alternatives

Some manufacturers have replaced old tests with less painful ones involving fewer animals. However, there are safe, economical, fast and humane alternatives which accurately predict the effect of a substance on humans without using live animals.

Currently, many accurate alternatives to the Draize and Lethal Dose tests utilize in vitro (in test tube or culture dish) technologies. In vitro tests use human or animal cell specimens, many of which can be grown and reproduced in the laboratory. These cell and tissue cultures can measure possible substance reactions on human skin or eye tissue, as well as potential toxicity. Human cell cultures provide a more accurate testing medium than do animal cells.

One popular alternative to the Draize involves exposing a synthetic matrix of proteins to the test substance. The synthetic proteins behave in much the same way as the protein in an animal's eye. Consequently, the test results provide the same information as the Draize, but without the Draize's inherent cruelty.

Other alternatives to irritancy and toxicity tests include using sheets of cloned human skin cells to predict skin irritation; creating mathematical and computer models to predict the reaction of tissue cells and organs to chemical substances; and using computer programs to predict human reactions to substances. The U.S. Food and Drug Administration and Environmental Protection Agency, as well as many corporations, use computer programs in place of animal testing. Furthermore, companies can use ingredients that are known to be safe, and they can perform literature searches which often eliminate testing by applying the results of previous experiments.

Animal-to-Human Organ Transplants Could Threaten Human Health

by John F. McArdle

About the author: *John F. McArdle is a scientific adviser for the American Anti-Vivisection Society, an animal rights organization.*

Throughout medical history charlatans have preyed upon the anxieties and fears of terminally ill patients, their families and friends by promoting a general retreat from rationality and substituting a variety of miraculous "cures." The modern incarnation of such quackery appears to be well represented by xeno-transplant researchers and surgeons.

Having failed to successfully scare the general population with dire predictions of death and devastation from such complex diseases as cancer and AIDS (both largely preventable and thus avoidable) and needing to justify inflated animal-based research budgets, the biomedical research/health care complex has prepared another threatening scenario, the so-called shortage of organs for use in transplantation. They also have a high technology solution, the use of various body parts, tissues and organs (xenografts) of healthy animals for implantation into unhealthy human recipients. This is the basic concept of the rapidly expanding field of xenotransplantation. It is also a realistic threat to the survival of many non-human primates and every human being.

Although there are only a handful of clinical research centers currently involved in planning and/or conducting xenotransplantation with human patients, researchers have found a gold mine of experimental possibilities, involving a wide variety of species, essentially every internal organ (except the brain), tissue (including the brain) and body part. The number of possible combinations of transplants, anti-rejection drugs and treatment protocols is endless. However, the current focus appears to be on using animal organs to compensate for a limited supply of suitable human organs, and using primate bone marrow to recon-

Excerpted from John F. McArdle, "Xenotransplantation: A Growing Threat and an Opportunity for Alternatives," a 1996 American Anti-Vivisection Society publication. Reprinted by permission of the author.

stitute the immune systems of AIDS patients. The same degree of research effort and money expended on overcoming hyperacute and delayed organ rejection from animal donors is not committed to solving related problems with using human sources.

No Shortage of Human Donors

In fact, there is no shortage of human organs for possible use in clinical transplantation. There is, however, a serious shortage of donors, as well as an inefficient and flawed system for selecting recipients. It is a sad commentary on our society that we routinely burn or bury more than enough viable organs to meet current legitimate needs. What is needed are new approaches to increase the number of donors. Less technologically advanced and more intuitively obvious alternatives to using animal organs and tissues in human clinical procedures exist. Based on successful experiences in other countries, there are numerous non-xenotransplant options which the federal government could take now to increase the supply of organ donors.

Despite the lack of realistic justifications, the research and treatment continues. This may be due to non-altruistic motives. If successful, xenotransplantation could involve up to 100,000 patients a year at a cost of thousands of dollars for each animal organ used, creating a new multi-billion-dollar animal exploitation industry. Additional billions would be earned by the xenotransplant medical professionals and supporting clinical research and treatment facilities.

Primate Donors

Which animals should be used for such medical procedures? Examination of the history of xenotransplantation shows Susan Ildstad's suggestion that "the optimum source for a donor would be the lowest on the phylogenetic trees, and possibly, one consumed as a food source" has not always been followed.

The first clinical use of animal organ transplantation was by French surgeon Princeteau, who in 1905 grafted a rabbit kidney slice into a child. In 1906

"The same degree of research effort . . . expended on overcoming . . . organ rejection from animal donors is not committed to solving related problems with using human sources."

Jabowlay implanted pig and goat kidneys into human patients. The use of primate organs was first tried in 1910, when Unger used a monkey kidney. Lastly, Neuhof, in 1923, utilized a lamb kidney for a similar operation. All of these xenograft recipients died quickly and the field was abandoned until the early 1960s.

During the 1960s and 1970s, more than 25 primate xenografts were conducted. In 1964 Dr. Keith Reemtsma started the current obsession with using primate organs by transplanting chimpanzee kidneys into six human patients. A single individual lived for nine months and served as the incentive for a rash of similar clinical trials. These involved several surgeons using chimpanzee hearts, kidneys and livers, and an entire series of baboon kidney xenotransplants by Thomas Starzl. As expected, none of these experiments was successful.

The rationalization offered in support of such experiments centered on the evolutionary proximity of humans, chimpanzees and baboons; the failure to establish viable human organ procurement programs; and, in the case of Reemtsma, the ready availability of non-human primate donors at the Delta Regional Primate Research Center.

Baby Fae

Due to consistent failures and the inability to control the rejection process, the field of xenotransplantation experienced a hiatus of nearly twenty years. Then, in 1984, Dr. Leonard Bailey conducted the infamous Baby Fae experiment, violating the basic medical credo, "Do no harm."

Baby Fae was born with a serious heart defect, which Bailey chose to treat by replacing her damaged heart with a healthy one from a baboon. This experiment is critically important since it provides a baseline for subsequent clinical xenotransplantation activities and a lengthy list of medically and scientifically inappropriate decisions. These include:

- Bailey's earlier experiments on heart transplantation in sheep and goats were privately funded, not subjected to peer review, and involved species that are genetically very similar.
- Bailey had virtually no experience with human heart transplantation.
- There are indications that truly informed consent was not given to the parents.
- No attempt was made to obtain a suitable human heart, although one was available the day of the surgery.
- A surgical technique existed to repair the damaged heart and could have kept the child alive until a suitable human heart became available.
- The baboon heart would not grow to adult human size, thus guaranteeing that the child would eventually need a human heart transplant.

Baboon Liver Transplants

It was a foregone conclusion that Baby Fae would not survive. A similar fate awaited the patients who received baboon liver xenotransplants in 1992 and 1993. Dr. Thomas Starzl and others rationalized such human experimentation by claiming that since some primates are resistant to human infections like hepatitis, the baboon livers could be used to replace human organs ravaged by the disease. The primate's natural resistance might prevent reinfection of the transplanted organ, a common but not universal problem associated with using human livers.

Infectious disease specialists, however, were appalled that Starzl chose xenotransplantation of baboon livers because of the known risk of transferring or creating a serious viral infection in the recipients. In fact, the Pittsburgh team did not inform the supplier of the animals that they would be used for clinical experimentation. Post-operative examination of the primate donors demonstrated that they were infected with at least four known primate viruses, with unknown consequences for human infection.

As with all examples of organ xenotransplantation, there was no evidence to indicate that the baboon livers would biochemically or physiologically function appropriately in a human recipient. Even Starzl admitted that "a baboon liver could impose on a human recipient lethal interspecies metabolic differences."

> *"There was no evidence to indicate that the baboon livers would biochemically or physiologically function appropriately in a human recipient."*

Dr. Hugh Auchincloss of Harvard Medical School, a strong supporter of xenotransplantation, summarized these baboon to human liver experiments by noting that "survival rates reported for allotransplantation (human to human) in those patients with hepatitis B is superior to that which we could expect from xenotransplantation."

Ironically, when biopsy specimens were taken from the transplanted baboon livers, one was positive for hepatitis B. This suggests that the original justification for the experiment, resistance to human pathogens, was not valid.

Although efforts to transplant primate hearts and livers into human patients are highly publicized, what is less obvious is the bewildering array of experiments conducted throughout the 20th century, with a major focus of activity within the last two decades. These usually involved transplanting organs between different species of non-human primates, transferring pig organs into baboons or other monkeys, these animals acting as surrogates for human patients; or general models of xenotransplantation with different types of rodents. In a surprisingly candid comment, Auchincloss also noted that "successful rodent experiments do not provide an adequate scientific basis for human experimentation." It should also be stressed that careful examination of the relevant scientific literature suggests that "successful" monkey and pig studies are also inadequate to predict the responses of human organ recipients.

Baboon Bone Marrow and AIDS

No xenotransplantation experiment has provoked more opposition and misinformation than that of Dr. Susan Ildstad. Because the immune systems of individuals with AIDS are destroyed by their HIV infections and baboons are supposedly not susceptible to the AIDS virus, she wanted to transplant healthy bone marrow stem cells from baboons into the bodies of terminally ill AIDS patients. In theory, these baboon cells would subsequently give rise to an entirely new, fully functional immune system, free of the AIDS virus. This is medical science fiction at its best.

Dr. Ildstad conducted a series of experiments involving rodents and primates. From that work she concluded that it was possible to graft immune cells from one species to another, without the long-term use of immunosuppressive drugs. In a study published in 1994, she and her co-workers acknowledged that the widespread clinical use of bone marrow transplantation had been limited by the general tendency of donor marrow to be rejected by a process called graft versus host disease, which usually kills the recipients. This would also likely be the case with humans and baboons, which are more similar to each other than either is to a rodent.

There was no reason to assume the baboon cells would function as planned in their new human host. With human to human, non-relative marrow transplantation, only 30 percent survive. Baboon to human would be less successful. In 1993 baboon marrow was given to an AIDS patient at the University of Pittsburgh. That attempt failed. Further, all of the previous rodent and primate experiments were conducted on healthy animals, not individuals who were terminally ill or with severely compromised immune systems. It is doubtful, even disregarding all of the other questionable biological and medical assumptions which characterized the project, that results from healthy animals would be relevant to either diseased animals or humans.

> *"Xenotransplantation experiments . . . could directly cause the creation of a new infectious disease more deadly than AIDS or Ebola."*

However, based on experiments involving mice, Dr. Ildstad also claimed the discovery of a new type of bone marrow cell (a facilitator) which, when mixed with typical stem cells from the marrow of a donor, allowed survival of the transplant and avoided the problems associated with graft versus host disease. She suggested that the use of these cells "may expand the potential application of bone marrow transplantation to disease states in which the morbidity and mortality associated with conventional bone marrow transplants cannot be justified." She also transplanted human bone marrow into baboons. This involved the use of immature cells, low levels of irradiation to prepare the recipient's bone marrow, and several days of immunosuppressive drugs. The result was a non-human primate whose immune system included 15 percent human cells, but with no evidence that these cells were functioning to support the needs of the baboon.

Unimpressive Results

Her bone marrow project received widespread criticism from physicians, immunologists, infectious disease experts, philosophers, animal protectionists, and other xenotransplant researchers. Apparently no scientists, other than Ildstad, were able to identify these special facilitator cells. In addition, baboon cells may not be resistant to HIV, foreign marrow cells may not function in an environment regulated by human hormones and physiology, and new immune cells may not be able to develop in AIDS patients with typically damaged thymus glands.

Stephen Rose, director of AIDS funding at the National Institutes of Health, was not impressed with Ildstad's experimental results. He noted that "having seen her data—there are no underlying data to make me believe this is going to be successful." David Sachs, Harvard University pro-xeno-transplant specialist, agreed, observing that "there was no evidence from the data she presented to show that facilitator cells were present in primates."

> *"Like primates, pigs have multiple endogenous retroviruses . . . , any one of which might cause an infection in human organ recipients."*

Others questioned Ildstad's motives for promoting such human experiments, since she had jointly patented the facilitator cells with the biotechnology company Genetic Sciences, and would likely make a considerable amount of money if the cells actually existed and the experiment worked.

Despite scientific skepticism about the validity of her hypothesis and the existence of her special facilitator cells, the major fear raised by these and other xenotransplantation experiments is that they could directly cause the creation of a new infectious disease more deadly than AIDS or Ebola, both of which probably were derived from non-lethal primate viruses transferred to new human hosts. Such concerns are widely expressed in the recent medical literature, but apparently ignored or diminished by supporters of xenotransplant research and federal regulatory agencies such as the Food and Drug Administration (FDA).

International Organizations Make Recommendations

Because of such clearly identified potential threats to public health, the American and British governments convened special committees to examine the relevant scientific evidence and make appropriate policy recommendations. In England, the Nuffield Council on Bioethics and official government Advisory Group on the Ethics of Xenotransplantation both considered the subject in great detail, included all interested parties, gave equal weight to ethical and medical issues, and produced comprehensive documents and recommendations for the possible use of animal organs in human patients. The primary suggestions were: (1) no human clinical trials until there is more knowledge concerning physiological, immunological and infectious disease risks; (2) use of non-human primates is ethically unacceptable; (3) use of pigs may be acceptable if welfare issues are addressed; and (4) much more effort must be taken to increase the number of human organ donors. The focus of these efforts was clearly the protection of public health, rather than the facilitation of xenotransplantation research and clinical trials.

In contrast, efforts in the United States appear to be little more than public relations campaigns to convince the media and general public that clinical use of animal organs and tissues is a safe, critically needed treatment option for terminal organ failure and AIDS.

The National Academy of Sciences' Institute of Medicine (IOM) held both public and private hearings and discussions on the issue of xenotransplantation, with only minor consideration of ethical issues, animal welfare and possible alternatives to increase human organ donations. Their published report was essentially a blanket endorsement of xenotransplantation. They suggested a need for some guidelines, but nothing that would restrict clinical experimentation or that would protect the general public from the potential disease risks.

Following the IOM effort, the FDA convened meetings of its own Biological Response Modifiers Advisory Committee (BRMAC), which included voting participation by many individuals who were either directly or indirectly involved with xenotransplant research and related commercial drug and therapy development. Although supposedly an open hearing, the only members of the public testifying were five individuals pre-selected by Jeff Getty, the intended recipient of baboon bone marrow cells. Neither the background nor advisory meetings included significant representation of public opposition.

> *"Xenotransplantation bypasses all of the body's natural defenses, which have thus far successfully prevented disease transmission."*

The final decision to support baboon bone marrow clinical trials was based more on politics and pressure tactics of AIDS activists than on sound medical and scientific evidence. As one member of the committee (Jonathan Allen) noted, "approval of the initial baboon bone marrow transplant rested more on the perceived needs of the AIDS patient rather than a clear indication that the procedure was safe from an infectious disease standpoint or that it had any clear scientific merit. Indeed, no convincing evidence has been presented to suggest that baboon bone marrow can be used safely and there are no data that would indicate any efficacy for ameliorating HIV infection."

Despite attempts by the FDA to represent the bone marrow experiments specifically and all xenotransplantation in general, as necessary and probably safe, the message was clearly delivered from other sources that such projects pose a serious threat to the health of all human beings.

Disagreement Among the Experts

From the IOM and advisory committee meeting, the FDA published a set of draft guidelines for clinical xenotransplantation, which were widely viewed as unlikely to protect the health of the general public, unable to prevent the spread of new infectious diseases, and more reflective of political and economic expediency than carefully considered clinical needs.

Due to the unexpectedly strident tone and extent of opposition to the guidelines within the infectious disease and medical communities, the FDA placed the guidelines on hold and decided to sponsor three more workshops on different aspects of xenotransplantation. The first of these brought together the world's leading experts on cross-species transmission of infectious diseases to discuss current knowledge on the health risks associated with xenotransplantation. Also present was a sampling of surgeons and researchers who specialize in the clinical use of animal organs. From the scientific presentations and discussions, it was obvious that these two groups had very different agendas and perceptions. Clinical, research and corporate supporters of xenotransplantation routinely promoted the use of non-human primate and pig organs and tissues. Due to the well-documented fears about creation of highly contagious and deadly new pathogens associated with using monkey or ape donors, none of the disease specialists were enthusiastic about this option. However, workshop presentations made it clear that pigs were likely to be equally unsuitable.

> *"Xenotransplantation of organs and tissues represents a major threat to future human health and little or no benefits."*

Evidence was presented that, like primates, pigs have multiple endogenous retroviruses (ERVs), any one of which might cause an infection in human organ recipients. These ERVs are non-pathogenic to the pigs and may even have adaptive value to them. For that reason, the ERVs should not be removed from the animals through genetic engineering and selective breeding.

A "Doomsday" Virus?

A major highlight of the presentations was one which noted that cells in all modern domestic pigs contain genetic material from the 1918 influenza pandemic, which killed millions of people and often acted more like an aggressive form of the disease Ebola than the flu. It was further noted that the use of pig organs in severely immunosuppressed human patients might facilitate the creation of the next world-wide outbreak of a deadly strain of influenza.

Although the probability that xenotransplantation would create a "doomsday" virus was described as low, none of the disease specialists ruled out the possibility. What if all went well until the 10,000th or 100,000th patient, when the medical establishment had already declared animal organs safe and controls (which may not work) became lax?

The surgeon-transplant research participants chose to deny the dangers enumerated by the scientific presentations. At the end of the workshop they proposed that, despite evidence to the contrary, clinical xenotransplantation should start now without so many restrictions. Their only defense offered to suggest that using animal organs is safe, was that humans and pigs have had close contact for thousands of years on farms and in slaughterhouses without the appearance of new diseases. This rationalization conveniently ignored the fact that xenotransplantation bypasses all of the body's natural defenses, which have thus far successfully prevented such disease transmission.

Throughout all of the hearings, workshops and scientific debates, the principal informed critic of the proposed non-human primate xenotransplantation experiments remains Dr. Jonathan Allen, from the Southwest Foundation (suppliers of baboons for use in xenotransplantation), an expert on primate viruses. He concluded

> *"There is no convincing evidence that the United States government ... [has] worked to increase the supply of human organs available for transplantation."*

that baboons were selected for these experiments because of their evolutionary closeness to humans, but "at the same time, any agent or pathogen that a baboon might harbor is also going to be more likely to be transmitted to humans." Further, he warned that it is "well-established that most new emerging human infectious diseases generally have their origins in other species." Baboons may be hosts for a variety of unknown viruses that, by themselves or in recombination with viral DNA already resident in humans, would be capable of creating a new disease. No guidelines or precautions currently being considered for such experiments can prevent the introduction or spread of such a virus into the general human population. The issue here is not the safety of the recipient, . . . but the future health and welfare of every other human that may be exposed to a new, deadly pathogen. This is not alarmist propaganda. It is very basic science.

A Major Threat to Human Health

Can primates or pigs be bred which are entirely pathogen-free? Probably not. A 1994 book by Richard Preston titled *The Hot Zone* was based on the 1989 discovery (in a primate supplier's holding facility in Reston, Virginia) of an Ebola-like virus. Although no humans died and all 450 of the monkeys were destroyed, the implications of the crisis did not end there. A subsequent survey of non-human primates in research facilities throughout the United States found that 10 percent of the animals then used in research were positive carriers of serious pathogens, including animals housed in colonies that had been quarantined for years.

All of the available scientific and medical information suggests that xenotransplantation of organs and tissues represents a major threat to future human health and little or no benefits.

In his concluding remarks to the FDA advisory panel, Jonathan Allen clearly summarized the basic problem with xenotransplantation in general and bone marrow experiments in particular. He cautioned that "to proceed with this kind of procedure in the face of knowing how AIDS is transmitted, is to repeat the past. . . . If you proceed with this, you need to understand that there is going to be a risk that you are not going to eliminate the risk of transmitting another virus that could be as deadly as the AIDS virus." These experiments "constitute a threat to the general public health and not merely a complication of the risk/benefit calculation for the individual xenogenic tissue recipient." In brief, "DO NOT use non-human primates as organ donors if you don't want to infect the human population."

Is all of this risk really an easier and better use of consumer and taxpayer dollars than working to increase the number of potential human donors? There is no convincing evidence that the United States government and medical communities have consistently and aggressively worked to increase the supply of human organs available for transplantation. Further, there is no unquestionable scientific or medical evidence that xenotransplantation clinical experiments will work as promised or should be conducted on human patients needing realistic and reliable treatment options.

The burden of proof that xenotransplantation is safe and needed lies with the transplantation community that is proselytizing for its approval and use in both clinical and biomedical research priorities. These individuals and organizations have failed to provide realistic assurances and scientific or medically convincing evidence that the process is safe, clinically efficacious and not a major threat to the future health and welfare of all humans.

Cloning Animals for Human Benefit Has Limited Justification

by Donald Bruce

About the author: *Donald Bruce is the director of the Society, Religion, and Technology Project of the Church of Scotland, an interdisciplinary association that studies the relationship between ethics and technology.*

Author's Note: From 1993–98, a working group of the Society, Religion and Technology Project (SRT) of the Church of Scotland examined the ethical issues of genetic engineering in non-human species, culminating in the recent book Engineering Genesis *by Donald and Ann Bruce (Earthscan Publications, November 1998, ISBN 1 85383 570 6). The inter-disciplinary group of experts included Roslin scientist Dr Ian Wilmut, head of the team which cloned Dolly. The following article by the Director of the SRT Project reflects on some of the ethical issues, straight from the sheep's mouth.*

Dolly and Her Applications

Dolly is the most famous sheep in the world. She looks much like any other sheep, but she has been cloned from another adult sheep. Scientists at the Roslin Institute in Edinburgh have rewritten the laws of biology. Her announcement in February 1997 led to an unprecedented media circus which caused as much confusion as it shed light. The attention focused mainly on speculations about the possibility, or otherwise, of cloning humans. In doing so, it missed the much more immediate impact of this work on how we use animals. It's by no means certain this would really lead to flocks of cloned lambs in the fields and hills of Scotland, or clinically reproducible cuts of meat on the supermarket shelves. But it does prompt us to ask questions about the way we are using animals with new technology, and the kinds of assumptions we make.

Reprinted from Donald Bruce, "Should We Clone Animals?" a Society, Religion, and Technology Project publication at http://webzone1.co.uk/www/srtproject/clonan3.htm, August 21, 1998, by permission of the author.

Cloning had already been done to a limited degree by splitting embryos, mostly in cattle, and raised ethical and welfare concerns in the process. But the Roslin work opens up the prospect of a far wider range of applications from adult animal cells. At the moment, there are only a few early results in sheep, and rather little is understood of how it has happened. Different farm animal species differ somewhat in their embryology. Now the technique has been extended to cattle and also mice, suggesting that it could be general in mammals. It remains to be seen to what extent the method would work in different animals without adverse effects. But assuming it could be applied more widely, what are the potential applications in animals?

Since 1986, [researchers at] Roslin have been genetically modifying sheep to produce proteins of therapeutic value in their milk. Successful as this has been so far, the present methods are very hit and miss, using perhaps 100 live animals to get just one right one. The original aim of Dr Ian Wilmut's nuclear transfer work was to find more precise methods [of] genetic modification, via a cell culture, if a way could be found to grow live animals from the modified cells. Their announcement in July 1997 of the transgenic cloned sheep Polly marked the first evidence of this principle. The fact it was a clone was, in a way, a side-effect. PPL Therapeutics, the Edinburgh firm behind the research, say they might clone 5–10 animals like this from a single genetically modified cell line, but then breed them naturally, as "founders" of a set of lines of genetically modified animals. There would be no advantage in cloning beyond the first point.

> *"It could be argued that to produce replica humans or animals on demand would be to go against something basic and God-given about the very nature of higher forms of life."*

But these medical applications on farm animals tend to be small-scale affairs. The amount of animals and the amount of milk is very small compared with conventional meat or bulk milk production. Imagine you are a commercial breeder of cows or pigs, and over many generations you have bred some fine and valuable beasts with highly desirable characteristics. One possible application of Roslin's work could be to clone such animals from the cells of one of them, and sell the cloned animals to "finishers"—those farmers who simply feed up the animals for slaughter, rather than breed them to produce more stock. Again, the breeder might want to clone a series of promising animals in a breeding programme, in order to test how the same "genotype" responded to different environmental changes. . . .

Ethics and Animal Cloning

Should this be allowed ethically? To look at this, here are several possible criteria—unnaturalness, diversity, fundamental concerns, animal welfare and commodification.

Is it unnatural? Many people say that cloning farm animals would be unnatural. Whereas in the plant kingdom cloning is a fairly common phenomenon, there are few animal examples and none in mammals or humans. Should we then respect this biological distinction, or should we celebrate our human capacity to override such limitations? It is hard to argue in an absolute sense that anything is unnatural, when so little remains around us that we might justifiably call natural, and nature itself is in constant motion. Yet many believe some technological inventions are now going too far to remain in tune with what we perceive "natural" to mean, despite how much we have intervened in nature to date. Is cloning animals a point to draw a line?

Would it narrow genetic diversity too far? This brings us to the question of diversity. One of the fundamental rules of selective breeding is that you must maintain a high enough level of genetic variation. The more you narrow down the genetic "pool" to a limited number of lines of, say, animals for meat or milk production, the more you run risks of problems from in-breeding. If that is the case with breeding, how much more is it true of cloning, where genetic replicas are involved. This means there are pragmatic limits to how useful cloning would be, but beneath the pragmatics there lies a deeper ethical concern. Does this reflect something fundamental about the nature of things?

Cloning and God's Creation

Is there a fundamental ethical concern? This is something for which Christian theology provides some insights. For the Christian, the world around us is God's creation, and one of its most characteristic features is variety. The biblical writers make repeated allusions to it, painting striking pictures of a creation whose very diversity is a cause of praise to its creator. It could be argued that to produce replica humans or animals on demand would be to go against something basic and God-given about the very nature of higher forms of life. Where God evolves a system of boundless possibilities which works by diversification, is it typically human to select out certain functions we think are the best, and replicate them? Deliberate cloning aims at predictability, replication, in order to exercise control, whose centralised, even totalitarian approach contrasts with God's command to animals and humans to "be fruitful and multiply". In the limit this argument would mean that cloning would be absolutely wrong, no matter what it was being used for. This intuition runs deep in many people. But there are also questions

> *"Nature is not ours to do exactly what we like with."*

of scale and intention to consider, and also what sort of application.

Justifiable uses of animal cloning? Cloning animals might be acceptable in the limited context of research or, where the main intention was not the clone as such but growing an animal of a known genetic composition, where natural methods would not work. Roslin's work to produce Polly the transgenic cloned sheep would be such a case, where the intention is not primarily to clone, but to find more precise ways of animal genetic engineering. Indeed, producing medically useful proteins in sheep's milk is one of the least contentious genetic modifications in animals, since the intervention in the animal is very small for a considerable human benefit. Careful scrutiny would be needed, to see that it was only applied to genetic manipulations that would be ethically acceptable, but that is a question we already faced before cloning.

> *"Most of the suggested applications relate to production improvements rather than clear human or animal benefits."*

Animal welfare concerns. We also need to be sure about the animal welfare aspects even of limited cloning. Questions have been raised about the number of failed pregnancies and unusually large progeny which appear to be resulting from Roslin's nuclear transfer experiments to date. In December 1998, the UK Farm Animal Welfare Council wisely recommended a moratorium on nuclear transfer cloning in commercial agriculture while these problems are investigated. While the suffering is not so great as to put a stop to the research, it is clearly necessary to understand the causes and establish whether the problems can be prevented, before the methods could be allowed for more general use. If after a reasonable time there seemed little prospect doing so, however, one would doubt whether it was ethical to go any further. This also points to the serious possibility that any attempt at human cloning could be extremely dangerous for both the foetus and the mother, a risk which would be medically unethical, regardless of all the other ethical concerns.

The extension of cloning to mice means that many more animals are likely to be used in research at a time when the trend is to reduce animal use. There is a difficult tension here.

Are There Unjustifiable Uses of Animal Cloning?

The discovery in 1998 that mice can be cloned suddenly opened up much wider possibilities to develop applications in animals and, potentially, humans. It is much easier to work with mice than farm animals, and many more laboratories can now jump on the cloning bandwagon, pushing cloning research forward much faster. This raises a question. What sort of research should it be used for? Roslin's work in sheep cloning has given a new and more powerful way of genetically modifying in animals. It is acceptable to use nuclear transfer cloning for pharmaceutical production in animal milk, but more controversial to extend it to other genetic applications such as modified pigs' hearts for human transplantation or cloned mice as models of human disease. These would need examining on their own merits.

Mixing Animal Species. More problematical still is US research where cow cells have been given the nuclei of sheep, pigs and monkeys and even humans.

There are deep intrinsic objections to this application of nuclear transfer. It violates the integrity of the animal at a very fundamental level far beyond genetic engineering practices, where only one or two genes are changed. There is no justification for such an intervention, regardless of whether the embryo was viable or not.

Cloning for Routine Animal Production. All these examples so far are indirect applications of cloning but serious ethical problems would also arise with applying cloning technology directly in routine animal meat and milk production, to accelerate or side-step natural methods. For many, this would be unjustifiable, quite apart from the welfare concerns. What's the problem, you might ask, since we already intervene so much in nature in animal. If most of our dairy cattle are produced by artificial insemination, where the semen from one select bull can service numerous cows, and embryo transfer extends this further. Isn't cloning just the logical next step?

Animals as supermarket commodities? What should we do with animals? Most of us eat them, but not everyone. Quite a lot of us enjoy them as pets and companions, or watching some of them in the wild. We used to use them to carry and haul for us, until technology made it redundant. But technology is now coming up with other ways of using the creatures we share the planet with, which pose important questions. And whatever use we find for animals, should we clone them so we can do so more efficiently?

One assumption is that the animal kingdom is there for us to use in almost any way scientists dream up or commercial companies see a market, short of inflicting gratuitous pain. The fact that we kill animals to eat them is taken to justify more or less any other use, especially if we can cite human medicine or job creation as goals. On this view, only if they are warm and furry, or primates, do we start to have some qualms, and even then, very selectively.

Many people would disagree. Nature is not ours to do exactly what we like with. On a Christian understanding, all creation owes its existence ultimately to God. This does not mean that we cannot use animals, but it does mean that humans have a duty of care and respect towards them, as creatures which exist firstly for God, and only secondarily may be used by us. Such use must be responsible and with a dignity due to another of God's creatures, and we should hold back from some uses. Is cloning then the point to say "no"?

Greater Restraint Is Needed

The suggestion that cloning is justified because we already intervene so much in animals can be an excuse for looking properly at the case in point. It also begs the question about what we are already doing. There are a number of techniques in regular use on farm animals which are ethically borderline, which illustrates a general problem. Both biotechnology and industrial production methods in agriculture carry over certain assumptions from the sphere of chemistry or engineering which, though scientifically applicable to animals, may not always be morally applicable to them. We see this in the animal welfare problems which conventional selective breeding has caused in some cases, such as poultry, from applying production logic too far.

Against that context, if anything, what is called for is greater restraint. Why would we want to clone meat-producing animals, anyway? Most of the suggested applications relate to production improvements rather than clear human or animal benefits. To create genetic replica animals routinely, for the sake of production convenience for the supermarket would be to apply a model derived from factory mass production too far into the realm of living creatures. In the limit, to manipulate animals to be born, grow and reach maturity for sale and slaughter at exactly the time we want them, to suit production schedules suggests one step too far in turning animals into mere commodities.

Chapter 3

Is Hunting Ethical?

The Ethics of Hunting: An Overview

by Ann S. Causey

About the author: *Ann S. Causey teaches philosophy at Auburn University in Alabama.*

The struggling fawn suddenly went limp in my arms. Panicked, I told my husband to pull the feeding tube out of her stomach. Sandy, as we called her, had by now quit breathing. I held her head down and slapped her back in an attempt to unblock her trachea. I turned her over in my arms and my husband placed his mouth over her muzzle. While he began blowing air into her lungs, I started squeezing her chest as a CPR course had taught me to do for human infants in cardiac arrest. After a minute or so I felt her chest for a pulse. Nothing at first, then, unmistakably, four weak beats in rapid succession. "She's alive! Keep breathing for her." My husband continued his efforts. I kept working her chest and began talking to her. "Come on Sandy, start breathing. Don't die."

Mourning Death

My husband, a wildlife biologist, and I had nursed over two dozen white-tailed deer fawns that summer. Most of the animals were in poor shape when we got them. People around the state found them, some actually orphaned, others mistakenly thought to be abandoned and "saved" by folks with good intentions. After two or three days of round-the-clock feedings, they would call their county conservation officer, who would in turn call us.

All the animals we raised required and received care and patience. We came to know each one as an individual with unique and often peculiar, but always endearing, personality traits and behavior patterns. Most lived to become healthy adults. Each fatality, no matter how merciful for the fawn, was a tragic loss for us. Though reason said these few fawns were not significant in the biological scheme of things, that all would have died anyway had we not intervened, we mourned each and every death.

The afternoon that Sandy died was not a convenient one for mourning. We

Reprinted from Ann S. Causey, "What's the Problem with Hunting?" *Orion,* Winter 1996, by permission of the author.

were going to a game supper that evening, and through my tears I made a marinade for the roast we had taken out to thaw. While the meat smoked over charcoal and hickory, we brooded over Sandy's death and tried to console each other.

At the supper, our moods brightened as our roast was quickly gobbled up, and we swelled a bit with pride when several guests declared that our roast was the best venison they'd ever eaten. We positively glowed. The best venison. The best deer meat. Part of an animal my husband, an avid hunter, had willfully killed and I had gratefully butchered, wrapped and frozen—a deer who once was a fawn, a unique individual with a personality and a will to live, an animal just like Sandy.

The Inherent Contradiction

If any one word characterizes the feelings of most people when they reflect on the morality of killing an animal for sport, that word is *ambivalence.* Thoughtful hunters concede the apparent contradiction between killing for sport and maintaining a reverence for life. Yet I know of few hunters who do not claim to have a deep reverence for nature and for all life, including the lives of the animals they seek to kill. It seems that this contradiction, inherent in hunting and increasingly the focus of hunting/antihunting debates, lies at the core of the moral conundrum of hunting. How can anyone both revere life and seek to extinguish it in pursuit of recreation?

None who know me or my lifestyle would label me "antihunting." Unwilling to either become a vegetarian or to support factory farming by regularly purchasing its products, most of the meat in my diet is game. I extol the virtues of the ethical hunter. I wax eloquent on the minimum environmental impact of hunters compared to that of other human omnivores, their intimate knowledge of natural systems, and their rightful claim to having practiced bioregionalism long before it became a buzzword. Many's the time I've defended hunting from the attacks of those who see all hunters as bloodthirsty, knuckle-dragging rednecks.

> *"If any one word characterizes the feelings of most people when they reflect on the morality of killing an animal for sport, that word is* ambivalence.*"*

Oddly, though, I have on recent occasion found myself with a new set of allies: the antihunters. My alliance with these folks has until now been uneasy and highly selective; my antihunting sentiments had been limited to opposing such blatantly unethical behavior as Big Buck contests, Coon Hunt for Christ rallies, and bumper stickers proclaiming that "Happiness Is a Warm Gutpile." Such crude displays, however, like racism and sexism, are increasingly unacceptable. Today, my tenuous occasional alliance with the antihunters has subtler and deeper roots. It stems, I believe, from my disappointment with the responses of many hunters and wildlife managers to the moral questions concerning hunting.

Ethics and Morals

Before looking into those moral questions, I would like to point out some errors—common to ethical reasoning and to the current debate—that hunters should avoid. The first is that of confusing prudence with morality. Prudence consists of acting with one's overall best interests in mind, whereas morality sometimes requires that we sacrifice self-interest in the service of a greater good. While thorough knowledge is all that is required to make prudent decisions, the making of a moral decision involves something more: conscience. Ethical hunters do not mindlessly follow rules and lobby for regulations that serve their interests; rather, they follow their consciences, sometimes setting their own interests aside. Guided by conscience, ethics gives us something to aim for beyond self-gratification.

Another important distinction is that of legality and morality. While many immoral activities are prohibited by law, not all behavior that is within the law can be considered ethical. The politician caught in a conflict of interest who claims moral innocence because he has broken no laws rarely convinces us. Nor should hunters assume that whatever the game laws allow or tradition supports is morally acceptable. The ethical hunter is obligated to evaluate the laws and traditions in light of his or her own moral sense. Conscience is not created by decree or consensus; morality is not determined by legality or tradition.

> *"Ethical hunters do not mindlessly follow rules and lobby for regulations that serve their interests; rather, they follow their consciences."*

One other point concerning the current debate deserves mention. It is all too tempting for hunters to dismiss the concerns of antihunters by questioning their motives and credentials instead of giving serious consideration to the questions they raise. Ethical hunters do themselves no favors by hurling taunts at their opponents. Hunters must stop their displacement behavior and begin to undertake the processes of deliberation and soul-searching that these moral questions demand.

Can Data Answer Moral Questions?

The most striking feature of the current debate is the debaters' vastly different understanding of the question, *Is hunting a morally acceptable activity?* Those who support hunting usually respond to this question by citing data. They enumerate the number of acres protected by hunting-generated funds; how many game populations increased due to management; how much the economy is stimulated by hunting; how effectively modern game laws satisfy the interests of the hunting community today while assuring surpluses of harvestable animals for the future. And, they assure the public that hunters, more than most citizens, care deeply about ecosystem integrity.

The above statements may be perfectly true. They also are almost totally irrelevant to the question at hand, for the antihunters are *not* asking whether hunting is an effective management tool, whether it is economically advisable, or whether hunters love and appreciate nature. Instead, they are asking, "Is it ethical to kill animals for sport? Are any forms of hunting morally right?" The hunter says yes; the antihunter says no, and yet they are answering entirely different questions. The hunter answers, with data, what he perceives as a question about utility and prudence; his opponent, though, has intended to ask a question about morality, about human responsibilities and values. It is as if one asked what day it is and the other responded by giving the time. While the answer may be correct, it is meaningless in the context of the question asked.

> *"Animal welfare proponents . . . are primarily concerned about the suffering and death inflicted on hunted animals and about the motives and attitudes of those who hunt."*

Moral debates are not debates about facts; they are debates about values. And, while factual reality certainly helps to shape our values, moral controversies cannot be resolved by examination of data or by appeal to scientific studies. That is why they are moral and not empirical questions in the first place.

Motives and Attitudes

An obsession with "sound, objective science" has led many hunting proponents to avoid the crucial issues, and in so doing fuel the fires of the antihunting movement. Animal welfare proponents and the general public are primarily concerned about the suffering and death inflicted on hunted animals and about the motives and attitudes of those who hunt. They are offended by references to game animals as "resources." They are angered by the sterile language and, by implication, the emotionally sterile attitudes of those who speak of "culling," "controlling," and "managing" animals for "maximum sustained yield." They are outraged by those who cite habitat protection and human satisfaction data while totally disregarding the interests of the sentient beings who occupy that habitat and who, primarily through their deaths, satisfy human interests. To them, these are not mere resources. They are living, feeling beings, individuals subject to fear and pain, with lives and interests independent of those of humans. Antihunters insist that nontrivial reasons be given for intentional human-inflicted injuries and deaths, or that these injuries and deaths be stopped. This is, in my view, an eminently reasonable request.

Defenders of hunting acknowledge that hunters feel an obligation to give back more than they take, and that they do. Granted, the overall benefits to humans and other species that accrue from hunting may outweigh the costs to the hunted. Nevertheless, this utilitarian calculation fails to provide adequate moral justification for hunting. Just as to kill a person but compensate the family does not constitute genuine reciprocation, the hunter and wildlife manager cannot give back anything to an animal once it is dead. Antihunters want to know why certain sentient creatures should be sacrificed so that sometimes apparently frivolous benefits may accrue to others: Should animals die to feed humans? To clothe them? To decorate their bodies and den walls? To provide entertainment and sport? It is a question of justice.

It does not suffice to charge opponents of hunting with scientific ignorance or biological naïveté, as these are not questions of science. Nor will charges of emotionalism quiet these accusers, since the emotions play an integral, valid part in value judgments and moral development. Anyway, both groups have members who are guided by their hearts, their minds, or both. Neither side has a monopoly on hypocrisy, zealotry, narrow-mindedness, or irrationalism. Opposition to hunting is based in large part on legitimate philosophical views.

The Thoughtful Hunter's Quarry

It has been said that hunting is the most uncivilized and primitive activity in which a modern person can legally engage. Therein lies ammunition for the biggest guns in the antihunters' arsenal; therein also lies its appeal to the hunter and the source of approval by many sympathetic nonhunters. Hunting is one of the few activities that allows an individual to participate directly in the life and death cycles on which all natural systems depend. The skilled hunter's ecological knowledge is holistic and realistic and involves all the senses. An ethical relationship with wildlife relies on an appreciation of ecosystems, of natural processes. Such an appreciation is gained through familiarity, over time, with effort, curiosity, humility, and respect. These are the lessons that hunting teaches its better students.

Ethical hunters have not only resisted the creeping alienation between humans and the outdoors, they have fought to resist the growing alienation between humans and the "nature" each of us carries within. Hunters celebrate their evolutionary heritage and stubbornly refuse to be stripped of their atavistic urges. As Aldo Leopold says in *A Sand County Almanac,* hunting in most forms maintains a valuable element in the cultural heritage of all peoples. But Leopold did not give a blanket stamp of moral approval to hunting, nor should we. Leopold recognized that some forms of hunting are not only not morally enriching, but are potentially morally depleting. We must ask ourselves, *what* forms of hunting *are* valid?

> *"Opposition to hunting is based in large part on legitimate philosophical views."*

Consider the following questions. To what extent is shooting an animal over bait, or out of a tree at close range after it was chased up there by a dog, a morally enriching act? Can shooting a captive animal enhance one's understanding of natural processes? Does a safari to shoot animals located for you by a guide honor your cultural heritage? Does killing an animal in order to obtain a

101

trophy demonstrate reverence? Which forms of hunting are nontrivial, meaningful, ecologically sound, and morally enriching?

Questions over Hunting Practices

All who hunt or support hunting must ask themselves the following: Does ignoring, downplaying, or denying the wounding rate in hunting, rather than taking all available measures to lower it, demonstrate reverence for life? Does lobbying for continued hunting of species whose populations are threatened or of uncertain status exemplify ecological awareness and concern? What about the hunting community's continued opposition to listing or upgrading any species in CITES (Convention on International Trade in Endangered Species) appendices if that species holds actual or potential value as a game animal? Is the continued hunting of some declining waterfowl populations, the aerial killing of wolves in Alaska, or the setting of hunting seasons that in some areas may sentence to slow death the orphaned offspring of their legally killed lactating mothers, consistent with management *by* hunters, or does it instead verify the anti-hunters' charges of management primarily *for* hunters?

These are only some of the questions around which the battle over hunting is taking shape. These questions and others have aroused fears, indignation, defensiveness, and denial. However, no proponent of ethical hunting has anything to fear from the questions. These are questions we hunters should have been asking ourselves, and answering, all along. The real threat comes not from outside criticism, but from the hunting community's mistaken belief that it must defend and protect *all* forms of hunting. Hunting is best viewed as a privilege, not a right. To protect the privilege of morally responsible hunting, the hunting community itself must attack and abolish the unacceptable acts, policies, and attitudes that threaten hunting as a gangrenous limb threatens the whole body.

> *"Hunting is one of the few activities that allows an individual to participate directly in the life and death cycles on which all natural systems depend."*

A Reverence for Life?

The battle cry "Reverence for Life" has been used by both sides, at times with disturbing irony. Cleveland Amory, founder of the Fund for Animals, described in the June 1992 issue of *Sierra* the ideal world he would create if he were appointed its ruler: "All animals will not only be not shot, they will be protected—not only from people but as much as possible from each other. Prey will be separated from predator, and there will be no overpopulation or starvation because all will be controlled by sterilization or implant." A reverence for life? Only if you accept the unecological concept of life as a characteristic of individuals rather than systems. On the other hand, not all who hunt

102

can legitimately claim to hold a reverence for life. In a video titled *Down to Earth,* a contemporary rock star and self-proclaimed "gut pile addict" exhorts his protégés to "whack 'em, stack 'em and pack 'em." After showing a rapid sequence of animals being hit by his arrows, the "master whacker" kneels and sarcastically asks for "a moment of silence" while the viewer sees slow-motion replays of the hits, including sickening footage of animals that clearly are gut shot or sloppily wounded. Such behavior demon-

> *"The real threat comes not from outside criticism, but from the hunting community's mistaken belief that it must defend and protect all forms of hunting."*

strates shocking irreverence and hubris. The hunter walks a fine line between profundity and profanity, and must condemn practices and attitudes that trivialize and desecrate hunting.

To be ethical, we must both act and think ethically. The hunting community has responded to its critics by trying to clean up its act. We less frequently see dead animals used as hood ornaments; those who wound more animals than they kill and recover are more reluctant nowadays to reveal it; and hunters avoid the term "sport." What's needed, though, for ethical hunting to flourish, is not just a change of appearance or vocabulary, but a change of mindset, a deepening of values. There are morally repugnant forms of hunting that are rightfully under attack. Hunters can successfully defend them only by sacrificing their intellectual and moral integrity. Hunters must reexamine and, if appropriate, give up some of what they now hold dear—not just because doing so is expedient, but because it is right. As T.S. Eliot, quoted by Martin Luther King Jr. in his "Letter from Birmingham Jail," reminds us: The last temptation is the greatest treason: To do the right deed for the wrong reason.

Is Hunting Ethical?

Can anyone give us a final answer to the question, "Is hunting ethical?" No. For one thing, the question, and thus its answer, depends heavily on how one defines "hunting." There are innumerable activities that go by this term, yet many are so different from one another that they scarcely qualify for the same appellation. More importantly, two morally mature people may ponder the same ethical dilemma and come to opposite and equally valid conclusions. The concept of ethical hunting is as hard to pin down as the definition of the virtuous person. Hunting proponents do not seek to impose a particular lifestyle, morality, or spirituality on all citizens; they *do* wish to preserve a variety of choices concerning responsible human recreation and engagement with nature. It is highly doubtful that any one system—whether it be "boutique" hunting, vegetarianism, or modern factory farming—is an adequate way to meet the ethical challenges of food procurement and human/nonhuman relationships in our diverse culture and burgeoning population.

The value of ethics lies not so much in the answers, as in the process of deep deliberation of moral issues. To offer valid, consistent *moral* arguments in support of one's conclusions calls for a level of soul-searching and critical thinking largely lacking on both sides of the current debate.

The Chinese have a wonderful term, *wei chi,* that combines two concepts: crisis . . . and opportunity. The term conveys the belief that every crisis presents a unique opportunity. The hunting community today faces its greatest crisis ever and, therein, its greatest opportunity—the opportunity for change, for moral and spiritual growth.

Hunting Is Ethical

by Lark Ritchie and Brian Douglas Ritchie

About the authors: *Lark Ritchie is a systems analyst and a hunting, fishing, and nature guide. Brian Douglas Ritchie is a software developer and a hunting guide.*

As a hunter, a hunting guide and a status Native American (read Cree Indian, Born, Chapleau, Ontario, Canada), I have been repeatedly challenged by the moral and ethical questions concerning hunting. Over some 40 years, I continue to arrive at a conclusion that hunting (and providing hunts for others) is a morally and ethically acceptable practice. Although a personal view, it is one I ask you to consider.

Providing a Definition

A clear argument for or against any issue requires definition of terms, and hunting, as defined in the dictionary, means to pursue game with the intent of capturing or killing. I add a further refinement: that of killing as an act of predation; as a means to food.

This refined definition makes it clear that we are concerned with hunting to kill; an act of predation, in which the game is consumed. While hunting to capture an animal may be another question for the moralists, it is distinctly set apart from the pursuit of game ending in death. Thus, I reformulate the question: "Is it morally acceptable to hunt and kill an animal as an act of predation?" I see three major perspectives: the issue of rights, the social argument, and the vegetarian arguments.

The animal rights activist and the anti-hunter offer us at least these three challenges as hunters. Each are briefly considered .

The Concept of Animal Rights

One argument touted is that when hunters kill an animal, they violate its right to life. This statement is logically and legally faulty.

The concept of rights is a legal principle, and in that legal sense, is not presently recognized for all creatures. Moreover, rights are an amorphous human concept developed within a culture and differ considerably, depending on the culture and society, and only defined and upheld within the laws and social conventions of a particular society.

When we leave this legal view, we enter an arena governed by personal, emotional and philosophical complications where no commonly accepted conventions dictate how we act or what is right. To use the concept of rights when speaking of animals means we must have laws in place under which we can make judgements. Without those laws we must face our own moral structures, and those of others.

> *"Hunting . . . is a morally and ethically acceptable practice."*

These legal, moral and philosophical details are complex, and a small example demonstrates the underlying reasoning.

When a wolf stalks and kills a rabbit, it is senseless to say that the wolf has violated the rabbit's right to life and freedom. In the wilderness there are no immoral acts or violation of rights since all events are by definition "natural." We can accept that in this event, there is no question of rights, other than a personal view. The event may be considered acceptable in that death is a part of natural wilderness life. Therefore the death of an animal caused by a hunter can only be examined in the human social or personal context.

Animals Do Not Have Legal Rights

My conclusion? In the present day, and in this country, legal rights are not granted to animals, hence there is no legal argument for, or against, taking the life of an animal, other than those laws and regulations governing hunting and humane practices. This may not be agreeable to some, but our system of laws are how we define our exact ways and behaviours. Without a law, we have to act within our own personal moral scope. And in hunting, we must bring ourselves to that moral mirror. Another challenge to the hunter is "An entire international industry is designed to raise domestic animals for consumption. You don't need to hunt."

This statement skirts the moral issue of killing and animal death and is, in effect, illogical when discussing predatory hunting. It actually accepts the death of animals, and makes a distinction only between domestic animals and wilderness animals.

Furthermore, it embeds a general and socially accepted assumption within; we are omnivores and by nature, part of our natural diet is the meat from animals, and eating meat is acceptable, and therefore killing of an animal is acceptable.

My conclusion? If the killing of a domestic chicken is considered acceptable, then we must also accept the killing of a bear, moose, grouse or trout as acceptable. With that acceptance, we are left to the present laws and to our personal choices and morals.What truly matters in the moral and ethical sense is motive and attitude.

A third challenge we hear today is the argument that we should not eat meat. To personally oppose the killing of any animal for consumption, one must profess himself a vegetarian, and when one is, then, and only then, is one remotely justified to reject animal death by himself or others. However, the ratio of vegetarian (or herbivore) human beings to non-vegetarians in our population is quite low, and although a minority has the right to an opinion and way of life, reciprocally, we have the right to hold our own opinions and way of life. The debate in this area will no doubt continue, until resolved by an act of legislation.

My conclusion? Realistically, one would have to accept that man is, either divinely, naturally or biologically designed to eat meat, as well as plants. Again we enter morals and ethics.

Summarizing: legally, animals are viewed differently when we speak of rights; objectively, there is no difference between a death of a domestic or wild animal; and socially, the majority of us accept the consumption of animals as food. It renders to moral and ethical issues.

> *"Because we are rational beings, we can make a free and informed choice to kill or not kill."*

The argument defending hunting and more generally, animal death, can be stated in one sentence. "People are naturally omnivorous and therefore it is natural for people to kill animals for consumption." Further, the act of predation (hunting) is no more than a variation on the more efficient practice of animal husbandry and subsequent killing for human consumption.

While this argument is simply stated, the moral implications are far reaching. The fact that man no longer considers himself apart from nature seriously complicates the matter.

Restrictions on Hunters

While it is not immoral for a wolf to kill a rabbit, even if it is the last one of the species, I consider it immoral for a hunter to knowingly threaten the sustainability of, or decimate a species.

Because we are rational beings, we can make a free and informed choice to kill or not kill the rabbit, where the wolf simply acts on instinct.

This ability to rationalize places a personal restriction and responsibility on the hunter to not knowingly deplete a species beyond a natural sustainable level. He or she must be an active part of a responsible resource management system. This implies that we adhere to high personal principles as well as legislated fish and game laws which, in terms of limits, are designed to maintain natural population levels.

A second restriction in the pro-hunting argument is that we may only kill animals as an act of predation (for food). While this argument does not seemingly condone sport or trophy hunting, it does not necessarily mean that one can't kill without eating the meat personally. In nature, animal mothers (and in the case of wolves, fathers) often kill to provide food for their young. The concept of killing to provide food for another is a natural occurrence. A suitable conclusion is that we are justified morally [to] hunt to provide food for others. However, to take more than that due a family would lead me to question the motives of the particular person.

A third restriction to the argument deals with motive. It is important that the motive of the hunt or the kill be an internal one. I maintain that there are two types of people who kill wilderness animals. I class them as internally motivated hunters and externally motivated killers. (I have been using these concepts since 1983: others have termed the same as 'intrinsically and extrinsically motivated.')

Internal and External Motivations

The basis of the hunting experience for the internally motivated, responsible hunter is the realization that he has met the challenges of the wilderness experience: hunting, killing and providing food for himself and others. He may also honour his animal by investing in the costs for a taxidermist to provide a memento of the experience. This in itself is not wrong.

The externally motivated killer, on the other hand, assumes that he is recognized more highly by others because of what he has done, interpreting the act of killing as symbolic of status and prowess. And, although very subjective on my part, I do not respect or condone the actions of this type of individual.

There is another sub-class within the externally motivated killers, the most dangerous of all, and these definitely should not be identified as hunters. I classify him or her as unthinking and opportunistic. He or she is the person who has no awareness of, or respect for, the animal pursued. This is the person who considers the case of two-four [Canadian colloquialism for a case of twenty-four bottles of beer] as part of essential hunting equipment, the person who risks the 200 yard shot, or the person who utters such terrible unfeeling words such as "that sucker" when recounting the experience. I personally do not respect such a person. The animal deserves to be honoured. As with the family dog who is humanely put down, or as with the chicken destined for the table, this should be done quickly, with respect, and with a minimum of pain. To achieve this objective, there is no moral argument for why an efficient tool should not be used to dispatch the animal. In fact, it is a legal requirement and strictly defined in our fish and game act.

> *"Hunting arose from natural predation and for many responsible people, is carried on as a tradition."*

Hunting Can Be an Important Experience

None of these ideas implies that we should not hunt for pleasure, as in the group experience. Hunting arose from natural predation and, for many responsible people, is carried on as a tradition. In earlier times, when a hunter killed an animal, there was rejoicing because he provided food for his family or tribe. There is, undeniably, a sense of pleasure and personal achievement and fulfilling tradition in such activity.

Therefore, there is a part of hunting which has developed into a social celebration in which one spends time with friends, talking, listening and learning. This is what I feel is the driving force for most true and honest hunters, what serious hunters desire to pass to their children, and is definitely the reason that I still hunt and provide hunting experiences.

There is an experience gained, even without a kill, that is almost beyond description. One realizes it at dusk, sitting around a late night fire, talking with new friends or maybe much later when one returns to regular and routine life. At many points a responsible hunter grows from the experience.

Serious hunters must be able to profess these thoughts clearly to make a distinction between themselves, the externally motivated hunter, and the unthinking opportunist who cares little for the game she or he encounters.

Hunting Keeps the Wildlife Population in Check

by Geoffrey Norman

About the author: *Geoffrey Norman is an editor-at-large for* Forbes FYI.

The white-tail is, generally speaking, what most people have in mind when they think of deer. It ranges across most of the United States but is concentrated most heavily east of the Mississippi. Wildlife biologists estimate that there are considerably more white-tail in North America now than there were when the first Europeans arrived. And there is no question that deer are vastly more numerous than they were twenty, thirty, fifty, or a hundred years ago. I can remember hunting deer in Alabama in the fifties with little hope of success. In those days, if a hunter killed a deer he could almost count on getting his picture in the local paper. The few deer left in the state lived back in the river bottoms, mostly, and they were hard to hunt. The season was short. The limit was one antlered buck per hunter.

A Population Explosion

Today, Alabama is thick with deer. The hunting season lasts several months, and there are so many special seasons—archery seasons and muzzle-loading seasons, for instance—that it is hard to know exactly how many deer a hunter can legally kill. A lot more than a hundred, but who's counting?

The deer, in the minds of many people, is an embodiment of wild, unsullied nature; the wary, graceful Bambi living nobly in the deep, primeval woods until man the killer and corrupter arrives and, naturally, shoots his mom.

The Bambi myth has much, if not all, of it wrong. Deer do not do so well in mature forests. In fact, unlike some species that truly are creatures of the wild and cannot exist in close proximity to man—the grizzly bear, for instance—the deer actually does better close to civilization. The deer population has exploded not so much in spite of man but because of him and his works—the crops he planted, the predators he exterminated, the logging he did, and the lawns and golf courses he built. Far from being a creature of the deep, primitive woods, the white-tail is a contented suburbanite. Deer are more abundant in West-chester County New York, than in the Adirondacks, the vast park with its thousands of acres of wilderness.

And this situation has led to some interesting developments. In America, there is just no escaping the deep cultural antagonisms between traditionalists and the new elites. They show themselves in loud national arguments over everything from abortion to movies to school choice to . . . well, even what to do about the common white-tail deer. One side believes in protecting every single deer; the other in killing just as many as necessary.

Deer Season

The deer is probably the archetypical American game animal, and the deer hunt is a kind of cultural ritual in many parts of the country. I can remember getting my face smeared, when I was 12 years old, with the blood of the first deer I ever killed. I killed that deer in an Alabama swamp very much like the big, epic woods where Ike McCaslin came of age in William Faulkner's *The Bear*, and I can still remember feeling some of the same mute and faintly melancholy awe that Ike experienced. It was one of the big days of my life.

In places like Pennsylvania and Michigan opening day is very close to a state holiday. Men who have dreamed of not much else for the last year go out into the woods wearing their hunter orange (which, by law, has replaced the traditional red and black) and carrying their Winchesters, Rugers, and Remingtons. They might stay in

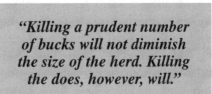

"Killing a prudent number of bucks will not diminish the size of the herd. Killing the does, however, will."

camps with a bunch of their buddies, or belong to clubs that have been in existence for several generations. These are generally men-only clubs, and some are dedicated to tall talk and heavy drinking more than serious hunting. Memberships are highly coveted.

In Vermont, where I now live, the deer season is treated with something close to reverence. There are all sorts of special community events, such as pancake breakfasts and game suppers to raise money for charity, built around the deer season. The local papers still run pictures of hunters standing next to a hanging buck. The typical greeting between men is a laconic, "Get yours yet?" And as newcomers to the state quickly find out, during deer season you cannot get a plumber to come fix a leaking faucet or a mechanic to work on your transmission. All the working men are out in the woods. Even my doctor takes opening day off and goes hunting.

Individuals Versus Populations

Vermont, of course, is within easy driving range of Boston and New York, and every year more people come to the state with the money and the attitudes they have accumulated in and around those places. They are opposed to hunting and they post their land. When they see deer struggling through the winter snow covering their yards, they take pity, and they feed them. Typically, they will put out hay which, according to biologists, can contain microbes that will explode a deer's stomach. Even if the feed put out by these compassionate people is okay (and they have been known to offer deer a peanut-butter sandwich), the simple act of feeding them is not. For one thing, it concentrates the

> *"In the absence of hunting . . . it does not take long for the deer population to explode."*

deer in places where they are vulnerable to what has become their most lethal predator—now that the wolves and mountain lions are gone—the domestic dog. Furthermore, death by starvation is what necessarily happens to some deer, every winter, in Vermont. Those deer become food for other species. The deer that die are, generally speaking, the older bucks who are past their prime and the weak fawns. The die-off keeps the herd strong. In the minds of these new Vermonters, however, it is the individual deer that is important. Hunters and people who work with deer, on the other hand, think in terms of populations. One tends to anthropomorphize the deer; the other considers deer a resource.

Where there is a strong, rural hunting tradition, the widespread increase in the number of deer is no problem. Most people, especially hunters, consider it good news since the wildlife departments establish longer hunting seasons and larger bag limits and will even do things to encourage the killing of females. Hunters traditionally want to kill bucks; partly for reasons of status—bucks are bigger, more wary, and they have those antlers—and partly for reasons having to do with conservation. Bucks will mate with as many does as they can, so if you kill one buck, another will move into his territory and impregnate the does there. Killing a prudent number of bucks will not diminish the size of the herd. Killing the does, however, will. In New Jersey, for instance, the regulations encourage the killing not of Bambi, who was a young buck, but of his mother.

But in the absence of hunting, with each doe typically bearing twins, and sometimes triplets, in the fall of the year, it does not take long for the deer population to explode.

A Danger to Humans

In some suburbs around New York, Washington, and other eastern cities, the deer are so numerous they have become not just pests but an outright danger to humans. Deer are largely nocturnal creatures and they act unpredictably around automobiles. They have a way of darting out of the shadows into the path of a car at night, giving the driver no chance to stop or swerve. The deer are usually killed in the resulting collisions and the cars are damaged. Drivers are sometimes injured and, occasionally, killed.

In Montgomery County, outside Washington, D.C., there were 782 automobile accidents involving deer in 1992. By 1995, the number was up to 1,244. Along some highways in New York and Pennsylvania, where the road crews have planted grasses the deer like to eat, the carcasses are everywhere, swarmed over by crows getting fat on the carrion. Princeton, New Jersey, passed a "no firearms discharge" ordinance back in the seventies and saw a 600 percent increase in the number of collisions between deer and vehicles. Lately, the town has begun to allow some hunting again.

Suburban deer are more than traffic hazards. They are very versatile eaters, with a special fondness for garden vegetables and ornamental plantings. People who have spent weeks putting in a garden often find that they are sharing it with the deer who come in at night. It does not take a few hungry deer very long to devastate a lovingly tended garden or a yard that has been carefully and expensively landscaped.

Last fall, when a friend who owns property in one of the New Jersey suburbs of New York learned that I like to hunt deer with a bow and arrow, he invited me down. Practically begged me. "Please come. I'll put you up. I'll show you the trails they use. You can kill as many as you want. Kill them all, if you can. Last winter, they ate $15,000 worth of landscaping."

The man was no hunter. The first year he owned the property, he said, he loved sitting in his living room, looking out the picture window, and seeing a deer, moving across the ground with that wonderful blend of poise and nervousness, stopping now and then to nibble at the tips of some shrub's branches. Now, he hated deer. They were utter pests—"rats with hooves," he called them—who made it impossible to garden or keep up the grounds. His wife would practically rage whenever she saw one.

But if suburban deer are a traffic hazard and a blight on the lawns, gardens, and golf courses of some of the country's more affluent communities, their status as a nuisance animal is made most secure by the fact that they spread disease. Lyme disease, specifically, which is carried by a tick that lives on the deer and will bite humans. The disease is spread by this bite. It causes fatigue and other, more severe symptoms, and can be especially debilitating, even fatal, to people who are very old, very young, or otherwise in poor health. It was difficult to diagnose

> *"Hunting took off . . . and when it did, . . . 'nuisance deer complaints dropped to the lowest level in twelve years.'"*

when it first began showing up, particularly in the Connecticut suburbs, a few years ago. But now, the disease has become so widespread that doctors know to look for it right away. Treatment with antibiotics works but not always. The disease is a bona fide health hazard. There were almost 500 cases reported in Maryland last year, the number growing along with the size of the deer herd.

So if an animal breeds so prolifically that it is a traffic and health hazard as well as an economic and aesthetic nuisance, what do you do?

The answer would seem obvious. And easy. Especially when the animal in question is a game species prized by hunters. You open a hunting season.

Problems with Other Methods of Deer Control

In Westchester County, celebrated rural bedroom community of New York City, the deer population was out of control and the landowners were complaining. A licensed hunter in New York may kill one deer, but the Department of Environmental Conservation (DEC) created a system under which a hunter who had killed a deer in Westchester (with a bow and arrow; rifle hunting would be unsafe in that kind of crowded environment) would be given a permit to take another deer from the county. And, if that second deer was a doe, he could take out a third permit. Hunting took off in Westchester and when it did, according to Kelly Stang of the DEC, "nuisance deer complaints dropped to the lowest level in twelve years."

There had been legal hunting in Westchester for years, however. Not enough hunters had taken advantage of it, and those who had were not killing enough deer. The special permit system changed that. But in communities where there is no legal hunting and there are too many deer, it isn't so easy.

One wonders why not. Can't you just open a hunting season?

"No," says Stang, "if enough people are against hunting, even when the deer are clearly out of control, you just can't get it done."

She cites the example of a community outside of Rochester that found itself infested with deer. So many people were opposed to hunting that the community was forced to come up with an alternative solution: something called "bait and shoot." Which is just about what it sounds like. Feed is put out to lure the deer to a spot where off-duty policemen and other officially sanctioned shooters are paid to kill them. The killing of deer is better and cleaner, presumably, if it is done by a bureaucrat. This solution recalls Lord Macaulay's famous line about how "the Puritan hated bear-baiting, not because it gave pain to the bear but because it gave pleasure to the spectators."

Still, that community is doing something. In other suburban communities, there has been a lot of talk but very little action. People are concerned but unwilling to bloody their hands. So there is talk of contraceptive programs where does are shot with darts that render them infertile. The problem is that it takes more than one shot, and you have to be able to mark the deer to keep track of which have been shot and which have not. It is unwieldy and expensive and hasn't worked well where it has been tried. It has also been suggested that deer be trapped and moved to more suitable neighborhoods. More suitable, that is, for the residents of the afflicted community. The deer like it just fine where they are. The problem, again, is cost. It is difficult and expensive to trap and move a deer. And sometimes a trapped deer never recovers from the shock and dies of something called "capture myopathy." Besides, there really isn't anyplace where there are too few deer. This is just a case of suburbanites shipping their

114

problems into somebody else's backyard, the way they send their trash and garbage to upstate landfills.

In addition to the talk about sterilization and transferring surplus deer, some communities have even discussed the possibility of bringing wolves back into the ecological mix. Wolves, in the suburbs of Washington and New York. It is almost too wonderful not to try it. The wolves would kill deer, of course. They would also terrorize and kill dogs and cats which is not, one suspects, what the suburbanites have in mind.

Finally, there are some communities that seem resolved to do . . . nothing. The small community of North Haven on Long Island is home to some 600–700 deer. The DEC estimates the optimum population at 60. The town has been browsed bare of vegetation, except where gardens and shrubs are protected by high fences. Drivers routinely collide with deer, and there

> *"For people who hunt, there is a kind of primitive joy in being the top predator."*

are so many carcasses left by the side of the road that the town has made a deal with a local pet cemetery to collect and dispose of the bodies. Some people in the town have had two or three bouts of Lyme disease.

On the occasions when hunting has been tried, local animal-rights people have worked to secure injunctions against the hunts—and when that has failed, they stalked the hunters, banging on pots and pans to alert the deer. Town meetings called to discuss the problem inevitably dissolved into acrimony. The activists believe, simply, that the deer are not the problem.

"Anyone that moves to the country and finds lots of deer shouldn't be surprised," one of them told a reporter. "Maybe we should just shoot anything that gets in our way, huh?"

The Deer Follow Humans

Or, as a *Washington Post* reporter wrote last September, after a harrowing collision with a deer, "Fifty years ago there was no deer problem; it is not the deer who overproliferated, building deer golf courses and low-slung deer ranch houses, and subways to permit deer to live farther and farther away from where they work, destroying the habitat of hapless humans."

The fact, of course, is that the deer follow the humans. The people have not come into some Edenic glen and disturbed the deer; it is the deer who have moved in on an environment created by humans because the pickings there are so easy. Life in the Adirondacks is much harder than life in the Hamptons—for both deer and humans.

But the spirit of the Hamptons is not the spirit of the Adirondacks. If man is descended of hunters, the suburbanites are ashamed of their ancestry. They will not kill for sport—though some of them will pay to have others kill nuisance animals for them—and they will not allow others to kill for sport. They will put up with deer populations that make highway slaughter inevitable before they will allow someone to go into the woods to stalk and kill a wild animal. They will even put up with disease before they will allow the killing of animals. Strange behavior in people who worry obsessively about their health, who are terrified of additives and pesticides, and would rather starve than eat red meat.

For people who hunt, there is a kind of primitive joy in being the top predator. For those who despise hunting, there is a kind of wonderful righteousness in standing up for innocent life. These are views that are fundamentally, almost theologically, in opposition. Even if the deer population is somehow regulated—and it probably will be, by disease or starvation or something—it is hard to imagine any kind of reconciliation between those who look at a deer crossing a highway and see "Bambi," and those who see the same animal and think "venison."

Limited Hunting Will Preserve Endangered Species

by *Economist*

About the author: *The* Economist *is a weekly English newsmagazine.*

An uncivil war is starting in the world of animals and people are having to take sides. In one camp are those who believe that more legal protection is needed to save the world's wildlife; they include fund-raising conservationists in the West, their allies in the media, and government officials almost everywhere. In the other camp are those who believe that greater protection is doomed to fail because it pits wildlife against indigenous people all over the world—be they Masai tribesmen, gamekeepers in Scotland or ranchers in Montana resisting the reintroduction of the wolf. The only hope, pro-hunters maintain, is to allow exploitation, so giving people an incentive to tolerate wild animals in their neighbourhood.

The debate is full of irony, not to say hypocrisy. In many countries, belief in free markets is spreading and confidence in government declining. Wildlife policy, by contrast is commonly moving in the opposite direction—towards stricter regulation. As western animal lovers let their heart-strings and wallets be plucked on behalf of endangered elephants, southern African ecologists are saying that in many places there are too many elephants. Old colonial right-wing whites embrace the cause of native blacks. Left-wing western whites stand accused of neo-imperialism on behalf of wild animals.

In central Asia, as in the Zambezi valley, wildlife is suddenly extremely valuable for its ability to draw well-heeled hunters from the West. The fee to kill a Marco Polo sheep in the high Pamirs now runs to more than $20,000. In Scotland, Britain's Conservative government has, in effect, nationalised the red deer and increased the powers of an agency (the Red Deer Commission) to cull them using helicopters. In the Rockies, the biodiversity of Yellowstone National Park steadily disintegrates as elk numbers climb unchecked. In India the tiger reserves are under great pressure from land-hungry people who object to being eaten.

Conservation Versus Exploitation

Should people manage wildlife? If so, should governments or private landowners do so? When conservation first became a priority in the middle third of the twentieth century, governments responded similarly all over the world by segregating humans from animals. They set aside publicly owned areas for game, drove out the indigenous people and passed laws protecting some species altogether. People and animals were to live in separate homelands. The policy was pursued most vigorously in Africa, where more than 48m hectares (120m acres) have been set aside for wildlife, a higher proportion than in other continents.

The flaws in this were soon apparent. The protected species were resented by local people, especially if they were dangerous (tigers in India) or fond of eating people's livelihoods (hippos in Africa; hen harriers in Scotland). Farmers whose mealies (maize) was destroyed by it viewed the elephant as a six-tonne cockroach. The protected areas, belonging to nobody, attracted corrupt profit-seekers. They also often proved too small to be ecologically viable. And the wildlife outside the parks—which is most of it in most countries—was left with no means of paying its way.

In Africa, where the row between the conserve-wildlife and the exploit-wildlife lobbies rages loudest, there is a startling contrast between the south and the east of the continent. East African countries, led by Kenya, rapidly nationalised their game. By 1976 they had, by and large, banned all hunting. Predictably, a corrupt free-for-all in ivory poaching soon developed, with a widespread but unproven suspicion that the profiteers included high-ups in the government. In 1989, with the charismatic Richard Leakey at their head, Kenyans led a fight to ban the international trade in ivory so as to save their rapidly declining and heavily poached elephant population.

> **"Safari hunting is good for wildlife."**

Another Tack

Southern African countries, led by Zimbabwe, took the opposite route. In 1975 Zimbabwe privatised wildlife, granting effective title to the landowner, though rearguard action by bureaucrats prevented this policy from coming fully into effect until the late 1980s. In 1989, led by Rowan Martin, Zimbabweans opened the fight against a trade ban on ivory, arguing that their elephant numbers were increasing to problem levels and destroying the cover essential for bush buck and other forest animals. The Zimbabweans further argued that profits from ivory and hide provided the best way to reconcile farmers with their damaging and dangerous pachyderm neighbours. The controlled trade in ivory was working relatively well in a relatively uncorrupt country.

Both Mr Leakey and Mr Martin have since lost their jobs and been accused of corruption, though few doubt their innocence. Mr Leakey won the trade ban, but many now think Mr Martin won the argument: Mr Leakey's successor, David Western, is trying to re-establish legal hunting in Kenya. Elephant poaching did fall immediately after the trade ban, but mainly be-

> *"Only in Britain and America do people mistake animal welfare for conservation."*

cause of a sudden and massive flow of aid money from the West to enforce anti-poaching measures. Since then, poaching has been increasing again, and even the Worldwide Fund for Nature (WWF) doubts that the ban has been responsible for a permanent decline in poaching.

The rhino precedent is not encouraging. Trade in rhino horn, which is used mainly to make medicines in East Asia and dagger handles for rich Arab youngbloods, has continued despite nine years of official banning under the Convention on International Trade in Endangered Species (CITES). Since one-third of doctors in South Korea believe there is no substitute for the horn as medicine, they are unlikely to persuade their patients to give up a remedy for their sick children in order to conserve a distant African animal.

An Imprecision

The parallels between elephant ivory and rhino horn are not exact: there are far fewer rhinos and they bring poachers far bigger rewards than do elephants. But they are close enough for many conservationists to have second thoughts about the current strategy for saving the rhino. This consists in trying to suppress poaching mainly in Africa, trying to stamp out the trade and trying to suppress demand in the consumer countries of Yemen, China and points east. It is not working. Black rhinos have declined from 12,753 in 1981 to 2,550 in 1993; white rhinos have increased from 3,561 to 6,784 but mainly in heavily guarded South African national parks.

As poaching increases, with automatic weapons widespread in nearby Mozambique and the South African government pressed by other priorities, nobody is especially hopeful for the white rhinos in South Africa's Kruger National Park. A Mozambican poacher can octuple his average annual income with one kilogram of rhino horn. When it reaches China that kilogram may be 100 times as valuable, at up to $18,000. The incentives driving the trade are huge.

In a book from the Institute of Economic Affairs, *Rhinos: Conservation, Economics and Trade-Offs* (1995), Michael 't Sas-Rolfes suggests a different strategy: legalise the trade again, auction some of the existing stockpiles of horn (many of which are derived from dehorning programmes), use the proceeds to pay for intensive protection measures for wild rhinos and rapidly build up the ranched population of privately owned rhinos whose horns can be painlessly cut off every few years for sale; and so in this way gradually drive down the price for horn (removing the incentive for poachers to take wild animals) and provide a steady income to protect the wild stock.

If this bold strategy is adopted, according to Mr 't Sas-Rolfes, the winners will be the countries that have rhinos, the consumers of rhino products, conservation agencies and their donors, taxpayers who pay for anti-poacher patrols—and rhinos themselves. The losers will be criminals, bureaucrats, politicians and environmental groups. Nearly everybody involved in wildlife in Zimbabwe believes that safari hunting is good for wildlife, and the facts bear them out. Since the partial privatisation of game in 1975, the area of private land devoted to wildlife in the country has almost doubled. Hunting brings money. To spend three weeks in the Zimbabwean or Tanzanian bush killing a lion, an elephant, a leopard and various antelopes will cost you nearly $50,000—not including air fares. For this sort of return a hunter, in a tent, leaves a smaller imprint on the landscape than thousands of tourists in minibuses. When Africans could sell furs, tusks and hides for good money they had less need to get the killing done by foreign rednecks. Now the most auctionable part of an elephant or a leopard is its death.

> *"Pragmatists would pursue [keeping as much land as wild as possible] through the market by providing real incentives for local people to prosper from wildlife."*

For most of Africa, in fact, the choice is less between hunters and tourists than between hunters and farming. For farming is not compatible with African elephants, Cape buffalo or lions. If Africa is to keep wild land, then it must pay its way in competition with cattle ranching. To do so, says David Cumming of the WWF in Harare, landowners need a "full range of options": hunting for meat and hides, sport hunting for fees, and photographic tourism. For an environmentalist, Mr Cumming is refreshingly candid about the need for blood to be spilled. There are no strong feelings against safari hunting in Africa, according to him. Only in Britain and America do people mistake animal welfare for conservation, he says, and to force western values on Africa is cultural imperialism.

Conservation Bwanas

If you give money to the WWF, at least it ends up in pragmatic hands in Africa. New, more radical organisations such as the Environmental Investigation Agency or the United States Humane Society are now big enough to buy considerable influence in Africa. Their dogmatic approach—that all killing is bad for wildlife—is widely resented by those who care about the welfare of the indigenous people.

If the dogmatism of the preservationists is unattractive, so too is the attitude of many hunters, who care little for their targets, let alone for the people in whose countries they hunt. Many tourists want a wilderness experience without a kill. They are increasingly prepared to pay well to be alone, or on foot, with wild animals rather than to watch lions from a queue of minibuses: to hunt with a camera. In the more scenic areas, hunting is already giving way to exclusive, 'non-consumptive' tourism.

The reason is simple enough. However well hunting pays, it cannot compete with tourism—in those few, special localities where tourists can be persuaded to come. Cattle ranching and game ranching both produce roughly about $5 a hectare. Sport hunting can double that yield to $10 a hectare. Exclusive tourism can raise that to $50 a hectare. And mass tourism, Serengeti-style, can double it again to $100 a hectare. Each tourist pays less than a hunter would pay, but the tourists make up for it in numbers. For obvious reasons, only a few hunters can be accommodated at any one time. Hunting preserves—which require minimal capital investment—are an intermediate stage. They will gradually evolve into private national parks.

Everybody in conservation wants as much land as possible kept wild. But dogmatic preservationists would achieve that aim entirely through regulation and public subsidy. Pragmatists would pursue it also through the market by providing real incentives for local people to prosper from wildlife. And those incentives would help the wildlife prosper too.

Hunting Is Immoral

by Fund for Animals

About the author: The Fund for Animals is an animal rights organization founded by author Cleveland Amory in 1967.

Hunting, it is true, is an American tradition—a tradition of killing, crippling, extinction, and ecological destruction. With an arsenal of rifles, shotguns, muzzleloaders, handguns, and bows and arrows, hunters kill more than 200 million animals yearly—crippling, orphaning, and harassing millions more.

The annual death toll in the U.S. includes 42 million mourning doves, 30 million squirrels, 28 million quail, 25 million rabbits, 20 million pheasants, 14 million ducks, 6 million deer, and thousands of geese, bears, moose, elk, antelope, swans, cougars, turkeys, wolves, foxes, coyotes, bobcats, boars, and other woodland creatures.

"Overpopulation" Is a Smokescreen

Q: Don't hunters mercifully shoot animals who would otherwise die a slow death from starvation?

A: When hunters talk about shooting overpopulated animals, they generally refer to white-tailed deer, representing only 3 percent of all the animals killed by hunters. Sport hunters shoot millions of mourning doves, squirrels, rabbits, and waterfowl, and thousands of predators, none of whom any wildlife biologist would claim are overpopulated or need to be hunted.

Even with deer, hunters do not search for starving animals. They either shoot animals at random, or they seek out the strongest and healthiest animals in order to bring home the biggest trophies or largest antlers. Hunters and wildlife agencies are not concerned about reducing deer herds, but rather with increasing the number of targets for hunters and the number of potential hunting license dollars. Thus, they use deer overpopulation as a smokescreen to justify their sport. The New Jersey Division of Fish, Game and Wildlife states that "the deer resource has been managed primarily for the purpose of sport hunting," and hunters readily admit, "deer hunters want more deer and more bucks, period."

Hunters shoot nonnative species such as ring-necked pheasants who are hand-

Reprinted, by permission, from "An Overview of Killing for Sport," a Fund for Animals publication at www.fund.org/facts/overview.html, 1997.

fed and raised in pens and then released into the wild just before hunting season. Even if the pheasants—native to China—survive the hunters' onslaught, they are certain to die of exposure or starvation in the nonnative environment. While hunters claim they save overpopulated animals from starvation, they intentionally breed some species and let them starve to death.

Q: Isn't hunting necessary for wildlife management?

A: Because they make their money primarily from the sale of hunting licenses, the major function of wildlife agencies is not to protect individual animals or biological diversity, but to propagate "game" species for hunters to shoot. State agencies build roads through our wild lands to facilitate hunter access, they pour millions into law enforcement of hunting regulations and hunter education, and they spend millions manipulating habitat by burning and clear-cutting forests to increase the food supply for "game" species such as deer. More food means a larger herd and more animals available as targets. They are out to conserve sport hunting—not wildlife.

For example, Michigan has a "Deer Range Improvement Program" (DRIP) that earmarks $1.50 from each deer hunting license sold into a fund specifically designed to increase deer reproductivity and to maximize sport hunting opportunities. According to a 1975 newspaper report, three years after the DRIP program began, "The DNR's Wildlife Division wants to keep clear-cutting until 1.2 million acres of forest land—more than a third of all of the state-owned forest—have been stripped . . . the wildlife division says it is necessary because a forest managed by nature, instead of by a wildlife division, can support only a fraction of the deer herd needed to provide for half a million hunters." Since that 1975 report, the number of hunters in Michigan has doubled and the state's deer herd has tripled.

> *"Hunters and wildlife agencies are not concerned about reducing deer herds, but rather with increasing the number of targets for hunters and . . . hunting license dollars."*

It is not just deer populations that wildlife agencies are trying to increase to provide more targets for sport hunters. Arizona's management plan for game species specifically states the goal is to "increase" pronghorn antelope and bighorn sheep "populations and provide recreational opportunity to as many individuals as possible," and to "maintain or enhance" cottontail rabbit and quail "hunting opportunity in the State by improving access to existing habitat."

Q: But animals can't feel pain, can they?

A: Scientists, biologists, veterinarians, and people who have lived with dogs, cats, or other animals, know that mammals and birds suffer fear and pain. All of our animal cruelty laws are based on this premise, as are all of the things we teach our children about kindness to animals. The ability of animals to suffer and feel pain is an accepted fact.

According to world-renowned scientists Carl Sagan and Ann Druyan, "From all criteria available to us—the recognizable agony in the cries of wounded animals, for example, including those who usually utter hardly a sound—this question [Do animals suffer?] seems moot. The limbic system in the human brain, known to be responsible for much of the richness of our emotional life, is prominent throughout the mammals. The same drugs that alleviate suffering in humans mitigate the cries and other signs of pain in many other animals. It is unseemly of us, who often behave so unfeelingly toward other animals, to contend that only humans can suffer."

The Brink of Extinction

Q: Do hunters kill threatened or endangered animals?

A: In the past, hunters have helped wipe out dozens of species, such as the passenger pigeon, the Great auk, and the heath hen. They have brought a long list of others, including the bison and the grizzly bear, to the brink of extinction. In fact, when Congress passed the Endangered Species Act (ESA) in 1973, the Senate Committee on Commerce stated, "The two major causes of extinction are hunting and destruction of natural habitat."

While the ESA has slowed killing of imperiled animals considerably, hunters continue to kill threatened and endangered animals every year, either for fun or for failure to identify them properly. In the last few years

> *"There is nothing fair about a chase in which the hunter uses a powerful weapon from the ambush and the victim has no defense except luck."*

alone, hunters have killed gray wolves, bald eagles, grizzly bears, and even such critically endangered animals as Florida panthers. While some species of squirrels and prairie dogs are candidates for listing under the ESA, state wildlife agencies keep them under the guns of sport hunters.

Q: But hunters aren't allowed to kill baby animals, right?

A: Some state wildlife agencies set hunting seasons on bears, squirrels, mountain lions, and other animals during the crucial months when they give birth and nurse their young. When a mother forages for food or searches for prey and she is killed by a sport hunter, her orphaned babies are certain to die of starvation or predation.

No Concept of "Fair Chase"

Q: Don't hunters try to be ethical and follow the concept of fair chase?

A: There is nothing fair about a chase in which the hunter uses a powerful weapon from ambush and the victim has no defense except luck. Furthermore, despite the hunting community's repeated rhetoric of "hunting ethics," they have refused to end repugnant practices that go above and beyond the cruelty inherent in all sport hunting. There is clearly no "fair chase" in many of the ac-

tivities sanctioned by the hunting community, such as:
- "canned hunts," in which tame, exotic animals—from African lions to European boars—are unfair game for fee-paying hunters at private fenced-in shooting preserves;
- "contest kills," from Pennsylvania's pigeon shoots to Colorado's prairie dog shoots, in which shooters use live animals as targets while competing for money and prizes in front of a cheering crowd;
- "wing shooting," in which hunters lure gentle mourning doves to sunflower fields and blast the birds of peace into pieces for nothing more than target practice, leaving more than 20 percent of the birds they shoot crippled and unretrieved;
- "baiting," in which trophy hunters litter public lands with piles of rotten food so they can attract unwitting bears or deer and shoot the feeding animals at point-blank range;
- "hounding," in which trophy hunters unleash packs of radio-collared dogs to chase and tree bears, cougars, raccoons, foxes, bobcats, lynx, and other animals in a high-tech search and destroy mission, and then follow the radio signal on a handheld receptor and shoot the trapped animal off the tree branch.

Q: Isn't hunting okay if they avoid high-tech weapons and use more natural techniques such as bows and arrows?

A: Bowhunting is one of the cruelest forms of hunting because primitive archery equipment wounds more animals than it kills. Dozens of scientific studies indicate that bowhunting yields more than a 50 percent crippling rate. For every animal dragged from the woods, at least one animal is left wounded to suffer—either to bleed to death or to become infested with parasites and diseases.

Q: Don't some people need to hunt for food?

A: A few Native cultures may still hunt to survive, but in the continental U.S. hunting is practiced primarily for sport. Several studies indicate that the average price of venison from deer shot in the woods—after calculating the costs of firearms, ammunition, license fees, travel expenses, etc.—is about $20.00 per pound. Clearly, there are more economic ways to eat than by spending $20.00 per pound for food.

Attempts to Recruit New Hunters

Q: Isn't it natural for humans to hunt?

A: If it were natural to hunt, more people would participate in the activity. Every year, the number of sport hunters decreases because fewer and fewer people are interested in killing animals for sport. According to the U.S. Fish and Wildlife Service, 10 percent of Americans purchased hunting licenses in 1975, approximately 7 percent in 1991, and approximately 5 percent in 1996. Leading researchers in hunting demographics indicate that if current social trends continue, sport hunting will be extinct by the year 2050.

To fight these trends, the U.S. Fish and Wildlife Service and most of our state wildlife agencies sponsor youth recruitment hunts on public land—some for children as young as 5 years old—taking kids into the woods and teaching them to kill. Similarly, most agencies have adopted the "Becoming an Outdoors Woman (BOW)" program in an effort to entice a segment of the population that traditionally has not been welcomed by the hunting fraternity, and thus, to increase sales of hunting licenses, firearms, and even new women's lines of outdoor clothing.

> *"Bowhunting is one of the cruelest forms of hunting because primitive archery equipment wounds more animals that it kills."*

Q: But don't hunters pay the bill for wildlife conservation?

A: When hunters talk about paying money for wildlife conservation, they generally refer to the "Federal Aid in Wildlife Restoration Fund," which Congress created in 1937 when it passed the Pittman-Robertson Act. The fund derives its revenues from an 11 percent excise tax on rifles, shotguns, ammunition, and archery equipment, and a 10 percent excise tax on handguns. Each year, the U.S. Fish and Wildlife Service collects the funds and distributes them to state wildlife agencies based on each state's geographical size and number of licensed hunters.

While hunters claim they foot the entire bill, anyone who purchases firearms or ammunition for activities such as gun collecting, target shooting, and self-protection contributes to the fund. In fact, according to the National Rifle Association there are nearly 70 million gun owners in the U.S., but the U.S. Fish and Wildlife Service reports there are only 14 million hunters.

Sadly, while hunters account for only one-fifth or 20 percent of those contributing to the fund, they benefit from nearly every expenditure of these monies. Of the revenue collected annually, about 25 percent is spent on hunter education, with the remainder spent on administration, research projects on "game" species, and manipulating lands to provide habitat favorable to "game" species—often at the expense of nongame and threatened and endangered species.

Funding Wildlife Programs

Q: What would happen to the animals if hunting ended tomorrow?

A: Realistically, hunting will not end overnight. The animal species that are nongame species have done just fine without sport hunting. Even if hunting did end tomorrow, people who purchase firearms and ammunition for target shooting, gun collecting, or personal protection would still contribute money to the Pittman-Robertson fund. Because the money would not be tied up in hunter education and stocking "game" species, the funds could be better spent on habitat protection and true conservation programs.

While only 5 percent of Americans hunt, more than 40 percent participate in nonconsumptive wildlife recreation, such as bird watching, wildlife photography, hiking, and camping. The loss of revenues from hunting license sales could be made up from other sources, such as a tax on tents, binoculars, and other outdoor equipment. Wildlife watchers spend $28.9 billion every year on their outdoor activities: $16.2 billion for equipment, $9.4 billion on transportation, lodging, and related items, and $3.2 billion on miscellaneous expenses.

Congress may soon consider a Teaming with Wildlife initiative which would levy a federal excise tax on nonconsumptive outdoors equipment. Such a measure would make state wildlife agencies less dependent on the dollars and the desires of sport hunters, and more receptive to the wishes of all their constituents. Missouri, for example, already has a one-tenth of 1 percent sales tax that funds the Missouri Department of Conservation. Every citizen of that state pays for wildlife management, not just the select few who use wildlife as targets.

Q: How can I help stop the war on wildlife?

A: Times are changing and state agencies are beginning to realize they have a growing constituency of nonhunters to whom they need to answer. Several recent studies indicate that 51 to 73 percent of Americans oppose hunting for sport or recreation. You, as a resident of your state, have a voice in how wildlife is treated. Become educated on the issue of hunting, contact your state wildlife agency, attend state wildlife meetings, and get involved in the decision making process.

Trapping Is Cruel and Inhumane

by Camilla Fox

About the author: *Camilla Fox is a staff writer for* Mainstream, *a quarterly publication of the Animal Protection Institute.*

In the National Trappers Association's video *Balancing Nature: Trapping in Today's World,* a fictitious state senator wonders if she should support a new trapping bill. To "get the facts from people who deal with these issues every day," she visits a sheep rancher, a state conservation officer, a wildlife biologist, a trapper, and her veterinarian. Wide-eyed and easily persuaded, the "state senator" blithely accepts the half-truths and distortions told her, and quickly "learns" the wonders of "regulated trapping as a necessary tool to manage wildlife populations." She even concludes that "trappers may be some of our best wildlife advocates."

A Desperate Attempt

Clearly a desperate attempt to combat the decline in the total sale of trapping licenses nationwide and the increasing public disapproval of trapping animals for fur, *Balancing Nature* was created, according to *American Trapper* magazine, "to inform the public, in a professional manner, about the need to manage furbearer populations through responsible, regulated trapping." The video took four years, three title changes, myriad target audience alterations, and more than $100,000 to produce. Tax-supported state wildlife agencies, mandated to conserve and protect the state's wildlife, supplied 60% of the funding. The rest came from state trapping associations.

This "soft sell" video is aimed at target audiences of "urban women ages 25–42, state and federal lawmakers and impressionable youth in 4th–6th grades," those people the trapping and fur industries believe will accept the message that "wildlife populations need to be professionally managed for their benefit and that the recreational and economic value of trapping provides the incentive for this management." Targets designated to receive the video include public

Reprinted from Camilla Fox, "What Trappers Won't Tell You," *Mainstream*, Fall 1997, by permission of the Animal Protection Institute. *Endnotes in the original have been omitted in this reprint.*

schools, universities, state and local libraries, civic groups, League of Women Voters branches, public TV, state Project Wild coordinators, and Community Education Councils.

What's Wrong with This Picture?

Balancing Nature carefully ignores the suffering of animals caught in traps. Instead, the video claims that trapping provides a quick, humane death. But any animal wandering into one of these traps faces terrible pain. Struggling for freedom, she may break bones, tear her flesh, and sever tendons. If she has young waiting for her return she may wring or gnaw off her paw to escape. If she cannot pay the horrible price for escape, she may starve or freeze to death before the trapper returns, or find herself the helpless prey of predators. If she is still alive when the trapper finds her, he will end her life with a blow to her head using a blunt instrument or a gun.

This suffering extends beyond the estimated 4.5 million animals that the 150,000 licensed U.S. trappers report catching for their fur each year. These numbers are misleading. Most state wildlife agencies rely on "fur dealer/buyer reports" to figure actual number of animals trapped in their state. Other states often obtain their data through random telephone or mail surveys, with response rates from 10% to 60%. State wildlife agencies then estimate the total numbers of animals trapped each year from these partial reports.

> *"For every 'target' animal trapped, at least two 'non-target' animals are trapped."*

In an April 1997 letter to API, the chief Furbearer Biologist of the Kansas Department of Wildlife & Parks admits that "numbers presented in these reports do not reflect the total take of each species either. We get a 20% response rate to our survey. Therefore, we infer our numbers based on who sent their surveys back. . . ."

The total numbers of animals state wildlife agencies estimate are trapped and killed do not include such "non-target" animals as cats, dogs, bald and golden eagles, hawks, rare and endangered species, and the "lucky" animals who chew off their paw to limp away on three legs. Dick Randall, a former government-employed trapper, testified before Congress in 1976 that for every "target" animal trapped, *at least* two "non-target" animals are trapped, which means that today the total number of animals trapped and killed each year for the commercial fur trade is closer to 13 million.

"Nature Is Cruel"

Balancing Nature repeats the trappers' argument that nature is cruel, and that trapping provides a quick death for animals who would otherwise die from starvation, exposure, disease or predation.

But cruelty is a human construct. Nature can be harsh and unrelenting, or indifferent, but not cruel. The natural cycle of life and death helps maintain genetic diversity and a strong gene pool in any given species population.

How "humane" are trappers? In *Get Set to Trap,* a publication distributed under various titles by nearly a dozen state wildlife agencies and provided to anyone interested in obtaining a trapping license, trappers are instructed to kill trapped animals with methods deemed inhumane by most agency standards: "Adequate tools are a heavy iron pipe or an axe handle. . . . Most furbearers can be killed by first sharply striking them on the skull. It is highly recommended that the animal be struck two times. . . . To ensure death, pin the head with one foot and stand on the chest of the animal with the other foot for several minutes . . . do not step off of an unconscious animal until it is dead."

> *"Nature can be harsh and unrelenting, or indifferent, but not cruel."*

The December 1996 issue of the *Trapper and Predator Caller,* a trapping trade magazine, instructs how best to kill a trapped fox. "There are several ways used by experienced trappers. I prefer to stun a fox by tapping it on the nose, hard, but not hard enough to draw blood. Quickly put one foot on its neck, to hold it down, and with the other foot press down hard on the chest area. Remain standing on the fox until it is dead which only takes a few minutes."

Many states allow nuisance wildlife control operators (NWCOs) to trap and kill so-called pests—which includes raccoons, skunks, and opossums—in any manner they desire. Some states do not even require that NWCOs have a trapping license. This practice is so unregulated that trappers may drown, poison, and fumigate animals to kill them with no legal restrictions.

Activists have begun to bring public attention to this common but often hidden animal cruelty issue, and to press for laws that would prohibit such inhumane practices. An August 1997 Connecticut law prohibits NWCOs from drowning animals, injecting animals with paint thinner, and using other cruel killing methods.

To argue that death by clubbing or suffocation is somehow more humane than a natural death for an animal is comparable to saying that as humans we should all shoot one another to avoid any pain and suffering we may experience as we grow old and infirm.

No Regulations

Alaska, Michigan, Montana, North Dakota, and Washington have *no regulations* requiring trappers to check their traps *at all.* Approximately 20 states allow animals to suffer in traps from 2 to 4 days. Only Georgia has laws designating how a trapped animal must be killed, in this case requiring that trappers kill all trapped animals with a .22 caliber rimfire rifle.

A number of states have no regulations restricting the types of traps allowed. Trappers may use any type of trap or snare desired, including steel-jaw leghold traps with teeth or serrated edges that prevent "pull outs" or "wring offs" (refer-ring to an animal that has chewed or twisted its own leg off and escaped from the trap on three legs). Few states require or offer any type of trapper education course, so most trappers learn "in the field."

Trappers (and *Balancing Nature*) claim that "only abundant species are trapped," yet an eight-year study in Minnesota found 32 bald eagles "inadver-tently" trapped in leghold traps set to catch other species. Most of the raptors died from the severe injuries caused by the leghold traps.

In March 1997 a U.S. District Judge found that the U.S. Fish and Wildlife Service (USFWS) had "consistently ignored the analysis of its expert biolo-gists" in 1994 to list the Canada Lynx under the Endangered Species Act. The biologists determined that "human activity results in the greatest mortality of lynx, principally through trapping" and that "86% of lynx mortalities was caused by trapping." One study showed that in Montana, where lynx are still legally trapped, "a dramatic decline has been attributed primarily to trapping as a result of the rising value of lynx pelts." Yet in July 1997, the Montana Wildlife Commission proposed allowing trappers to kill more lynx each year. Only a few hundred lynx remain in the lower 48 states, inhabiting small pockets of Maine, Montana, Washington and Idaho.

Besides the Canada Lynx, many furbearing species—including the sea otter, kit fox, wolverine, river otter, marten, and wolf—are now either extinct or en-dangered in a number of states where they were once abundant. Such popula-tion declines can be directly attributed to commercial trapping and hunting of these species in the 1800s and early 1900s.

"Good Management Tool"

Another claim of trappers and wildlife managers is that without trapping, our cities and towns would be overrun with animals. This argument is contrary to management practices of state wildlife agencies, which regulate the trapping and shooting ("taking") of animals so that a large, healthy population will pro-vide trappers and hunters with plenty of targets. A constant supply of healthy furbearing animals whose pelts can be commercially sold means that trappers will continue to buy trapping li-censes each year and put money into the coffers of state wildlife agencies. If population reduction were the aim of these agencies or of trappers, ran-dom trapping of animals would not be considered a viable wildlife man-agement "tool."

> *"Many furbearing species . . . are now either extinct or endangered in a number of states where they were once abundant."*

Nor does trapping help reduce furbearer populations. Many wildlife species have internal biological mechanisms that increase their reproductive rate to compensate for any population decrease caused by external factors.

David Macdonald, a leading authority on the red fox, writes (in *Running with the Fox*), "If the spring population is reduced, the surviving foxes, either through having a greater share of the food supply and/or through the disruption of their social system, will probably produce young at a faster rate; in other words a reduction in numbers of foxes can increase their productivity."

> *"Trapping is anything but an effective wildlife 'management tool.'"*

America's century-long war on coyotes has only helped this resilient, highly intelligent species to prosper throughout North America. Trapped, poisoned, and shot by the hundreds of thousands each year by the federal government in the name of "livestock protection," the coyote has resisted eradication efforts by increasing reproductive rates and litter sizes in the face of persecution. Because the older coyotes are frequently killed, the remaining coyote population will be younger, more inexperienced, and prone to create more "problems" than adult coyotes. Recent research indicates that effectively decreasing the number of coyotes in a specific geographic location would require removing at least 70% of the population. Random trapping only serves to stimulate reproduction and often results in a net increase of individual species in a given population.

Fewer animals competing for the resources of a habitat area means an abundance of food and cover for the remaining individuals. With plentiful resources, the population produces more young per breeding female, more animals survive to maturity, and the population increases.

Trapping is anything but an effective wildlife "management tool."

Trapping Increases Disease

The veterinarian in *Balancing Nature*—who apparently never treated a dog or cat caught in a leghold or other cruel trap—repeats the trappers' argument that trapping helps control the spread of rabies and other diseases. Biologists refuted this claim decades ago. Rabid animals do not travel or eat as much as healthy animals, and therefore are less inclined to wander toward a baited trap. In 1973 the National Academy of Sciences subcommittee on rabies concluded, "Persistent trapping or poisoning campaigns as a means to rabies control should be abolished. There is no evidence that these costly and politically attractive programs reduce either wildlife reservoirs or rabies incidence. The money can be better spent on research, vaccination, compensation to stockmen for losses, education and warning systems."

Today a raccoon rabies epidemic is spreading north and west from its center in West Virginia. The Centers for Disease Control and other authorities attribute this epidemic directly to trappers and hunters who translocated more than 3,000 raccoons from Florida to West Virginia in 1977 to provide additional targets for their so-called "sports." At that time this strain of raccoon rabies was restricted to Florida. Some of the animals translocated to West Virginia were infected with the strain and raccoon rabies has since spread across much of the northeast and to the Canadian border.

Researchers following this epidemic have determined that trapping actually *increases* the spread of the disease by removing older, naturally immune animals and by opening up habitat, thus encouraging larger litters in a disease-stricken area. The younger animals born in the next breeding season are more susceptible to disease, setting up a new cycle for rabies outbreaks.

Despite all evidence countering claims that trapping is an effective method of rabies control, trappers continue to argue that they provide a public service by removing diseased animals from the wild. And taxpayer-supported state and federal agencies encourage trappers to trap and kill animals for their fur in the name of "disease control."

Without a Clue

In 1996/97, Congress directed the USFWS to survey the status of trapping on the 511 National Wildlife Refuges (NWR) throughout the United States. These pristine wilderness areas, encompassing more than 92 million acres in all 50 states, were specifically set aside as sanctuaries to protect wildlife and wildlife habitat.

API found that the USFWS official in charge of managing the NWR division had no idea how many wildlife refuges allow trapping, even though federal law requires each refuge regional director to compile an annual environmental analysis (EA) if trapping is done on the refuge. Also, before trapping is allowed on a refuge, the refuge manager must develop a "trapping plan," with input from the public. When API contacted the USFWS refuge division, not a single EA or "trapping plan" for any of the refuges could be found.

When our federal government doesn't even know if trapping is allowed on our nation's National Wildlife Refuges, no one can truthfully claim that "trapping is regulated and only abundant species are trapped."

"Humane" Traps

U.S. trapping associations argue that traps used today are humane, indicating the "padded" leghold trap as a commonly used humane alternative to the steel-jaw version. Yet the only distinctive difference between the two traps is that the padded leghold trap has a thin strip of rubber attached to the trap jaws.

Padded leghold traps not only cause significant injuries to animals, but fewer than 5% of U.S. trappers even own padded leghold traps. Only California and Tennessee require that padded leghold traps be used, and this provision only applies to leghold traps set on land.

Many studies testing padded traps have shown that these devices can cause severe injuries to their victims. In a 1995 study by the federal Animal Damage Control agency, padded leghold traps were tested on coyotes. Nearly all (97%)

of the animals trapped experienced severe swelling to their legs and 26% of the coyotes suffered from lacerations and fractures. In a similar study using red foxes, of 55 red foxes trapped in padded leghold traps, 25 suffered severe swelling, 23 suffered lacerations, 17 suffered tooth fractures (from biting the traps), and 13 suffered severance of tendons, abrasions or fractures.

Even trappers themselves admit that "padded" leghold traps cause severe injuries to animals.

Career Opportunities

Another pro-trapping claim is that "trapping provides a viable income for many trappers," yet in trade publications trappers complain that trapping hardly pays for itself.

In the June/July 1996 issue of the *Trapper and Predator Caller,* one trapper admits, "At my age, for the last five years, I have caught a lot of fur for an old geezer, but if I had counted all my time, car parts, gasoline, and other expenses, I doubt if I made a dollar an hour. I could have made more money picking manure with the chickens."

API conducted a national survey in Spring 1997 to find the average annual income of trappers in each state. State wildlife agencies that responded indicated that income from trapping was either extremely low or non-existent. The California Department of Fish and Game reported that "the average income per successful trapper in 1995–1996 was $240." The head Furbearer Research Biologist with the Kansas Department of Wildlife & Parks wrote, "Variability among trappers is too great to provide any form of estimate of income. The time and expenses incurred while trapping would need to be accounted for (equipment, vehicle use and gas, time invested, etc.) to provide a reliable estimate of a trapper's expenses. *Income derived from these calculations have indicated that trappers lose money* [italics added]."

> *"Even trappers themselves admit that 'padded' leghold traps cause severe injuries to animals."*

A 1992 Missouri Department of Conservation study found that "Approximately 30% of all trappers in 1991 reported no household income from trapping. . . . Only 5% of trappers in this survey reported obtaining at least 20% of their total household income from trapping. Most trappers reported earning small incomes from trapping. This suggests that motives other than monetary gain are also important to trappers. The average cost of trapping per day was $30.67."

The Bureau of the Census reports that only 2,099 individuals earned their living by hunting and/or trapping in the U.S. in 1990. Of this total, probably no more than 20 individuals actually make their living as full-time trappers in the lower 48 states, given the ratio of trappers to hunters in the U.S.

In 1994, the total value of U.S. fur exports (including trapped and "ranched" animals) was $225,410,580. Whole fur skins accounted for $166,017,000 or 74% of the total. What this means is that fur manufacturing is taking place in countries outside the U.S. where labor is cheap. The fur coats are then re-imported into the United States for retail sale. Simply put, most fur industry related jobs are exported to cheaper labor markets, refuting any claims that this industry provides significant employment opportunities for Americans.

Animals as Resources

Trappers today see furbearing animals only as "resources" to be killed for their fur and otherwise discarded. They fail to see the intrinsic value every living creature has in its own right. It is especially disturbing when our state wildlife agencies publish and disseminate information that contains such sentiments. *The Role of Trapping in Wildlife Conservation in Illinois,* a brochure issued by the Illinois Department of Conservation, says, "Just as the trees of a forest are a renewable resource that can be cropped on

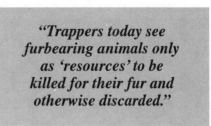

"Trappers today see furbearing animals only as 'resources' to be killed for their fur and otherwise discarded."

a sustained yield base, so are wild fur-bearing animals a renewable resource."

But animals are not resources or pieces of property to be used, tortured, and worn on our backs, not if we, as part of the animal kingdom ourselves, wish to evolve into a more compassionate, empathic species. Needed is a paradigm shift in human consciousness that instills an appreciation for other beings with whom we share this earth and an understanding that every animal is a being with a life and interest independent of ours.

The Run

The shift toward an appreciation of the right of animals to live without interference from humans has begun. The number of animals trapped for the U.S. commercial fur trade has declined by nearly 75% since 1988. Today, the official count is approximately 4.5 million animals a year—including foxes, bobcats, raccoons, coyotes, muskrat, beaver and mink—trapped for their fur, compared to 17 million animals in 1988. The number of licensed trappers has declined also, from 330,000 in 1988 to about 150,000 today.

Much of this decline can be attributed to the success of the anti-fur movement. Through public education we have changed public attitudes about trapping and exposed its cruelty. A December 1996 national Caravan Opinion poll showed 74% of Americans now believe leghold traps should be outlawed. In a 1997 poll conducted in California, 83% of voters said they oppose the trapping and killing of animals for the commercial sale of their fur. Similarly, a 1995 Associated Press poll found that 59% of Americans believe that "killing animals for fur is always wrong."

Through public policy efforts, legislation, litigation, grassroots activism, and ballot initiatives, we have succeeded in banning or reforming trapping in a number of states, cities, and municipalities. Trapping has been banned in Arizona, Colorado, and Massachusetts through the ballot initiative process. API in a coalition with six other national organizations is working to place an initiative on the 1998 ballot in California that would severely restrict commercial trapping and ban two poisons used to kill predators.

As we continue our fight to stop trapping at the local, state, national, and international levels, we will be faced with an increasingly articulate, media-savvy opposition. We must be prepared to challenge the myths, the lies and the media ploys, such as the *Balancing Nature* video, that trapping proponents will use to maintain their cruel, unsporting practice of killing and skinning animals for their fur.

Hunting Needs Reform

by Ted Kerasote

About the author: *Ted Kerasote is the author of* Bloodties: Nature, Culture, and the Hunt *and* Heart of Home: Essays of People and Wildlife.

In America, and in general, we dislike hunters. We dislike them because they use tools of destruction. And we dislike them because they kill beings who more easily win our affections—mammals rather than fish. Even those who want to engage the values of primalness often dislike hunters because they insist on getting blood on their hands whereas most of us are satisfied with less graphic measures—songs, drums, a simple walk through the trees. Most importantly, though, we dislike hunters for their dishonesty—for how their actions do not live up to their claims that hunting is a noble and conscientious activity.

Some hunter advocacy groups claim that these accusations are no more than perceptual problems, rooted in animal rights rhetoric and urban people's diminished connection to firearms as useful tools, to land and animals and to natural cycles. Such arguments have a shade of validity as well as a great deal of smoke screen behind which to avoid the truth: the hunting community has denied the character of many of its members, and until very recently has refused to address—deeply, committedly, and spiritually—what constitutes appropriate behavior toward animals.

The Dominionistic Hunter

This denial is no longer being tolerated, just the way our nation, in fits and starts, will no longer tolerate racism, the actions of the alcoholic behind the wheel, abuse within the home, or the unsustainable use of the commons. Intolerance of the hunting community comes about not only because trophy hunters make headlines for violations of the Endangered Species Act, or hunters in the pay of sporting goods manufacturers are convicted of shooting elk in Yellowstone National Park while making hunting videos. Rather it is how, on a thousand days in a thousand ways, we witness what Steven Kellert has called the "dominionistic/sport hunter" act with a callousness that debases everything hunters say about hunting's being a sacred connection to our Paleolithic roots.

Reprinted from Ted Kerasote, "To Preserve the Hunt," *Orion*, Winter 1996, by permission of the author.

Kellert's 1978 survey sampled hunters across the nation and found that nearly forty percent (38.5 percent) were what he termed the "Dominionistic/Sport Hunter." Often living in cities, these hunters savored competition with and mastery over animals in a sporting contest. "Utilitarian/Meat Hunters"—those interested in harvesting meat much as they would a crop of wheat—made up 43.8 percent of the sample. The remaining 17.8 percent Kellert called "nature hunters"; the youngest segment of the hunting population, these individuals knew the most about wildlife and their goal was to be intensely involved in nature through hunting.

> *"Whereas the hunter was once the teacher and shaman of his culture, he is now the boor."*

Unfortunately, it has been dominionistic/sport hunters, even though they represent less than forty percent of America's hunters, who have often set the image for the rest of the hunting community. Despite hunters' best efforts at educating the public about the hunter's role in conserving habitat and species, it is this group's behavior that the public remembers when they hear the word "hunting."

Indeed, they may represent a great many nonhunters. Developers who fill wetlands, homeowners who spread toxic herbicides on their lawns, every one of us who supports monoculture forests, agribusiness, and animal factory farms participates in a type of dominionistic mastery over wildlife and nature. Often, because the effects of such practices occur far away from our daily lives and in the form of what economists call "externalities"—birds, small mammals, and reptiles gobbled up by combines and poisoned as nontarget casualties of pesticides—we overlook their enormous destruction. On the other hand, the dominionistic hunter's actions are visible, premeditated, and often discomforting, but they are in keeping with the fundamental beliefs of the culture that has bred him. When his worst colors show, he can easily become our scapegoat, one that, like an oft reprimanded child, seems to revel in ever more unruly behavior.

The Use-It-Up-and-Move-On Ethic

As a committed hunter, I say this with regret. I say this with embarrassment. And I say this with frustration. Whereas the hunter was once the teacher and shaman of his culture, he is now the boor. And I'm forced to emphasize this point because on so many days in the field I myself have seen the average hunter bend the rules of fair chase and even the laws of the land—spotting game from aircraft, chasing animals with vehicles, or shooting on the evening before the season opens. On so many occasions such dubiously taken animals end up in the record books, our record-keeping organizations paying only lip service to the standards that they have set. I have seen downed hen mallards left to float away so they wouldn't be included in the day's bag limit, and hunters only grudgingly retrieve them when their obvious disregard has been pointed out. Some of my own neighbors have taken bucks on their girlfriends' tags; around my home two mule deer, an elk, three antelope, and a black bear with triplets have been poached during the last few years; several coyotes have been hung on a fence to rot because they were, well, "just coyotes"; and most recently one of Yellowstone's reintroduced wolves was shot because it was "just a wolf." But these aren't the real hunters, goes the hunting community's old saw, these are the lawbreakers, these are the people who indulge in inappropriate behavior.

On the contrary, I believe that these individuals *are* hunters and that their attitudes are founded in the same values that Americans have held about the commons—namely, take as much as you can before it's used up. For a century and a half, starting slowly with the writings of Henry David Thoreau and gathering speed with the forest and park campaigns of John Muir, the American conservation movement has tried to alter the consciousness of use-it-up-and-move-on. For hunting, this change in consciousness was initiated by Theodore Roosevelt in 1887, with his founding of a club of ethical hunters called the Boone and Crockett Club. Their invention of the idea of "fair chase" began to create a genuine hunting ethic, the rough design for what Aldo Leopold would later call "the land ethic," and what I'm calling appropriate and compassionate behavior toward nature.

An Exhausted Myth

However, a hundred years after Roosevelt transformed the nation's leading hunters into some of its most effective conservationists, the most compelling ideas about our evolving relationship with animals comes not from hunters but from nonhunters and even antihunters. Indeed, the story of the modern hunter as the best of conservationists often seems, at least to this hunter, like an exhausted myth.

In part, this myth says that it is hunters who are active and fit, and who know nature and wildlife best. However, if you visit the forests during hunting season, you find the roads full and the backcountry largely empty, many hunters "camped" in RVs full of amenities. When hunters are asked to support the creation of legally designated wilderness areas in which hardy recreation takes place (and the

> *"[If] the hunter is a disciplined, reluctant taker of life, . . . why are so many of my nonhunting neighbors afraid to go into the woods during hunting season?"*

places that are irreplaceable wildlife habitat), they often choose to side with the so-called wise use movement and others who want to build roads through the last remaining wild country.

The old hunting myth goes on to say that the hunter is a disciplined, reluctant taker of life. Yet, if this were the case, why are so many of my nonhunting neighbors afraid to go into the woods during hunting season? Perhaps it's because there are too many hunters who resemble the fellow I met several years ago on a trail. I asked how he had done. He replied that he hadn't seen any elk but that he had taken "a sound shot." His disregard for the suffering he might have caused was borne out a few years later when, not far from my house, one elk hunter shot and killed his good friend when the friend bugled.

> *"Actions speak louder than words when it comes to the hunter's relationship with the animals he or she kills."*

The myth goes on to say that hunting is a courageous and sometimes dangerous activity. The sporting press has been particularly fond of painting this picture. However with the advent of nature documentaries and adventure travel, millions of people have witnessed the behavior of wildlife that is not being threatened. After you have fished fifty feet from several brown bears in Alaska, and come to no harm, it is difficult to believe that shooting one is either a courageous or dangerous activity.

Hunters Are Depending on Technology, Not Skill

The myth goes on to say that hunters hunt to return to a world of origins, simplicity, and honest interaction with nature. But when you look at hunters, especially bowhunters, in the pages of sporting magazines, in the equipment catalogues, and in the woods, they look like a cross between Darth Vader and a commando. If you go to one of the annual trade shows that display new outdoor equipment, a hundred people a day will try to sell you a new hearing aid, a new camouflage pattern, a new scent, cartridge, or bow that will improve your chances of getting game, and too few hunters question the replacement of skill and intuition by gadgets.

Of course, using improved technology to enhance survival has been one of the hallmarks of our species since ancient times. Does this inventive tradition mean that we are permitted no room to discriminate between laser sights and atlatls? Developing codes that distinguish appropriate from inappropriate technology is one of the challenges hunters need to face and have not.

All these examples show the discrepancy between who hunters claim to be and who their actions demonstrate that they are. Many outdoorspeople, including backpackers, canoeists, climbers, and skiers, have noticed that hunters haven't cornered the market on nature lore, woods savvy, or hardihood. In fact, they are frequently lacking in them.

The Hunter's Relationship with Animals

Actions also speak louder than words when it comes to the hunter's relationship with the animals he or she kills. When the hunting community, believing that it can't relinquish any form of what it calls "hunting," refuses to denounce such activities as shooting live animals for target practice or for competition, its moral stature vanishes.

The image of the hunter as a far-seeing conservationist also comes into question when hunters and the agencies that represent them refuse to consider the idea that some wild species, not typically eaten as food, might no longer be hunted for sport. These would include brown bears, wolves, and coyotes. Hunters tend to reject such proposals as radical, yet, they are increasingly being floated by sportsmen themselves. Indeed, they evolved out of the ideas of some far-seeing hunters at the end of the nineteenth century, who suggested that certain bird species would remain immune from pursuit. In its time, this suggestion seemed ridiculous to some of the hunting community. It is now unquestioned.

Finally, American male hunters have been resistant to incorporate women into their ranks, mostly because women have stricter rules about which deaths are necessary for the procurement of food, and which are no more than gratuitous, based on fun, or the gratification of ego. Men fear women hunters would close down the sorts of hunting that can't be morally justified.

Is Hunting Worth Reforming?

Given this list of grievances, is it possible to reform hunting? One must also ask the larger question: Is hunting *worth* reforming?

The first question is one of logistics, the second one of sentiment. Logistically, hunting can be reformed, given what reforms most things—energy, time, and money. However, the real answer to the question of whether hunting is worth reforming depends on how you feel about animals. If you believe that humans can exist without harming animals—that we can evolve to the point that death is removed from the making of our food—then hunting is indeed a relic. If you believe that human and animal life is inextricably linked, and that the biology of the planet demands and will continue to demand that some life forms feed others, then hunting is not only part of that process but also has the potential to serve as a guide to how that process might be most conscientiously and reverentially undertaken.

> *"Hunting can be reformed and is worth reforming."*

How to Reform Hunting

I believe that hunting can be reformed and is worth reforming, and I offer these suggestions on how to do it.

First and foremost, the hunting community must provide more rigorous hunter education programs. Biology, forest management, expert marksmanship, and ethics would be covered in far greater depth, and a stiff field and written test administered before a hunting license was issued. Part of this course would examine the pros and cons of ecosystem management and wilderness designation, so that hunters might become a constituency for keeping habitat undeveloped. This will be an extremely difficult task given that a more stringent program will eliminate some hunters, which of course will decrease funding for agencies and profits for the sporting industry.

Nonetheless, there are ways to overcome the loss of revenue associated with a reduction in the hunting population. A hunting license remains one of the most inexpensive ways to participate in the outdoors in North America today. If, for argument's sake, the number of America's hunters was reduced by half, couldn't license prices be doubled to make up the difference? A deer license that was $17 would become $34 and still be a bargain.

Could gun, clothing, and outdoor equipment manufacturers raise their prices twofold and maintain sales? Unlikely. But outdoor equipment could be taxed, as guns and fishing tackle now are, to produce revenues for wildlife that isn't hunted. As well, a small income tax could be levied for wildlife care and research.

> *"Hunters need to speak out against competitions that involve shooting animals. . . . Such gaming shows a gross disrespect for animals, and has nothing to do with hunting."*

Second, deemphasize the record book and the pursuit of trophies for the trophy's sake. This is not to say that animals will no longer be admired and taxidermists put out of business. Rather we would stop valuing animals by so many inches of horn or antler. I would also suggest that if records must be kept as a way of honoring animals that only animals are listed, not hunters. In addition, hunters might initiate a completely new form of record keeping, one that honored the greatest amount of wildlife habitat conserved.

Third, hunters need to speak out against competitions that involve shooting animals—deer, pigeons, coyotes, prairie dogs, you name it. Such gaming shows a gross disrespect for animals, and has nothing to do with hunting.

New Terminology Is Needed

Fourth, managers and communicators need to reshape their terminology. *Sport* and *recreation,* the terms that distinguished conservationist hunters like Roosevelt from the market hunters who participated in the decimation of buffalo and waterfowl, have become pejorative terms when used with reference to killing animals. They are unacceptable to many in the environmental movement, who are not opposed to hunting if it is done with care, and many nonhunters, including vegetarians, who have been ambivalent about hunting but who can understand the activity as a "least harm option" when compared to agribusiness and the domestic meat industry. Perhaps hunters can call themselves simply *hunters.*

Likewise, the words *consumptive,* which has been used to describe hunters, and *nonconsumptive,* which has been attributed to birdwatchers and backpackers, need to be discarded. *Consumptive* and *nonconsumptive,* like *sport* and *recreation,* aren't the most precise terms with which to conceptualize these issues. Should the hunter who hunts a deer ten miles from his home be called a *consumptive* resource user, and his neighbor who flies ten thousand miles to Antarctica to watch penguins be termed a *nonconsumptive* user of the planet's resources? The entire hunting debate needs to be reframed in terms of an individual's impacts on regional, national, and global wildlife.

Fifth, the hunting community must open its doors to women: in its practice, in its ideas, and in its administration. "Man the hunter" has been a great sound bite for anthropologists who believe that hunting has been one of the primary shapers of human character, but women—helping to stampede bison and mammoths over cliffs, skinning animals, making clothing, and gathering vegetables and herbs—work just as hard, if not harder, to keep the species alive. Indeed, if women anthropologists had been doing most of the research, hunting peoples over most of the temperate globe might have been more accurately labeled "gatherer-hunters" rather than "hunter-gatherers." Either way you read it, both genders contribute to the evolution of our species, and it would be healthy if, today, they participate more equally in all the tasks of living, from raising children to growing and killing food. Until women restore their sympathies to hunting's fundamental life-giving, life-respecting aspects, and have a hand in reducing its elements of machismo and competition, hunters will be fighting an uphill and losing battle. It is women who will vote hunting out of existence.

> **"Sport *and* recreation . . .** *have become pejorative terms when used with reference to killing animals."*

Sixth, hunters need to participate in more realistic population planning and immigration policy. At current birth rates, along with legal and illegal immigration, the United States will have 400 million people by 2080. There will be almost no room left for wildlife. We need to examine our policies on tax credits for bearing children, on teenage sex education, and on the availability of birth control. Ignoring the issue of population control, as most everyone in North America does, will lead to the inexorable loss of wildlife habitat, wildlife, and public hunting as we know it.

A Cost Accounting of Diets

Seventh, hunters need to publicize a more accurate cost accounting of American diets. Millions of North America's hunters hunt locally and put a substantial amount of food, in the form of venison and birds, on their families' tables. In terms of their consumptive effect on the total environment, some of these hunters—who don't use large amounts of fossil fuel to go hunting—can incur less ecological impact than supermarket vegetarians whose entire diet consists of products from America's intensively managed and fossil fuel-dependent industrial farms, causing wildlife to suffer from pesticides, combining, and habitat loss.

To illustrate this idea one can compare the kilocalorie cost of different diets. An elk shot near a hunter's home in the Rocky Mountains incurs a cost to planet Earth of about 80,000 kilocalories. This includes the energy to produce the hunter's car, clothing, firearm, and to freeze the elk meat over a year. If the hunter chooses to replace the amount of calories he gets from 150 pounds of elk meat with rice and beans grown in California, the cost to planet Earth is nearly 500,000 kilocalories, which includes the energy costs of irrigation, farm equipment, and transportation of the food inland from the coast. It does not include the cost to wildlife—song birds, reptiles, and small mammals—who are killed as a result of agribusiness. Their deaths make the consumer of agribusiness foods a participant in the cull of wildlife to feed humans.

> *"If hunters are going to preserve hunting, they must re-create it as the disciplined, mindful, sacred activity it once was for our species."*

Even when we understand these tradeoffs, it's not always easy to make clear or compassionate choices about our diets. The elk shot in the forest, the tuna netted at sea, the rabbits lost as the combines turn the fields to provide us with our natural breakfast cereals, as well as the Douglas fir hidden in the walls of our homes, and the wildlife displaced to light and heat our buildings with fossil fuels or hydropower are all foreclosures. Every day, consciously or not, we close down one life over another, a constant, often unwitting choice of who will suffer so that we may continue living. Given this condition (what one animal rights scholar has called "the condition of being an imperfect being in an imperfectible world") and the difficulty of our escaping from it completely, we may attempt to do the least harm possible to other life. Virtually always, this means finding our food more locally. In some home places such a discipline would still include hunting, in other home places organic farming, in some places both.

Hunting Image Must Be Re-Created

In spite of our differing sentiments about animals, hunters and nonhunters remain in this dynamic system together. All the accusations that may be fairly leveled against the American hunter—greedy, thoughtless, lazy, consumptive, sexist—can also be brought against our culture at large. How can we expect more of the average American hunter, or for that matter inner city gangs or junk bond dealers, when they are products of a society that, in its films, politics, work ethic, and recreation, frequently displays these very negative characteristics and in the main has lost a sense of attention, discipline, care, practice, respect, and quality?

This impoverished state exists because we have lost our reachers and our holy people. Hunters ought to be in the ranks of both, but unless they find impeccable ways to restore what was a sacred activity, it will be, in its depauperated condition, rightfully disparaged and lost. Going out to have fun, I'm afraid, will no longer cut it. In fact, it never did. The humble, grateful, accomplished emotions that surround well-performed hunting cannot be equated with *fun*, that which provides amusement or arouses laughter. By fun I mean the cruel delight that comes at another's demise, not the celebratory joy inherent in well-performed hunting that produces the gift of food.

If hunters are going to preserve hunting they must re-create it as the disciplined, mindful, sacred activity it once was for our species. They will also need to help redeem the culture in which they have grown and which finds fun at the expense of others. This is a job for hunters not only as hunters but also as citizens—an ongoing task to define appropriate behavior between person and person and between what Black Elk, the Oglala Sioux holy man, called the two-leggeds and the four-leggeds. I would say that this definition will have much to do with the notions of kindness, compassion, and sympathy for those other species with whom we share this web of life and upon whom we depend for sustenance, the very notions—and I might add restraint—that informed the lives of many hunting peoples in times past.

Such a reformation—a return to older principles of mutual regard between species—will be a profound undertaking, for it is based on the pre-Christian belief that other life forms, indeed the very plants and 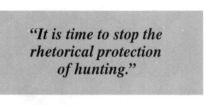 earth and air themselves, are invested with soul and spirit. If we must take those spirits, it can only be done for good reason and then only if accompanied with constant reverence and humility for the sacrifices that have been made. Whether we're hunters or nonhunters, meat eaters or vegetarians, this state of heart and mind compels us to say an eternal grace.

Not an Easy Task

Facing up to this basic and poignant condition of biological life on this planet—people, animals, and plants as fated cohorts, as both dependents and donors of life—wasn't easy ten thousand years ago and won't be today. Of course, we can back away from the task, but I think the result would be either a world in which people continue to dominate nature, or a world in which simplistic notions of how to reduce pain sever the bonds between people and nature. In either case we will remain distant from the complex burdens and daily sympathy that ancient hunters considered the basis for a loving community of people and animals.

Can this reformation really be accomplished without the participatory context of gathering and hunting that informed our species for thousands of years? Can we know the old knowledge of hunting times even though many of us spend lives far from the animals and plants who sustain us? I doubt it, unless we attempt to restore participation. Many of us may never have the privilege to thresh wheat we have grown, skin a deer we have killed, or filet a fish we have caught. Virtually all of us, though, have a window and a piece of sky. We can choose to grow salad greens or a few herbs. Though a small gesture of participation in the world that feeds us, putting one's hands in a small pot of dirt, emblem of the original ground from which we have sprung, is a powerful thing to do and a beginning.

It is time to stop the rhetorical protection of hunting. It is time to nurture and restore the spirit that informed it. Such a commitment, if followed diligently, would certainly close down hunting as a sport. It would maintain it, though, as one of our important and fundamental weddings with nature.

Chapter 4

Should Animals Be Bred for Human Consumption?

Chapter Preface

The controversy over whether animals should be bred and raised for human use has its roots in the issue of whether animals have rights. Animal rights activists maintain that because animals are sentient and can feel pain, they have the same right to live as humans do. These advocates assert that it is therefore unacceptable for humans to exploit animals for their own uses, which includes killing them for food, using their skin or fur for clothing, or, according to some animal rights extremists, even owning animals as pets. According to the novelist Alice Walker, "The animals of the world exist for their own reasons. They were not made for humans any more than black people were made for whites, or women for men." Animals have the right to be treated with the same respect as that given to people, Walker contends.

Others maintain that sentience and feeling pain do not give animals the same rights that are enjoyed by humans. The fact that animals can feel pain requires only that they be treated humanely, they assert; it does not mean that animals may not be used for their fur or their milk or their meat or their companionship. These supporters contend that animals were put on the earth to meet the needs of humans, a view that some contend is based on God giving Adam dominion over the earth and all its inhabitants. Author L. Neil Smith explains this belief: "Animals are groceries. They're leather and fur coats. They're for medical experiments and galloping to hounds. That's their *purpose*."

Whether raising animals for their meat and fur is cruel and inhumane or justified and necessary is among the topics examined by the authors in the following chapter.

In Defense of Killing Animals for Meat

by Stephen Bodio

About the author: *Stephen Bodio is the author of several books on hunting, falconry, and the outdoors.*

> How, given the canine teeth and close-set eyes that declare the human animal to be a predator, had we come up with the notion that oat bran is more natural to eat than chicken?
>
> —Valerie Martin, *The Great Divorce*

My life has been built around animals and books about them. They have been in every book I've written and most of my essays. I was imprinted on the *Jungle Books* and Peterson's *Field Guide* before I was four, fated to be a raving biophiliac as long as I lived. I fed myself a constant diet of books with animals—Charles Darwin, William Beebe, Konrad Lorenz on the one hand, Rudyard Kipling, Ernest Thompson Seton, Albert Payson Terhune, Jim Kjelgaard on the other. I read bird guides like novels and novels about pigeons. As long as I can remember I kept snakes, turtles, insects, pigeons, parrots, fish; bred them all, learned falconry and dog training, kept life lists, raced pigeons, hacked falcons for the Peregrine Fund, did rehab, joined conservation groups, supported veterinarians, partnered for life with bird dogs. I would say I "loved" animals but for the fact the word is so worn out in our culture that I distrust it. (Valerie Martin again: ". . . a word that could mean anything, like love. At dinner last night Celia had said, 'I love pasta. I love, love, love pasta, and then to her father who had cooked the pasta for her, 'And you Dad. I love, love, love you.'") Suffice it to say that some animals are persons to me as well as points of focus, subjects of art, objects of awe, or quarries.

And . . . yet? . . . I eat meat, and always will. Which today is not only becoming vaguely suspect in some civilized quarters but also might be my one point of dissension with what I understand of Buddhism. Although I also take a quote from a modern Buddhist everywhere I wander about this subject—at a book-

Excerpted from Stephen Bodio, "Strange Meat," *Northern Lights*, May 1996. Reprinted by permission of the author.

store, Gary Snyder once grinned as I handed him my copy of *Turtle Island* to autograph, opened to the poem "One should not talk to a skilled hunter about what is forbidden by the Buddha."

I recently announced too loudly at a dinner that I would no longer write anything with the purpose of convincing anyone to do anything. If writing essays means anything to me it is as an act of celebration and inquiry, like, if lesser than, poetry and science. With that in mind, let this be an inquiry into meat and, as my late friend Betsy used to say of the Catron County Fair, "a celebration of meat." I will try to be honest, even if it means admitting to crimes. Maybe this is about love after all.

A Family History

Personal history does shape us all. I was born to blue-collar stock in the post-War suburbs. My mother's people were Irish and Scottish and English and German. Some had been farmers and many had been fishermen, but by the time of my birth, they had escaped the land and become respectable, things my animal-obsessed intelligence rejected without analysis. McCabes tended to react with disgust to the messier parts of life. I still remember with delight my outspoken little sister Anita, who used to help me clean game, when she came to visit me with our grandmother and found me making a study skin from a roadkilled woodpecker. She was all of eleven at the time, when many little suburban girls think they must be fastidious, but she scooped up the carcass and tossed it in the wastebasket. "You'd better get that covered up," she giggled, "or Nana Mc-Cabe's gonna puke all over the kitchen floor."

But the Bodios, who came over from the Italian Alps in their and the century's late teens, were from another planet than the lace-curtain Irish. My father had a furious drive toward WASP respectability, but his folks were Italian peasants who happened to live in Boston. Less than ten miles from downtown, they maintained until the ends of their long lives what was almost a farm. I believe their Milton lot contained a half-acre's space. On it they had twelve apple trees, grapevines, and a gigantic kitchen garden. They also kept a few pigeons and rabbits. (No chickens—even then Americans objected to the happy noise that half the planet wakes up to.)

> *"Some animals are persons to me as well as points of focus, subjects of art, objects of awe, or quarries. And . . . yet? . . . I eat meat, and always will."*

Nana McCabe could cook pastries and cakes, but the Bodios *ate*. Eggs and prosciutt' and parmesan, young bitter dandelions and mushrooms picked almost anywhere, risott' and polenta that, when I was very young, would be garnished with a sauce I learned ("don't tell nobody") was made from uccelini, little birds—I suspect sparrows, bush-whacked in the pigeon house. Eels, and mussels—which, back then, had to be gathered rather than bought. I tasted real vegetables there, not like the canned ones at home—tomatoes and corn eaten in the garden, warm from the sun, with a shaker of salt, zucchini and eggplant breaded and fried in butter like veal. Tart apples, stored in the cool cellar where Grandpa kept his homemade wine. That wine, served at every meal, to kids and adults alike.

The Delight of Strange Meat

And, of course, meat, interesting meat. My father hunted and fished and kept racing pigeons, but has always been indifferent to food. I suspect that, until his own old age, he found his parents' food too "ethnic," too reminiscent of the social barriers he wore himself out trying to transcend. As for my mother, she *hated* game—the mess of cleaning and its smells, the strangeness of its taste. She passed this down to most of the kids; my sister Wendy so abhorred the idea of venison that my brother and I would tell her steak and veal were "deer meat" so we could get her portion, a subterfuge so effective that she would leave the kitchen, claiming to be nauseated by the imagined smell.

So the good stuff often went to the Bodios by default. *Really* good stuff—black ducks with a slight rank taste of the sea, ruffed grouse better than any chicken, white-tailed deer that would hang swaying in the garage until the meat formed a dry crust and maybe a little mold. Bluefish, too rich ("fishy") for my mother's taste, and fifty-pound school tuna.

> *"The movement against meat and the 'Animal Rights Movement' are largely a creation of American . . . culture, which doesn't have the world's richest culinary tradition."*

I don't know if my parents ever realized that I, tenderest-minded and softest and most intellectual of their kids, was also the one being trained to the delight of strange food, strange meat, even if the eating of it conflicted with my other "principles." My father would snap a pigeon's neck without a thought if it was too slow in the races, but he wouldn't eat it. I would cry when he "culled" (never "killed") a bird, then eat it with delight at my grandparents'.

I thought then that I was weird, and felt guilty. Now I think it's my father who was weird, and my tender-minded sisters, who would be vegetarians if they had to kill their meat. They "love" animals, deplore my hunting. Only one of the six of them keeps animals, which are messy and take work to keep and know.

Living Off the Land

All these as yet unexamined attitudes and preferences came with me when I left home at seventeen. I became *seriously* weird at that point—to my parents, of course, because I grew my hair long and cultivated a beard and disagreed with them on sex, religion, politics, drugs, and money—but also, to my surprise, to many of my new friends. They of course shared my beliefs about all of the above. But at that time I usually lived in freezing shacks in seaside outer suburbs like Marshfield, with trained hawks and my Dad's old .410 and 16-gauge shotguns, and "lived off the land" in a way rather unlike that of rural communards. I spent so much time in the salt marshes that one girlfriend called me, not without affection, "Swamp Wop."

I shot ducks and geese all fall, gathered mussels and quahogs and soft-shelled clams. You could still free-dive for lobsters then without being assaulted by legions of vacationing boat thugs. Squid swarmed in the summer and would strand themselves in rock pools on the spring tides. In summer we—my uncivilized blue-collar work mates and I, not my friends who agreed with me on art and politics—would use eelskin rigs and heavy rods to probe for stripers in the Cape Cod Canal. Winter would find us on the sandbars, freezing but happy as we tried for a late season seaduck for chowder or an early cod on a clam bait for the same.

Gradually I achieved some small notoriety—not just as some sort of nouveau primitive, but as a guy who could serve you some serious food. In the late seventies I was a staff writer for a weekly post-counter-culture paper in Cambridge and began to introduce occasional animal and/or food pieces to its pages. We had entered the age of debate on these subjects, but I still had fun. Just before the paper died, the food writer Mark Zanger, who still writes under the nom-de-bouffe "Robert Nadeau," and I were going to do a game dinner extravaganza, to be titled "Bodio Kills It, Nadeau Cooks It," complete with appropriate wines and between-the-courses readings from my game diary. But the owners folded the paper and I left for New Mexico, a more hospitable ecosystem for my passions.

A Paradox

I present the above as a partial recounting of my bona fides, but also to present you a paradox. America and American civilization are still "new" compared to, say, France, Italy, China, Japan. The movement against meat and the "Animal Rights Movement" are largely a creation of American or at least Anglo Saxon culture, which doesn't have the world's richest culinary tradition, to say the least.

My friends considered me a barbarian, yes, but also a cook.

France and Italy and China (and even Japan—fish, after all, is meat, the "meatless" Fridays of my youth notwithstanding) eat *everything*. They eat frogs and snails, eels and little birds, dogs and cats (and yes, deplorably, tigers and bears), snakes, whales, and poisonous puffer fish. They actually eat less bulk of meat than our sentimental in-denial culture of burger munchers, but they are in that sense more carnivorous—or *omnivorous*—than we are.

> *"Hunter-gatherers know animals are persons, and eat them."*

People who eat strange meat are considered "primitive" by our culture, whether or not theirs has existed longer than ours, or created better art, and happier villages.

So are our oldest ancestors, hunter-gatherers, who eat thistles and birds and eggs and grubs, roast large game animals and feast on berries like the bears they fully realize are cousins under the skin. Hunter-gatherers know animals are persons, and eat them.

Can it be that we are the strange ones? We, who use up more of the world's resources than anyone, even as we deplore the redneck his deer, the French peasant his *grive?*

> *"If we weren't supposed to eat meat, why does it smell so good? Honest vegetarians I know admit they can be forced to drool by the sweet smell of roasting birds."*

Can it be entirely an accident that in the wilds of southern France the wild boar thrives in the shadow of ruined Roman coliseums? That carefully worked out legal seasons for thrushes exist alongside returning populations of griffon vultures, lammergeiers, peregrines? That you can eat songbirds in the restaurants and look up to see short-toed eagles circling overhead? Just over the border, in Italy, they still have wolves, while in wilderness-free England and Brussels, Euromarket bureaucrats try to force the French to stop eating songbirds.

French Hunters

In 1993 I spent a month in the little Vauclusien village of Serignan-de-Comtat. . . .

One morning at dawn I came over a little rise and surprised two middle-aged men in camo fatigues loading two hounds into the back of a 2CV. The larger man was moon-faced and moustached. The smaller, like many Provençals, could have been a blood relative of mine; he was dark and wiry, with curly black hair. Both smoked unfiltered cigarettes; the black tobacco was pungent in the still sweet morning air. The short hunter's dog was sleek and black with long bloodhound ears, not unlike a black-and-tan coonhound; the big man's dog was also huge, white and shaggy, with a whiskered muzzle like a terrier's.

They replied curtly to my cheery "Bonjour," but I was fascinated. "Je suis un chasseur Americain," I began: I'm an American hunter. . . .

The transformation was instantaneous; they both shook my hand and began speaking over each other in quick French made even tougher to understand by their heavy local accents. "You're *American*, that's good. . . . We thought you were from Paris . . . those northerners, they think they're better than us. They don't hunt, they hate hunters . . . they are all moving down here to their summer houses.". . .

I realized that, unlike in England and Germany, *everybody* hunts in France—the butcher and baker and mechanic as well as the local personages. Maybe it's the French Revolution, maybe the Mediterranean influence. I doubt that the sign on the tank, posted by my new friends and their fellow members of the

Serignan hunter's society, would have appeared in England or Germany or the U.S.: "Nature est notre culture." Nature is our culture, our garden, if you will.

Nature *is* our culture. Our "permaculture," if you will; something a part of us, that we're a part of. Nobody in rural southern France is ignorant of what food is, or meat.

I had been trying to live something like this for as long as I had been conscious. I hunted, and gathered, and gardened, and liked it all. I spent my rather late college years in rural western Massachusetts, put a deer in the freezer and cut cordwood, some of which I sold to professors. I ate roadkill for two years, cruised the roads at dawn for carcasses of cottontail and snowshoe hare and squirrel, praising whatever gods when I found a grouse (I barely had time to hunt except during deer week), learning you could cook snake and make it good. I even ate a roadkilled hawk once—it was delicious. . . .

Celebrating Meat

Food should be delicious, and inexpensive, and real, which last two keep it from being mannered or decadent. My hunting and gathering and husbandry are driven both by principle and by pleasure—why should they not be driven by both? But because the "good people" in our northern protestant civilization-of-the-moment are so often gripped by a kind of puritanism even as their opposite numbers rape the world with greed (did I write "opposite"? I wonder. . . .) most writers do not write of the sensuous pleasure of food. OK, a few: M.F.K. Fisher, first and always; Patience Gray; Jim Harrison; John Thorne. But even they don't write enough about the pleasure of *meat.* So before we return full circle to principle, to guilt and remorse, to "why," let's take a moment to celebrate the delights of our subject.

If we weren't supposed to eat meat, why does it smell so good? Honest vegetarians I know admit they can be forced to drool by the sweet smell of roasting birds. No food known to humans smells quite as fine as any bird, skin rubbed with a clove of garlic, lightly coated with olive oil, salted, peppered, turning on a spit over a fire. . . .

> *"Vegetarians kill too . . . do they seriously think that farming kills nothing?"*

Why do we Anglo Saxons overcook our meat? Another residue of puritanism, of fear of the body, of mess, of eating, of realizing that death feeds our lives? Do we feel that guilty about not photosynthesizing?

Nobody could tell me wild duck tastes "of liver" if they cooked it in a 500° oven for fifteen or twenty minutes.

No one could say that venison does, if they dropped thin steaks into a hot skillet, turned them over once, and removed them and ate them immediately.

Hell, nobody could tell me *liver* tastes "like liver" if they did the same, in bacon fat, with onions already well-cooked piled around it.

154

A cowboy I know used to say he hated "nasty old sheep." We changed his mind when we bought a well-grown lamb from the Navajos, killed and skinned and gutted it, and let it soak for a day in a marinade of garlic, honey, chiles, and soy sauce, turning it frequently. Then Omar and Christine, Magdalena's prime goat and lamb roasters, cooked the legs and ribs over an open fire, until a crust formed over the juicy interior. The smell could toll cars passing in the street into Omar's yard. Omar and I, especially, are known to stab whole racks of ribs off the grille with our knives and burn our mouths, moaning with pleasure.

> *"I am determined . . . to remind myself that death exists, that animals and plants die for me, that one day I'll die and become part of them."*

Stock: I put all my bird carcasses in a big pasta pot with a perforated insert. I usually don't add vegetables. I cook them for ten to sixteen hours, never raising the stock to a boil . . . *never.* The result perfumes the house, causes shy friends to demand to stay for dinner, ends up as clear as a mountain stream but with a golden tint like butter. Then you can cook the risotto (we say "risott," like northern peasants, to distinguish it from the yuppie version) with it. But you only need a little—the real stuff uses more wine or even hot water, and a lot of parmesan. . . .

I love my pigeons, but have you ever eaten "real" squab, that is, five-week-old, fat, meltingly tender pigeon? I keep a few pairs of eating breeds for just that. You could cut it with a fork. . . .

How about real turkey, the wild kind? It actually tastes like bird, not cardboard, and has juice that doesn't come from chemical "butter." Eat one, and you'll never go back.

How about the evillest meats of all, the salted kind? How about prosciutt', with its translucent grain and aftertaste like nuts? How about summer sausage? Old style hams with a skin like the bark of an oak? How about real Italian *salame,* or capicolla?

Good things could be said about vegetables too, by the way. We here at the Bodio household actually eat more veggies than meat; meat is for essence and good gluttony, not for bulk. We eat pasta and rice and beans, cheese, good bread, garden vegetables by the ton, *roast* vegetables, raw ones. But these things don't need a defender. Meat, improbably to me, does.

Turning Animals into Meat

Let's veer in through that sensuousness once more. Last month I was preparing five domestic ducks for a feast with friends. To cook it the best way the breast meat had to be blood-rare, the legs well-done with a crispy skin. Which of course involved totally dismantling the ducks, hard work. You had to partly cook them, then skin them, getting seriously greasy. (The skin would become crackling, or as Libby called it, punning on the pork-crackling *chicharonnes* of New Mexico, "pata-ronnes.") You had to fillet the breast meat from the bone, and disjoint the legs. The carcasses had to go back into the oven for browning, and then into the stock pot. You ended up physically tired, sweaty, with aching hands, small cuts everywhere, and slime to your elbows. You felt good, accomplished, weary. But it was hard to avoid the idea that you had cut up an animal, or five.

Or take a *matanza*, a pig killing, in Magdalena. After shooting the pig in the head (if you do it right, the other pigs watch but nobody, even the hero of the feast, gets upset), it's work, work that will give you an appetite. The pig is carried out on a door, wrapped with burlap sacks boiled in one half of a fifty gallon drum, scraped, hung up. It is eviscerated, and the viscera are washed and saved. The bulk of the "real" meat, all that will not be eaten that day, goes to the freezer. The chicharonnes are cut up and heaped into the other half of the drum, to sizzle themselves crispy in their own fat. Everything steams in the cold air—the fires and vats, your breath, the pig's innards. Those innards are quickly fried with green chiles and wrapped in fresh flour tortillas so hot they'll burn your tongue, to give you energy to rock that carcass around, to stir the chicharonne vat with a two-by-four. The blood is taken in and fried with raisins ("sweet blood") or chiles ("hot blood") and taken out to where you are working. By afternoon you

> *"I suspect the culture would be saner if we all lived a bit more like peasants, . . . killed our own pigeons and rabbits, ate 'all of it' like bushmen or . . . the Chinese."*

are as hungry as you have ever been. You eat like a wolf. You also can't avoid the idea that you have taken a life. Afterwards, you all lie around like lions in the sun.

I once mentioned a matanza in a piece I wrote for the Albuquerque *Journal*. An indignant letter writer (from Massachusetts!) called me "refuse" for my "Hemingwayesque" love of "blood, hot and sweet," which he assumed was a grim metaphor rather than a rural delicacy. He hurt my feelings. But maybe he was right, in a way he hadn't intended.

Death and Cruelty

So, OK, *death*. And cruelty.

Deliberate cruelty is inexcusable; I won't say much about it here. As I get older I actually use bigger calibers and gauges than when I was young; I can't stand wounding anything.

But death? We all cause it, every day. We can't not. Tom McGuane once said, "The blood is on your hands. It's inescapable." Vegetarians kill too . . . do they seriously think that farming kills nothing? Or maybe they're like the Buddhist Sherpas that Libby used to guide with, who would ask her to kill their chickens and goats so the karma would be on *her* hands.

Let me pause for a moment to quote from two books. From Allen Jones's *A Quiet Violence,* a philosophical investigation of hunting: "The vegetarian does have good intentions. He or she is making an honest attempt to relate more directly to the natural world. The irony, of course, is that in denying their history they have placed themselves farther away from the process. . . . When death is seen as evil, or if pain is something to be rejected at all costs, then nature itself is in danger. If most animal rights activists had their utopias, neither ecology nor evolution would exist."

> *"I should sometimes kill some beautiful animal and eat it, to remind myself what I am: a fragile animal . . . who eats and thinks and feels and will someday die."*

And from Mary Zeiss Stange's *Woman the Hunter:* "Far from being a mark of moral failure, this [hunter's] absence of guilt feelings suggests a highly-developed moral consciousness, in tune with the realities of the life-death-life process of the natural world."

An acceptance of all this is not always easy, even for the hunter and small farmer, who usually know animals far better than the vegetarian or "anti" or consumer. I find that as I get older, I am more and more reluctant to kill anything, though I still love to hunt for animals, to shoot, and to eat. Still, I am determined to affirm my being a part of the whole mystery, to take personal responsibility, to remind myself that death exists, that animals and plants die for me, that one day I'll die and become part of them. "Protestant" "objectifying" "Northern" culture—I use those inverted commas because none of those concepts is totally fair or accurate, though they do mean something—seems to be constantly in the act of distancing itself from the real, which does exist—birth, eating, juicy sex, aging, dirt, smells, animality, and death. Such distancing ends in the philosophical idiocies of the ornithologist Robert Skutch, who believes sincerely that God and/or evolution got the universe wrong by allowing predation and that he, a Connecticut Yankee, would have done better.

A Reasonable Life

I, on the other hand, don't feel I know enough about anything to dictate to the consciences of others. I certainly don't think that anyone *should* kill, so long as they realize they are no more moral than those who do; I can find it hard enough myself. While I suspect the culture would be saner if we all lived a bit more like peasants, grew some veggies out of the dirt, killed our own pigeons and rabbits, ate "all of it" like bushmen or Provençal hunters or the Chinese, I have no illusions that this is going to happen tomorrow. I can only, in the deepest sense, cultivate my garden, sing my songs of praise, and perfect my skills. I'll try to have what Ferenc Mat calls "a reasonable life," strive to be aware and compassionate and only intermittently greedy, to eat as well as my ancestors, to cook well and eat well as a discipline and a joy. The French say of a man who has lived well that "Il bouffe bien, il boit bien, il baise bien": he eats well, he drinks well, he [in this context] fucks well." Sounds like a life to me.

And in living my good and reasonable life, I suspect I should sometimes kill some beautiful animal and eat it, to remind myself what I am: a fragile animal, on a fierce fragile magnificent planet, who eats and thinks and feels and will someday die: an animal, made of meat.

Slaughtering Can Be Humane

by Temple Grandin

About the author: *Temple Grandin is an animal scientist who has designed one-third of all the livestock processing facilities in the United States, including humane handling chutes for slaughtering cattle.*

Language-based thought is foreign to me. All my thoughts are full-color motion pictures, running like a videotape in my imagination. It was always obvious to me that cattle and other animals also think in pictures. I have learned that there are some people who mainly think in words and I have observed that these verbal thinkers are more likely to deny animals' thought; they are unable to imagine thought without words. Using my visual thinking skills, it is easy for me to imagine myself in an animal's body and see things from their perspective. It is the ultimate virtual reality system. I can imagine looking through their eyes or walking with four legs.

My life as a person with autism is like being another species: part human and part animal. Autistic emotion may be more like an animal's. Fear is the dominant emotion in both autistic people and animals such as deer, cattle, and horses. My emotions are simple and straightforward; like an animal's, my emotions are not deep-seated. They may be intense while I am experiencing them but they will subside like an afternoon thunderstorm.

Since the early 1980s, I have designed chute systems for handling cattle in slaughter plants. The conveyorized restraint system I designed is used in slaughtering one third of all the cattle in the United States.

Cattle are not afraid of the same things that people fear. The problem is that many people cannot observe this because they allow their own emotions to get in the way. To design a humane system I had to imagine what it would be like if I were the animal. I had to become that animal and not just be a person in a cow costume.

Cattle and people are upset by different things. People are repulsed by the

Reprinted from Temple Grandin, "Thinking Like Animals," in *Intimate Nature: The Bond Between Women and Animals*, edited by Linda Hogan, Deena Metzger, and Brenda Peterson (New York: Ballantine, 1998). Reprinted by permission of the author.

sight of blood, but blood does not bother cattle. They are wary of the things that spell danger in the wild, such as high-pitched noise, disturbances of the dirt, and sudden jerky movements. A high-pitched noise may be a distress cry, and dirt or grass that is displaced may mean that there has been a struggle to avoid being eaten. Abrupt motion may be associated with a predator leaping onto its prey. These are all danger signals.

Many times I have observed cattle balking and refusing to move through a chute at a slaughter plant. They may balk at a jiggling gate, a shadow, a shiny reflection, or anything that appears to be out of place. A coffee cup dropped on the floor can make the cattle stop and turn back. But cattle will walk quietly into a slaughterhouse if the things they are afraid of are eliminated. Solid sides on chutes prevent them from seeing people up ahead and muffling devices lessen the shrill sounds that alarm them.

Cattle are sensitive to the same things that disturb people with autism. Immature development in the lower brain systems causes some people with autism to have a heightened sense of hearing, and an intense fear is triggered when anything in their environment is out of place. A curled-up rug, or a book that is crooked on the shelf, causes the same fear as being stalked by a predator. The autistic brain is acutely aware of details that most other people ignore. Sudden high-pitched sounds in the middle of the night cause my heart to race as if a lion was going to pounce.

Like a wild animal, I recoil when people touch me. A light touch sets off a flight reaction and my oversensitive nerve endings do not tolerate hugging. I want the soothing feeling of being held, but the sensations can be too overwhelming, so I pull away. My need for touch started my interest in cattle.

A Firm Touch Is Calming

Puberty began the onslaught of hormones that sensitized my nervous system and started the constant fear and anxiety. I was desperate for relief. At my aunt's ranch I observed that when cattle were placed in a squeeze chute for their vaccinations, the pressure from the side panels squeezing against their bodies relaxed them. Pressure over wide areas of the body has a calming effect on many animals. Pressure applied to the sides of a piglet will cause it to fall asleep. Firm touch has a calming effect, while a light tickle touch is likely to set off a flight reaction.

> *"Cattle are not afraid of the same things that people fear."*

Many parents of autistic children have observed that their child will seek pressure by getting under sofa cushions or a mattress. Therapists often use deep pressure to calm autistic children. I decided to try the squeeze chute and discovered that the intense pressure temporarily made my anxiety go away. When I returned home from the ranch I built a squeezing machine. Early versions pressed against my body with hard wood. When I first started using the machine I flinched and pulled away from it like a wild animal. As I adjusted to being held I used less intense pressure and I remodeled the side panels with foam rubber padding to make the machine more comfortable.

As I became able to tolerate being held I became more interested in figuring out how the cattle felt when they were handled and held in squeeze chutes at the feed yards. Many of the animals were scared because people were rough with them. They chased them, yelled at them, and prodded

> *"Death at the slaughter plant is quicker and less painful than death in the wild."*

them. I found that I could coax most cattle to walk through a chute to be vaccinated by moving them quietly, at a slow walk. When an animal was calm I could observe the things that would catch his eye, like shadows or people leaning over the top of the chute. The leader would look at the things that concerned him. He would stop and stare at a coffee cup on the floor or move his head back and forth in time with a small chain that was swinging in the chute. Before moving forward he had to carefully scrutinize the things that attracted his attention. If the handlers tried to force him to move before he had determined that the chain was harmless, he and all the other cattle would panic. Cattle moved quietly and quickly through the chutes as soon as the swinging chain was removed.

Gentle Pressure Is Best

I found that the animals were less likely to resist being held by the squeeze chute if pressure was applied slowly. An animal would panic if suddenly bumped. I also discovered the concept of optimum pressure. The chute must apply sufficient pressure to provide the feeling of being held but not cause pain. Many people make the mistake of mashing an animal too tight when it struggles. And the chute always needs solid sides, so that the cattle do not see people deep inside their flight zone. The flight zone is the animal's safety zone. They become anxious and want to get away when people get too close.

Years later, when I designed a restraint chute for holding cattle for slaughter, I was amazed that the animals would stand still and seldom resist the chute. I found that I could just ease their head and body into position by adjusting the chute. When I got really skilled at operating the hydraulic controls, the apparatus became an extension of my arms and hands. It was as if I could reach through the machine and hold each animal very gently. It was my job to hold the animal gently while the rabbi performed the final deed.

The Right Attitude

During the last ten years, more and more women have been hired to handle cattle and operate chutes in both feed yards and slaughter plants. At first the men were skeptical that women could do the work, but today progressive managers have found that women are gentler and work well with the animals. Some feed yards now hire only women to doctor sick cattle and vaccinate the new arrivals. In slaughter plants, two of the best operators of kosher restraining chutes are women. They were attracted to the job because they couldn't stand to see the guys abusing cattle.

When I first started designing equipment I thought that all the problems of the rough treatment of animals in slaughter plants could be solved with engineering. But engineering is only part of the equation. The most important thing is the attitude of management. A strong manager acts as the conscience of the employees in the trenches. To be most effective in maintaining high standards of animal treatment the manager has to be involved enough to care, but not so much that he or she overdoses on the constant death. The managers who are most likely to care and enforce humane handling are most likely to have close associations with animals, or are close to the land.

Nature Can Be Harsh

I am often asked how I can care about animals and be involved in their slaughter. People forget that nature can be harsh. Death at the slaughter plant is quicker and less painful than death in the wild. Lions dining on the guts of a live animal is much worse in my opinion. The animals we raise for food would have never lived at all if we had not raised them. I feel that our relationship with animals must be symbiotic. In nature there are many examples of symbiosis. For example, ants raise aphids and use them as "dairy cows." The ants feed the aphids and in return they provide a sugar substance. It is important that our relationship with farm animals is reciprocal. We owe animals a decent life and a painless death.

I have observed that the people who are completely out of touch with nature are the most afraid of death, and places such as slaughter houses. I was moved by Birute Galdikas's book on her research on orangutans. The people in the Borneo rain forests live as a part of nature and have a totally different view of life and death. To the native people, "death is not separate from life." In the jungle they see death every day. Birute states, "For me, as for most middle-class North Americans death was just a tremor far down, far away at the end of a very long road, not something to be lived with every hour of every single day."

> *"The animals we raise for food would have never lived at all if we had not raised them."*

Many people attempt to deny the reality of their own mortality. When I designed my first system I had to look my own mortality straight in the eye. I live each day as if I could die tomorrow. I want to make the most of each day and do things to make the world a better place.

Fur Farms Are Humane

by American Legend Cooperative

About the author: *American Legend Cooperative is a marketing company owned by North American mink farmers.*

Furbearing animals have been raised on farms in North America since shortly after the Civil War. Today's farm-raised furbearers are among the world's best-cared-for animals. Good nutrition, comfortable housing and prompt veterinary care have resulted in domestic animals very well suited to the farm environment. Precise attention to animal care has enabled North American farmers to produce the finest quality fur in the world.

In 1994, family fur farms in North America produced approximately 3.8 million mink and fox pelts with a value of nearly $113 million. The U.S. produces about 10% of the world's mink supply, while Canada accounts for another 4%. Much of this fur is exported to other parts of the world.

There are about 1,200 mink and fox farms in North America. Many more mink are raised than foxes, and mink farms are generally larger operations than fox farms.

Fur farms in North America were the first in the world to develop black mink. This color is quite rare in nature. Breeding stock was sold to Scandinavian countries, the Soviet Union and countries in the Far East. Using special selective breeding programs designed for domestic mink and fox, North American fur farmers have developed the wide variety of pelt colors used in manufacturing fur garments today, including many shades of brown, gray, blue and white to complement the black (standard) pelts which are popular throughout the world.

Most fur farms in North America are family businesses, often operated by two or three generations of the same family. Today's young fur farmer generally has a college or university degree in agriculture, biology or business. Virtually every fur farmer begins by serving at least a one-year apprenticeship on a well-established farm to learn the complete annual fur production cycle.

North American mink and fox farmers are strongly committed to the ethic of humane care. To promote good animal husbandry and humane farm management practices, they have developed comprehensive standards of practice. Created in

Reprinted, by permission, from "Facts About Fur Farming," an American Legend Cooperative publication at www.seattlefur.com/alcfacts.html.

consultation with veterinarians and animal scientists, the standards contain guidelines for:

- Farm management
- Accommodations (site, sheds and pens)
- Food (nutrition, preparation, distribution)
- Watering systems
- Health and disease control
- Environmental quality (sanitation, water quality)
- Transport of live mink
- Euthanasia

The standards are administered in the United States by the Animal Welfare Committee of Fur Commission USA (FCUSA), and in Canada by the Canadian Mink Breeders Association. They are periodically revised to reflect the most current knowledge of animal care and the most humane management techniques.

Humane Euthanasia

Humane euthanasia techniques practiced on fur farms are those recognized by the American Veterinary Medical Association in the United States and by the Guelph University Research Facility in Canada.

The only method of euthanasia for mink certified by the FCUSA Animal Welfare Committee is pure carbon monoxide or carbon dioxide bottled gas. The animals are placed in a special airtight container which has been prefilled with gas. The unit is mobile and is brought to the cages to minimize any stress from handling. The animals are immediately rendered unconscious and die without stress or pain.

> *"Today's farm-raised furbearers are among the world's best-cared-for animals."*

Due to the larger physical size of fox, the American Veterinary Medical Association approves lethal injection as the most humane method. This method causes instant cardiac arrest. Lethal injection is the only fox harvesting method recommended by the FCUSA Animal Welfare Committee.

Fur Farming's Role in Agriculture

In the United States, the U.S. Department of Agriculture (USDA) includes fur farming in annual agriculture production statistics and reports, as do most state agriculture departments. In Canada, fur farming is licensed and regulated by the provincial departments of agriculture.

Fur farming plays an important role in the agriculture chain. Furbearers are fed mixtures of fresh meats and meat byproducts, fish, eggs, poultry and pork byproduct, and grains. Over a billion pounds of these byproducts are consumed each year on fur farms. In coastal regions with access to fish processing plants, diets are likely to be based more extensively on fish. In other areas, there is more reliance on byproducts from meat and poultry processing facilities. Mink and fox also consume prepared rations produced by commercial animal feed companies.

The feed byproducts described here are inappropriate for human consumption. If they weren't consumed by furbearers, they would require disposal, probably in scarce landfill space, as solid waste. By purchasing offal which would otherwise be discarded, fur farmers provide a source of revenue for other agriculture producers, effectively subsidizing lower food costs for consumers.

"Fur farming plays an important role in the agricultural chain."

Beautiful, warm, durable fur is just one of the byproducts of fur farming. After fur pelts are harvested, carcasses are processed to become protein meal, a basic ingredient in pet and animal feeds. In mink, the layer of fat between the pelt and the carcass produces mink oil, an important ingredient in hypoallergenic soaps, cosmetics and hair care products. Mink oil is also used as a lubricant for fine leathers to keep them soft and supple. Nutrient rich manure from fur farms, an environmentally preferable alternative to chemicals, is in heavy demand as a natural fertilizer for crop fields.

The Role of Farmer Associations

State and provincial fur farming associations, together with the Fur Commission USA, Canada Mink Breeders Association, the U.S. Fox Shippers Council and others, promote sound and humane farming practices. They accomplish this by administering comprehensive standards for farm management and organizing seminars, field days, local meetings and live mink and fox shows.

Gunnar Jorgenson, head of research for the State Animal Husbandry Station in Hilleroed, Denmark, where many mink and fox are raised, has written:

> Farm produced furbearing animals are for the most part beasts of prey, namely mink and foxes. It is characteristic of beasts of prey that they cannot develop or reproduce normally if conditions are not optimum with regard to cages, food and care. . . .
>
> As far as nourishment is concerned, furbearing animals have a very low level of tolerance. Consequently, modern fur animal production is based not only on optimum supply of specific foodstuffs, but also on the fact that the foodstuffs comprise a combination of high quality ingredients and low contamination level.

Sven Wahlberg, General Secretary of the World Wildlife Fund (Sweden) and Gunnar Krantz, Chairman of the Swedish Federation of Animal Protection Societies, described the commitment of farmers to proper animal care:

> Only a person who is interested in animals and who likes them becomes a fur farmer. These criteria are essential for two reasons: working with furbearing animals is no easy job; it is both hard and time-consuming. They are live animals and must be cared for and fed every day—weekday, weekend or public holiday. It takes a real interest in animals to work up the best material. The

farmer who has no real interest in his animals or feeling for their welfare soon suffers himself, in the form of poor financial return.

Recognizing that the future of fur farming depends on maintaining the highest standards of care, most associations conduct continuing education programs to keep farmers fully apprised of new techniques and changing technologies. Topics regularly addressed include disease control, nutrition, genetics, husbandry methods and reproduction. These programs are farmer supported and are not based on government study.

The Merit Award Certification Program

This Merit Award certification seal is awarded to fur farms which meet the criteria set forth by the FCUSA Animal Welfare Committee in its "Standard Guidelines for the Operation of Mink and Fox Farms in the United States."

After inspection by an independent, licensed veterinarian to verify compliance with Commission standards, farms that are certified are authorized to use the Merit Award certified seal until the next mandatory reinspection.

The Merit Award seal is an honor for commitment to humane treatment in all aspects of fur farming:
- Vigilant attention to nutritional needs
- Clean, safe and appropriate housing
- Prompt veterinary care
- Consideration for the animal's disposition and reproductive needs
- Elimination of outside stress

Humane fur farming practices have positioned North American fur at the top of the world market, annually attracting buyers from across the globe to auction houses in the United States and Canada. Producing the world's best fur does not happen by accident. It's a reward for years of conscientious attention to providing the best possible animal care.

The Case for Vegetarianism

by Egypt Freeman

About the author: *Egypt Freeman is a freelance writer who has been a vegan for several years.*

First of all, let's get one thing straight. I am not a health nut. With all the fat in a nut, I'd much rather be called a health plum or carrot or lemon—well, edit that last one. Call me what you like now, but when I'm 45 and looking 25, you won't have to call and ask me how I did it. When you finish this article you'll know.

Diet and Disease

You'd have to be truly out of the loop if you haven't heard that hypertension, along with cancer, heart disease and diabetes, are among the leading causes of death among Americans, especially African-Americans. What you may not know is that, according to the latest research, most—if not all—of these health problems are entirely controllable, and even preventable, with the proper diet.

What is the proper diet? Unfortunately, chances are—if you're like most African-Americans—you're not on it.

"The present American diet, with its emphasis on dairy, meat, fish, chicken and oils, accounts for 75 percent of our diseases," says Dr. Caldwell Esselstyn Jr., head of thyroid and parathyroid surgery at the Cleveland Clinic Foundation. "Namely, heart disease; stroke; hypertension; adult-onset diabetes; obesity; breast, prostate, colon, and ovarian cancer; gout; and osteoporosis."

The standard American dinner consists of a slab of meat, a potato, and something green. To that, add eggs and bacon and a glass of milk for breakfast and two pieces of nutrient-free white bread with meat or fatty peanut butter and sugary jelly. Taken together it all adds up to a diet too high in fat, cholesterol and protein.

"If you want to be as strong as an ox, eat what the ox eats—don't eat the ox," says Dr. Agatha Thrash, health lecturer and author of 15 books on nutrition. She teaches health and nutrition to medical missionaries at the Uchee Pines School in Seale, Ala., where they have helped people control and even reverse many medical afflictions such as heart disease and cancer. They have even had suc-

Reprinted from Egypt Freeman, "The Meat of the Matter," *HealthQuest*, February 28, 1995. Reprinted by permission of *HealthQuest: Total Wellness for Body, Mind, & Spirit*, the first health magazine for African Americans.

cess at keeping the immune systems of AIDS patients functioning strongly, thanks to immune-strengthening foods you can get at your local grocery or health-food store.

Dr. Thrash calls the amount of protein in the average American diet "toxic." What's to blame? Meat, she says.

Too Much Meat

"The average meat-eater gets 50–150 grams of protein daily when you can get by on a lot less." Too much protein increases the risk of kidney and liver failure, cancer and osteoporosis—a bone-thinning disease. "Alaskan Eskimos lead the world in cases of osteoporosis," Dr. Thrash points out, "mainly because of a diet far too rich in protein."

Echoing Dr. Thrash's concern is Dr. Neal Barnard, president of the Physicians' Committee for Responsible Medicine and a professor at the George Washington School of Medicine. As far as protein is concerned, "Americans consume more than twice of what they need," he says. " A high protein intake is detrimental to bone strength and overworks the kidneys." Like Dr. Thrash, Dr. Barnard blames it on meat.

In addition to introducing too much protein into the diet, meat, poultry and fish also supply too much fat and cholesterol. According to an August 1991 article in *Vegetarian Times*, "Americans currently get close to 45 percent of their daily calories from fat, and most of that fat comes from meat." The National Academy of Science recommends that no more than 30 percent of daily caloric intake come from fat. Many leading medical professionals suggest an even lower amount of fat, especially for people with health problems.

Dr. Dean Ornish, director of the Preventive Medicine Research Institute in Sausalito, Calif., has reduced fat in the diets of his heart-disease patients to less than 10 percent by placing them on strict vegetarian diets. The results: "We found reductions in blood-cholesterol levels that were comparable to what can be achieved with cholesterol-lowering drugs," Dr. Ornish reports. His diet program is so effective that Mutual of Omaha reimburses its policyholders for the cost of Dr. Ornish's services, making the Ornish program the first alternative therapy for heart disease to gain approval by a major insurance company.

"In addition to introducing too much protein into the diet, meat, poultry and fish also supply too much fat and cholesterol."

"Getting animal fat out of the diet has a dramatic effect on cholesterol levels," explains Dr. Barnard. "But don't get the idea that trimming the strip of fat off the outside of a cut of meat will eliminate the animal fat. In the leanest cuts of beef, about 30 percent of the calories are from fat, and in the leanest of chicken, the amount is about 20 percent."

Chapter 4

The Skinny on Fat

There are two main types of fat—saturated and unsaturated. Saturated fats are solid at room temperature whereas unsaturated fats are liquids. Saturated fats stimulate your liver to make more cholesterol, while unsaturated fats do not. Even if no cholesterol is eaten, however, the liver already produces as much cholesterol as the body needs. Adding to your cholesterol level by consuming foods high in saturated fat (meats and dairy products, for example) only proves detrimental to your health.

Are meat and dairy products really all that bad? Well, it depends on who you ask. Almost every leading health and nutrition expert will tell you to at least monitor your consumption of animal products—to eat leaner meats and use low-fat milk. But the National Live Stock and Meat Board—the organization representing the nation's producers, processors and marketers of the nation's meat supply (minus poultry and fish)—says not to worry, your diet's just fine as it is.

In a brochure called "Exploring Meat and Health," the Meat Board emphasizes balance, variety and moderation for people seeking the proper diet. "When meat is not a part of the diet, as in the case of vegetarians, food choices must be carefully planned so that an adequate supply of the essential nutrients is consumed," the brochure says.

This opinion is mainly based on the belief that meat is the only source for essential and nonessential amino acids, the "building blocks" that make up protein. (Amino acids en-

"Meat, poultry and fish are not all they're cracked up to be when it comes to nutrition."

able vitamins and minerals to perform their jobs properly and are necessary for the functioning of the central nervous system and the growth of bones.) However, according to the November 1993 edition of the *American Dietetic Association Journal*, "whole grains, legumes and vegetables all contain essential and nonessential amino acids. Conscious combining of these foods within a meal is unnecessary," which means vegetarians don't have to count amino acids or be any more careful about meal planning than anyone else.

Traditionally, meat has been considered an excellent source of protein, iron, zinc and other vitamins and minerals. It is now known that meat supplies more protein than a healthy diet needs. As far as iron is concerned, the Meat Board explains that "iron is the nutrient most frequently in low supply in the American diet." No one disagrees with the Meat Board's insistence that "children, athletes and pregnant, nursing and premenopausal women have increased iron needs." But "many people falsely conclude they are iron-deficient because of the popular myth linking fatigue and iron," says Dr. Randall Lauffer, a biochemist at Harvard University and author of "Iron Balance."

Meat contains "heme iron," which is more easily absorbed by the body than "nonheme iron," which is found in fruits, vegetables, grains and dairy products. The absorption of iron more readily from meat was once thought to be an advantage meat had over other foods, but it is now known that more people get into trouble because of iron overload. Iron is needed to carry oxygen in the blood, but in excess, iron is a catalyst for the formation of free radicals—unstable molecules that attack the cells of the skin, heart, brain and other organs.

"Grains, legumes, fruits and vegetables . . . contain carbohydrates, protein, fiber and essential vitamins and minerals."

"Iron-catalyzed free-radical damage is now thought to be a spark that can set off both heart disease and cancer," Dr. Lauffer explains. "In general, as you age, you accumulate iron in your body where it stays, waiting to cause trouble."

In sum, because meat contains iron that is easily absorbable—in addition to its high saturated fat and cholesterol content—"every bite of meat is contributing to two problems in the body, both of which lead to heart disease and possibly other chronic diseases," Dr. Lauffer says.

Fish and Fowl?

Are poultry and fish healthier than the hard-core hoofed meats? "Fish and light-meat poultry do contain less saturated fat than beef or pork," says nutrition expert and author Ellen Hodgson Brown in her book *With the Grain*. "But," she continues, "in studies in which poultry and fish have replaced red meat in the diet, no significant lowering of cholesterol has resulted." Contrary to popular belief, then, beef, pork, poultry and fish all contain about the same amount of cholesterol, she concludes.

There are also the man-made problems to consider. Toxic chemicals and other pollutants from the water can soak into fish and be passed on as the bigger, already-contaminated fish eat the small, also-contaminated fish. This is an especially notable problem for shellfish (shrimp, scallops, etc.), which Washington, D.C., vegetarian chef Trinna Moore graphically dismisses as "the vacuum cleaners of the sea."

Chicken's man-made problems stem from antibiotics used to make chickens grow larger from every pound of feed they eat. Whatever is in the chicken's system before the kill remains there for us to digest, along with additional bacteria that settles in as the no-longer-with-us chicken slowly decomposes while awaiting purchase.

OK, OK, enough already, you say. No more scare tactics. You get the point: Meat, poultry and fish are not all they're cracked up to be when it comes to nutrition.

But before you trade your succulent Kentucky Fried Rotisserie Gold chicken leg for a spinach salad, sans bacon, you need to know more than the downside of being a meat-eater. You need to know the upside of moving—gently, now—toward a vegetarian diet.

Consider the health benefits. "Studies of vegetarians indicate that they often have lower mortality rates from several chronic diseases than do nonvegetarians," according to the American Medical Association. Vegetarians have lower cholesterol levels and lower rates of hypertension, heart disease, cancer and other degenerative diseases.

What makes vegetarians healthier than their nonvegetarian counterparts? It's all in the food.

The New Four Food Groups

Grains, legumes, fruits and vegetables—the staples of a vegetarian diet and the New Four Food Groups recommended in 1991 by the physicians' Committee for Responsible Medicine—contain carbohydrates, protein, fiber and essential vitamins and minerals. Building your diet around these groups will ensure you plenty of energy (from complex carbohydrates) and regularity (thanks to plenty of fiber), making certain that harmful toxins are cleared out of your body before they can cause disease. Fiber not only keeps you regular, but it helps prevent colon cancer, lowers cholesterol, helps prevent dramatic fluctuations in blood sugar and helps you feel satisfied after eating. Overall, the combined effects of less total fat, no animal fat, fewer contaminants, more fiber and more cancer-fighting vitamins and minerals make the benefits of eating only from these groups enormous.

Based on these New Four Food Groups, approximately half of daily calories should come from grains—whole grains, that is. Whole grains, also known as unrefined grains, are better for you than refined grains, which have had all the nutrients bleached out. An emphasis on whole grains means choosing 100 percent whole-wheat over white bread, brown rice over white rice, or natural pastas homemade or from health-food stores over the bleached grocery-store pastas made from Semolina, a refined wheat. The grain group also includes corn, oatmeal, rye, oats, millet, barley, buckwheat and quinoa. Nutritionally, these foods will give you lots of fiber, complex carbohydrates, important vitamins and a healthful amount of protein.

Like whole grains, fruits and vegetables are loaded with carbohydrates, fiber and minerals, and are excellent sources of vitamins A and C—important for strengthening the immune system. Plus, fruits and vegetables are naturally low in fat. (Remember, pouring on salad dressings with a high saturated fat content or sautéing in oils adds a lot of fat to otherwise healthy salads and vegetables.) Recognizing the health benefits of fruits and vegetables, the

> *"It is best to eat fruits and vegetables as fresh as possible and avoid overcooking."*

U.S. Department of Agriculture stresses that you should eat at least five servings daily. Some health officials even suggest seven servings, since studies have shown that people who eat large amounts of fruits and vegetables have lower incidences of some cancers and other diseases.

It is best to eat fruits and vegetables as fresh as possible and avoid overcooking. Yemi Bates-Jones, herbalist and wellness counselor at Alabama's Cottonwood Health Spa, notes that overcooking is a particular problem in African-American diets. "Overcooking kills the nutrients in food," she explains. "Food is at its highest level of nutrients when it is raw." She recommends eating foods closer to their natural state and advises African-Americans to move away from salt and black pepper and season instead with natural herbs and spices, such as cayenne, basil, ginger, garlic, etc.

Legumes include beans, lentils and peas. These foods, nutritiously rich sources of protein, may be purchased at your local grocery store dried, canned, frozen or dehydrated. Dried beans should be soaked before cook-

> *"Changing your diet is not like giving up smoking. Cravings are minimal and pass. Taste buds quickly adapt to change."*

ing to get rid of dust and other particles that may have settled on them. Soaking improves digestibility and decreases cooking time, as well as cutting down on the gas-producing tendency of beans. (Yes it's true: beans, beans, good for your heart. The more you eat them . . . well, you know the rest.)

There are many myths about vegetarianism. While protein, iron, calcium and other essential nutrients are readily available in any balanced vegetarian diet, vitamin B-12 is a genuine nutritional issue for vegetarians.

B-12, which helps maintain healthy blood and nerves, is not produced by plants or animals, but by bacteria and other one-celled organisms, and is easily found in meat. The body can store B-12, so it is not necessary to have it every day. Every few days, however, vegetarians should be sure to have some in their diet. Sources of B-12 are the Asian foods miso and tempeh, due to the bacteria used in their production. Some breakfast cereals are also enriched with B-12, as are multivitamins. (Look for the words cobalamin or cyanocobalamin, the chemical names for B-12, on labels.)

Making That Change

Knowing what you know now about health and nutrition, you may be inspired to rush to the freezer and throw out all the meat and other products that are potential hazards to your health. You may want to jump in the car and go buy up fruits and beans galore and every green leafy vegetable you can find. And you'd be doing yourself and your family a great service.

Tameca Tucker, a vegetarian for the past three years and a cashier at Atlanta's Sevananda Health Food Co-op, became a vegetarian after reading *Dick Gregory's Natural Diet for Folks Who Eat: Cookin' with Mother Nature.* Before changing her diet, Tucker says, "I used to get sick all the time, but now I find that I don't get as many colds, my skin is a lot clearer, mental capacity is more focused, and elimination is better." She adds, "I just feel good all over." Many vegetarians (myself included) can second that emotion.

Chapter 4

Culturally speaking, vegetarianism is no longer as weird as it used to be. With the ever-growing interest in health and nutrition, as well as the continued spread of cultural consciousness in the African-American community, vegetarianism is seen as a way to get closer to our natural heritage. With that said, however, taking your new eating habits home to Mom and Dad or explaining to your grandmother why you no longer eat her Thanksgiving ham—even with the pineapples and cherries on top—the best advice is to plan ahead. Before a confrontation, bring up the issue for discussion, perhaps in a phone conversation or letter. Addressing things ahead of time will give your family a chance to think about your choice and perhaps prepare a special dish for you. Catching your family off-guard with a sudden announcement as dinner is being rolled in is a sure way to gain a grimace.

Going out to eat is less of a problem for most vegetarians since many restaurants now offer vegetarian options. Avoid restaurants with names like the Steak House or Piggy's. Ethnic eateries—such as Indian, Chinese, Italian and Japanese restaurants—are better choices.

For many of us, however, change is not always easy. That "F" word gets in the way every time—FEAR. But rest assured. Changing your diet is not like giving up smoking. Cravings are minimal and pass. Taste buds quickly adapt to change. Give up salt today, and in three weeks, you'll hardly remember what it tastes like, let alone miss it.

If you don't want to drop everything at once, try gradually improving your diet. One less steak or hamburger will be a little less fat and cholesterol. And adding more fruits and vegetables will mean added protection against diseases, thanks to increased immune strength.

When most of us think of improving our diets, we think of restrictions. Instead, focus on adding a plentiful supply of nutritious, whole foods. You can balance these additions against some of the goodies that you know contribute to poor health. So, if a completely meat-free diet sounds unappetizing, try to limit your meat consumption to fish and chicken (which can contain less saturated fat then beef or pork) once or twice a week. Trim the fat and learn to broil and bake, adding these more healthfully cooked versions to your dinner menu, as broiling and baking cut down on the amount of fat and cholesterol your poultry and fish soak up from cooking oils. Also, add a dark green leafy salad to your lunch or dinner, remembering to eat the salad first, before you embark upon the cooked food. Rediscover brown rice, whole-wheat flour and legumes, then add them to your daily eating plan.

Ultimately, according to the experts, these small steps could add years to your life. Call me when I'm 45—or, better yet, 75—and I'll prove it to you.

Factory Farms Are Cruel and Inhumane

by Lorri Bauston

About the author: *Lorri Bauston is the president of Farm Sanctuary, the first and largest sanctuary for animals abandoned by factory farms.*

Hilda was loaded onto a truck with hundreds of other sheep. The sheep were severely overcrowded in accordance with standard livestock marketing strategy to get more dollars per load, even though some animals inevitably die from the stress. After discovering an ailing Hilda on a pile of dead animals behind the Lancaster (Pennsylvania) Stockyards, investigators from Farm Sanctuary rushed her to the nearest veterinarian. Twenty minutes later she stood up and started eating and drinking.

While Hilda regained her strength, Farm Sanctuary launched an investigation to determine who had abandoned her. The stockyard records revealed that she had been on the deadpile for 16 hours. The trucker who was responsible admitted that he had dragged her off the truck and thrown her on the pile because she couldn't walk. With both a personal admission and evidence of blatant cruelty and neglect, it seemed certain that local authorities would prosecute the trucker and stockyard for cruelty to animals. However, this was not the case. Law enforcement officials claimed this common livestock practice was legal because "normal animal agriculture practices" were exempt from Pennsylvania's anti-cruelty laws, and dumping live farm animals on deadpiles was considered "normal."

Inhumane Conditions

Every year, more than seven billion animals are raised, transported, and slaughtered under grossly inhumane conditions. Animals are crammed into small crates, dragged to auctions with chains, and slaughtered while they are fully conscious. All of these practices are considered "normal agricultural operation" and have become business as usual in a system driven by profit. The food animal industry treats animals as commodities, not as living, feeling animals. Economic priorities, not humane considerations, determine industry practices in

Reprinted from Lorri Bauston, "Seven Billion Reasons to Go Vegetarian," *The Animals' Agenda*, July/August 1996. Reprinted with permission from *The Animals' Agenda*, P.O. Box 25881, Baltimore, MD 21224, USA.

all aspects of animal agriculture, from production and transportation to marketing and slaughter.

The misery begins at the production or breeding facility. The vast majority of animals used for food production are raised in intensive confinement operations, commonly called "factory farms." Overcrowding is one of the most common techniques. In hog production, for example, the pork industry readily admits that "overcrowding pigs pays—if it's managed properly," according to *National Hog Farmer* magazine. To produce pork profitably, thousands of pigs are stacked in rows of crates and crammed into giant metal warehouses. Feeding, watering, and manure disposal are completely automated, and the animals do not receive individual care.

> *"Every year, more than seven billion animals are raised, transported, and slaughtered under grossly inhumane conditions."*

The Land O' Lakes corporation's hog division estimates that "a hog needs just 12 minutes of human attention during its four months" in a confinement operation. Breeding sows spend most of their adult lives pregnant, confined in gestation or farrowing pens measuring just two feet by six feet long. The sows cannot walk, turn around, or even lie down comfortably. When the piglets reach three weeks of age, they are taken from their mothers and crowded into finishing pens until they reach slaughter weight. According to hog industry reports, more than 70 percent of pigs in intensive confinement system suffer painful foot and leg injuries, irritating skin mange, and chronic respiratory diseases. Conditions are so harsh that every year millions of pigs die before reaching the slaughterhouse.

Severe animal suffering has also resulted from reproductive and genetic manipulation. Dairy cows live a continuous cycle of impregnation, birth, and milking. Cows are milked for ten months of the year, and are pregnant for seven of these months. Calves are taken from their mothers soon after birth so that the milk can be sold for human consumption. Modern dairy cows are under constant stress, pushed to produce as much as ten times more milk than their bodies would naturally. Increased milk production, intensified with the use of bovine growth hormone (BGH), leads to increased incidences of painful udder infections, lameness, and other ailments. After four or five years of intensive production, worn-out and unproductive dairy cows are slaughtered for ground beef (a large proportion of hamburger comes from former dairy cows).

Factory farms vary in size and standards, but they have in common severe animal deprivation, cruelty, and neglect. Such blatant abuses as overcrowding, excessive reproduction, genetic manipulation, and severe confinement are standard (and legal) meat industry practices. Currently, no federal or state laws prohibit any of them. Animals used for food production are specifically excluded from the federal Animal Welfare Act, and most state humane laws exempt livestock and poultry.

Going to Market

After production, animals are either shipped directly to slaughter or are trucked to livestock marketing facilities such as stockyards and auctions. During transport, animals are loaded into severely overcrowded trucks and suffer from stress, inadequate ventilation, and trampling. As with production practices, transportation overcrowding is deliberately done to increase profits. In *Lancaster Farming* magazine, a Pennsylvania swine specialist admitted, ". . . over 250 hogs show up dead at packing plants every day. Death losses during transport are too high . . . but it doesn't take a lot of imagination to figure out why we load as many hogs on a truck as we do. It's cheaper."

Death, injury, and disease are standard during transporting and marketing. Every year, hundreds of thousands of animals collapse from the cruel conditions and can no longer stand. The meat and dairy industries call these animals "downers." Such animals can be sold for human consumption as long as they are still alive. Downed animals are often left in alleys or on loading docks, without food, water, or veterinary care, until it's convenient to take them to slaughter, usually the next day. Many die of neglect. Injured animals are typically dragged with chains or pushed with tractors or forklifts, practices that cause injuries ranging from bruises to broken bones. Downed animals who are no longer profitable are abandoned to die slowly and painfully, since most stockyards and auctions do not humanely euthanize unwanted animals.

Most laws do not adequately protect animals from transportation and marketing abuses. Federal law allows animals to be transported for up to 36 hours without food or water, and does not address overcrowding. Legislative and enforcement efforts are just starting to address the treatment of downed animals. In 1995, California enacted the Downed Animal Act to prevent cruelties at stockyards and slaughterhouses. On March 15, 1996, a stockyard and its manager were convicted of cruelty under this law. . . .

The final horror for animals raised for food production is the slaughterhouse. Stunning is not required for most animals, and when it is used, industry reports indicate a high failure rate. The industry uses three methods: captive bolt stunning (a gun shoots a bolt into the animal's brain); cardiac arrest electrical stunning; and head-only electrical stunning. All three methods can cause tremendous pain and suffering. If captive bolt guns are improperly placed, or if the gun is poorly maintained, the animals are not stunned

"Factory farms vary in size and standards, but they have in common severe animal deprivation, cruelty, and neglect."

and will be in severe pain from partial impact. Cardiac arrest stunning, which can cause animals to feel painful heart attack symptoms, kills the animals by stopping the heart. Insufficient stunning can result in paralyzed animals who feel everything. Many small slaughtering plants use head-only stunning because they lack restraint equipment. This type of stunning is reversible, and animals regain consciousness when they are not bled to death immediately. The most severe stunning problems occur in calf slaughterhouses. According to Temple Grandin, a livestock industry consultant, "Approximately half of the calf slaughterers in the U.S. shackle calves while they are still alive," despite the fact that this is illegal. Under the federal Humane Slaughter Act, animals are supposed to be stunned before slaughter. The law specifically excludes poultry (which comprise more than 90 percent of animals slaughtered for food) and ritual slaughter, such as kosher and halal. At hundreds of ritual slaughterhouses, a chain is wrapped around one of the animal's rear legs and the frightened, conscious animal is hoisted into the air, kicking and thrashing. Large animals such as cattle are particularly prone to torn ligaments and broken bones. Grandin, who has been allowed to visit ritual slaughter plants, wrote in *Moment* magazine: ". . . after visiting one plant in which five steers were hung up in a row to await slaughter, I had nightmares. The animals were hitting the walls and their bellowing could be heard in the parking lot. In some plants, the suspended animal's head is restrained by a nosetong . . . stretching of the neck by pulling on the nose is painful. Suspension upside-down also causes great discomfort . . . ."

Stop the Abuse

The raising, transporting, and slaughtering of animals for food is a nightmare for billions of animals. As in other countries, for example, Sweden and the United Kingdom, legislation must be passed and legal actions initiated in the United States to ban cruel confinement systems, downed-animal cruelties, and slaughterhouse abuses. Every individual must take action to stop the use of animals for food production. There are seven billion reasons to stop eating animals and animal by-products—just ask Hilda.

Killing Animals for Their Fur Is Inhumane

by Betsy Swart

About the author: *Betsy Swart is the national program director of Friends of Animals, an international animal rights organization.*

Wild animals are trapped, clubbed, strangled, and stomped by the millions every year to serve the relatively few people who wish to wear fur coats. Animals killed for fur in the United States include raccoons, red and gray foxes, beavers, otters, coyotes, wolves, lynxes, bobcats, opossums, badgers, nutria, and muskrats. It takes between 30 and 60 of these beautiful animals to make one fur coat.

Most wild animals killed for fur are captured in steel-jaw leghold traps. Although 64 nations have banned the use of these cruel and indiscriminate traps, the powerful U.S. fur lobby has limited regulation to just a handful of states. The steel-jaw trap is legal in all but 11 states.

The consequences for wildlife have been devastating. For every "target" animal caught in a trap, two to ten times as many "non-target" animals (including squirrels, hawks, owls, dogs, cats, and songbirds) are killed in the same trap. Some animals manage to free themselves by chewing off their trapped legs, only to die later from shock and blood loss, or as the crippled victim of a hungry predator. Called "wring-off," this horrible act of self-mutilation illustrates the incredible pain and terror experienced by trapped animals.

Fortunately, trapping is on the decline. According to pelt auction sales reports and annual state trapping records, at the height of U.S. retail fur sales in 1988, approximately 17 million animals were trapped for their skins. In 1994, however, about 2 million were trapped.

Fur Farms

Fur-farming methods are designed to maximize profits at the expense of the animals' health and comfort. Foxes are kept in cages approximately two feet square, with up to four animals per cage. Minks suffer from similar confinement, often developing self-mutilating behaviors. Cages are usually kept in

Reprinted from Betsy Swart, "The Fight Against Fur," *The Animals' Agenda*, July/August 1996.
Reprinted with permission from *The Animals' Agenda*, P.O. Box 25881, Baltimore, MD 21224, USA.

open sheds that provide little protection from harsh weather. Summer heat is particularly hard on minks because they lack the ability to cool their bodies without bathing in water. In the wild, minks spend most of their time in water. But on fur farms, where little water is available, their salivation, respiration, and body temperatures increase to unnatural and painful levels. An investigation by Friends of Animals revealed that in 1987, about 450,000 minks died on American fur farms due to heat stress alone.

Animals live in filth on fur farms and are often victims of disease and pests. Farmed animals are fed meat by-products such as cattle lungs and chicken entrails that are often so gristly that they are unfit even for the pet food industry. Bacterial contamination from such a diet threatens the health of the animals, particularly newborns.

Contagious diseases such as viral enteritis and pneumonia, as well as bladder and urinary tract infections, are also prevalent on fur farms. Fleas, ticks, lice, and other insects are attracted by the piles of excrement under the cages. These piles are often left for months, long enough for insects to infest the animals.

Even death does not come easy on a fur farm. There are no humane slaughter laws to protect the animals. Farmers have devised hideous killing methods that do not damage the animals' pelts but can cause excruciating pain. Small animals are often killed in makeshift boxes pumped with hot, unfiltered engine exhaust. Sometimes they are

> *"No regulations protect animals on fur farms."*

still alive (although unconscious) when the hose is turned off, and wake up while being skinned. Foxes and other large animals are killed by anal electrocution (the insertion of a metal rod into the anus) or in decompression chambers; others have their necks broken.

No regulations protect animals on fur farms. The growing consciousness about the cruelty inherent in fur production is helping to decrease the number of fur farms in the United States. For example, in 1988, about 6 million animals were raised and killed on American fur farms. In 1994, the number declined to about 2.5 million. In 1988, there were 1,027 mink farms registered with the U.S. Department of Agriculture; today there are 457.

Industry Scare Tactics

Faced with growing opposition, the American fur industry has resorted to misleading campaigns to sway public sentiment. Some advertising campaigns aimed at women encourage them to assert their "freedom of choice" in regard to fashion. The industry is also touting fur to middle-income women and men by marketing lower-quality furs at cheaper prices. Still, according to a 1995 Associated Press poll, 59 percent of the U.S. public believes that "killing animals for fur is always wrong," reflecting a 13 percent increase from a 1989 American Broadcasting Company poll. Furthermore, many notable designers (including

Giorgio Armani, Bill Blass, Calvin Klein, Carolina Herrera, and Todd Oldham) refuse to create fur fashions. Dozens of influential models and celebrities also shun fur.

European Union Passes Law Against Cruel Traps

In November 1991, the European Union (EU) enacted a landmark law against the steel-jaw leghold trap (EU Regulation 3254/91). Phase I of the law prohibits the use of leghold traps within the EU. Phase II bans importation of fur from badgers, beavers, bobcats, coyotes, ermines, fishers, lynxes, martens, muskrats, otters, raccoons, sables, and wolves into the EU from countries that have not banned leghold traps or adopted "internationally agreed humane trapping standards." In January 1995, Phase I of the law went into effect for all 15 member nations of the EU. A one-year delay was granted for Phase II.

A political struggle to gut the EU regulation then began. According to a chronology compiled by the Animal Welfare Institute, in August 1995, U.S. Trade Representative Mickey Kantor (and the former Secretary of Commerce) agreed to "cooperate" with Canada if Canada decided to bring a challenge against the regulation before the World Trade Organization, the successor to the General Agreement on Tariffs and Trades. Animal protection groups, aghast at the buckling of the Clinton administration under fur industry pressure, worked furiously to persuade the United States to change its position. But in November 1995 there was more bad news. The European Commission announced its decision to propose a delay of Phase II. The European Parliament, however, voted to reject the Commission's position. Then the Commission presented the Parliament with changes in the regulation that would completely destroy the original intent of the law and indefinitely delay the import ban.

The struggle to implement the EU regulation continues. On January 1, 1996, Phase II went into effect for all 15 nations of the European Union, but only the Netherlands currently enforces it.

The International Fund for Animal Welfare and the Royal Society for the Protection of Cruelty to Animals are attempting to compel the British government to enforce the regulation if imports of the prohibited furs are not refused entry into the United Kingdom. In the United States, a coalition of groups continues to work hard to prevent the U.S. government from pressuring the EU to overturn its law.

Based on industry reports, it would appear that animal rights advocates are having a definite impact on the fur industry. Since 1988, U.S. retail fur sales have fallen from $1.85 billion to $650 million, while the average price of a mink coat has dropped from $7,200 to $2,700. Legislation has been introduced in the Congress to end the use of the steel-jaw leghold trap in the United States. Clearly, although the battle is not over and much work remains, the animal rights movement has more than just a foothold in the fight against fur.

Raising Sheep for Wool Is Inhumane

by Jennifer Greenbaum

About the author: *Jennifer Greenbaum is a freelance writer and animal rights activist.*

Woven into socks, sweaters, and blankets, wool fiber has all the strength, warmth, and softness that once grew on a sheep. So pleasant are the associations we have with wool that it is rarely thought of as anything other than store-bought comfort, or something "borrowed" from a sheep through a friendly hair-cut. But a closer look at the shearing to shipping experience reveals an unpleasant reality.

Long a part of human history, the domesticated sheep has endured centuries of careful breeding for optimum wool production, quality of carcass, hardiness in harsh weather, and prolificacy in ewes. And the cost has been the animals' health. Merinos, bred in Australia, are a particularly egregious example of the problems that selective breeding has caused. To provide more surface area for wool, meaning more wool for greater profits, Merinos were bred for excess skin wrinkles, but extra skin meant new health problems.

Merinos are extremely difficult to shear without cutting the skin. They may suffer blowfly maggot infestations within the moist folds of their skin; the extra wool covering their eyes often makes them "wool blind"; and the extra wool they carry can bring on heat exhaustion.

In the United States, because lamb meat and mutton are more profitable, wool is a by-product. The slaughterbound sheep who produce wool are treated the same as any other commercial farm animal. Their tails are docked; they are impregnated, castrated, sheared, prodded, packed, shipped and slaughtered. Adult sheep are kept alive to produce wool and lambs, year after year, until they are too old to be cost-effective and are sent off to slaughter. Every year, ewes experience the labor of lambing, the love of mothering, and the loss of their frightened babies when they are taken away and sold to the local butcher or nearest

Reprinted from Jennifer Greenbaum, "What's Wrong with Wool?" *The Animals' Voice Magazine,* July/August/September 1996. Reprinted by permission of the Animal Protection Institute.

slaughterhouse. And every year the ewes are impregnated all over again. Every year, lambs experience harsh weather, body mutilations, separation from their mothers, and slaughter. To buy wool is to support the slaughter of lambs and sheep, and to contribute to the meat industry by purchasing a by-product of its main harvest.

We'd like to believe that wool harvesting causes little or no discomfort, that the wool is shaved from the outside of the sheep, much like a haircut, leaving the animal cool and comfortable for the summer. After all, wild sheep have the ability to shed their own wool during the warm months and retain it during the winter. But shearing is nothing like shedding. The sheep are thrown on their backs and restrained while a razor is run over their bodies. Whether sheared manually or mechanically, cuts in the skin are very common. Careless shearing can injure teats, pizzles, other appendages, and ligaments. Sheep are held in restraints with tight clamps on their faces when they're mechanically sheared. Naked to the world, sheep are put back out to pasture where they can suffer severe sunburn or freeze as the heat is drawn from their bodies. Death can occur when the shearer is rough and twists the sheep into an organ-damaging position, when the health of the sheep is already poor, or when being stripped of wool is a shock to the sheep's system.

Lamb Mortality

The losses in sheep production are mostly through lamb mortality. Some lambs, born on the range, are vulnerable to lethal hypothermia. Another common cause for lamb death is diarrhea, often caused in U.S. lambs by the *E. coli* bacteria, a bacteria that thrives in filth. Cold, damp lambing quarters and improper or erratic feeding of ewes usually play a part in the outbreaks.

Before the male lambs even leave the barn or pasture, when they are usually just a few days old, their tails are docked and they are castrated. Removal of the tail is a routine procedure on sheep farms that serves to maintain the quality of the wool around the back end of the sheep. Rich feeds give the sheep loose stools which soil the wool. Instead of solving the problem, the tail is cut off to help prevent messes and fly problems. The rubber

> *"To buy wool is to support the slaughter of lambs and sheep, and to contribute to the meat industry by purchasing a by-product of its main harvest."*

ring method, a common practice, involves fastening a thick adhesive band at the base of the lamb's tail. After days of painful circulation-loss, the tail dies and falls off. This method of docking is usually accompanied by rubber ring castration, a similar procedure involving the scrotum.

Docking and castration leave lambs with open wounds that are common sites for bacterial infections. If sickness is not prevented on the farm with vaccinations or treated immediately upon discovering the sick sheep (which is difficult when thousands are present), the animal is likely to die within a few days. Tetanus is one common disease that occurs in lambs after castration and docking, especially when the rubber ring method is used.

Lambs who survive long enough with their mothers are soon taken away by the farmer to be weaned early and fattened. The lambs are moved into feedlots and "finished" on forages and cereals that increase their growth rate. Some ewe lambs are retained to be used as replacement ewes. They are fed highly nutritional feed to push them into puberty at seven to eight months of age, and are not even fully grown before they are mated.

Living Conditions

Most of the sheep in the United States reside in Western ranges in flocks of 2,000 to 15,000. These range-fed sheep are constantly moving, grazing on new grasses and vegetation every day. They are not brought in for shelter, except when a ewe is lambing. Sheep are left outside to stand through the worst weather conditions, from scorching heat to pouring rain to blowing snow. They are especially sensitive to changes in temperature after shearing.

In the cold winter months, sheep are usually left standing in their pasture during a storm, since it is too difficult to bring the animals inside. To keep the freezing snow from stinging their faces, sheep turn their backs to the wind and often head away from it altogether. When they come to a barrier or fence and cannot go any further to escape the wind, the sheep pile up on one another, and are eventually buried by the snow. In this "sheep pile," the buried animals at the bottom die from suffocation or freeze in the snow.

> *"Animals produce their coats not for the benefit of humans, but for their own survival."*

Although sheep suffer for consumer demand, that can change. All products derived from sheep can be avoided, such as wool, lamb, mutton, lanolin (an oil extracted from wool), or products made from sheep's milk such as Romano cheese. The use of wool for textiles has declined dramatically in the past few decades and is almost entirely due to the increasing supply of natural and synthetic fibers.

Alice Walker wrote, "The animals of the world exist for their own reasons. They were not made for humans any more than black people were made for whites, or women for men." Animals produce their coats not for the benefit of humans, but for their own survival. Removal of their hair, feathers, fur, leather and wool is often hazardous, painful, and deadly. Sheep, ducks, and geese need insulation, silk worms need to fulfill their life cycles, and cows would obviously need their own skins if they were not slaughtered for their flesh. If you wish to leave cruelty to animals out of your lifestyle, then leave wool, down, silk, and leather behind in the stores. Leave what rightfully belongs to animals on the animals and in so doing, you help eliminate their suffering.

Chapter 5

Are Animals in the Entertainment Industry Abused?

Chapter Preface

The Iditarod Trail International Sled Dog Race is a 1,150-mile competition held in early March over Alaska's frozen tundra from Anchorage to Nome. First run in 1973, the Iditarod re-creates the 1925 journey in which sled dog teams carried much needed diphtheria serum 674 miles from Nenana to Nome. It took twenty teams of sled dogs six days to transport the serum to Nome. In today's lengthier race, under optimum conditions, the top teams of sixteen dogs run the race in less than ten days.

Some animal rights groups argue that the Iditarod and other sled dog races like it are not competitions, but a form of animal abuse. They cite the fact that thirty-two dogs have died running the Iditarod since 1990 and dozens more have dropped out due to injuries such as sore feet, sprains, fractures, and exhaustion. In 1994 the Humane Society of the United States (HSUS) publicly opposed the race because of the dog injuries and fatalities in the name of entertainment. Wayne Pacelle, an HSUS vice president, contends that many of the dogs' deaths were due to overexertion. "The race pushes these animals beyond their physical limits, and some of them suffer and die during the race," he says. The animal rights group People for the Ethical Treatment of Animals (PETA) is unequivocally opposed to sled dog races. "Basically, our organization is opposed to the use of animals in any form. They weren't put on this Earth for human purposes. Using them to race in zero or below-zero weather is inhuman," maintains Chris Kohl of PETA.

Supporters of the sled dog race contend that the charge that the dogs are run to death is an exaggeration. The animals are bred for speed and endurance, they assert, and the dogs love to run. Race officials and supporters enumerate how the health and welfare of the dogs is protected during the race: The dogs' feet are protected from the cold and rough terrain with polar-fleece booties and wrist wraps; the dogs are fed 10,000 to 11,000 calories a day; and the animals and their handlers are subject to mandatory rest periods during the race. In addition, race advocates point out that race rules require that all dogs be examined by a veterinarian at each rest stop to ensure they are fit to continue running. Any dog that is determined to be unfit is removed from the race. Supporters also contend that dog fatalities during the race, while tragic, are to be expected when one thousand dogs are exercised over a period of two weeks.

Running dogs in an endurance race is just one example of the many ways that animals are used for sport and entertainment. The authors in the following chapter debate whether other entertainment venues are abusive and harmful to animals.

Zoos Preserve Endangered Species

by Charles Hirshberg

About the author: *Charles Hirshberg is a staff writer for* Life *magazine.*

Once upon a time, not so long ago, zoos were little more than jails. Animals were kidnapped from the wild and imprisoned in bleak cells. Inbreeding was so common that their offspring rarely survived.

Today, zoos are being reinvented, revolutionized. Old cages are being knocked down and replaced with lush habitats. And thanks to an ingenious breeding program, baby animals are busting out all over.

Kejana and Baraka are two bright-eyed young gorillas, full of curiosity and mischief. As Lisa Stevens watches them bound from branch to branch in Washington, D.C.'s National Zoo, she shakes her head: "I cannot believe how far we've come."

Stevens, curator of the zoo's primates (except, of course, its humans), remembers a time, not even 15 years ago, when baby gorillas were almost as rare in zoos as the dodo bird.

She smiles as Kejana pokes his mother in the back with his toe. Then, one by one, Stevens begins ticking off the old errors: In the wild, gorillas usually live in groups of several females to each male, but zoos were keeping them either alone or in pairs. In the wild, gorillas spend hours foraging through thick vegetation for low-calorie, high-fiber food, but zoos kept them in stark concrete bunkers and fed them large servings of prepared foods that they devoured in ravenous gulps. In the wild, many of a gorilla's most important social behaviors are developed by rearing its young, but on the rare occasions that a birth occurred in a zoo, the baby was quickly removed and hand-raised by humans. Feeding, housing, rearing . . . wrong, wrong, wrong!

What made it right was the Species Survival Plan program, an effort by 175 North American zoos and aquariums to save threatened animals and their habitats from extinction. In a very real sense, SSP is a parent not only of Kejana and

Baraka but of all the animal babies on these pages. The program has much to do: Conservationists warn that within a generation, one out of five species living on earth today may be gone forever. For all too many animals, zoos may be the last best hope.

The Sloth Who Was Poked to Death by Umbrellas

Most early American zoos were showcases of mankind's mastery over nature. The creatures were stolen from the wild by hunters who stalked and slaughtered animal mothers—elephants, hippos, tigers—and then snatched their young, a practice that continued well into the 20th century. According to Vicki Croke, whose book, *The Modern Ark*, [came] out in [June 1998], zookeepers knew almost nothing about their unfortunate prisoners (one European zoo fed its gorilla sausages and beer), and visitors showed scant respect for these dazed, broken specimens. Shortly after the Philadelphia Zoo opened in 1874, a sloth was poked to death with canes and umbrellas by visitors who couldn't understand why the nocturnal tree-dweller insisted on sleeping during the day. Incredibly, most zoos didn't even employ full-time veterinarians until the 1950s.

There were exceptions: The Bronx Zoo is largely responsible for saving the American bison. But as a rule, enlightenment came slowly. Then, in 1979, a bomb exploded in the form of a scientific paper called "Inbreeding and Juvenile Mortality in Small Populations of Ungulates." (Translation: "Incest and Baby Death in Little Groups of Hoofed Critters.")

The report revealed that zoo-born baby animals were dying at a shockingly high rate. The reason: Since each zoo housed only a few representatives of each species, keepers were breeding fathers with daughters, and brothers with sisters. At the same time, animals were disappearing from the wild. America's zoos wanted to help. They needed to help. Without animals they couldn't survive.

The Alligators Who Honeymooned on the Bayou

Meanwhile, one solution to the breeding problem was being cooked up by, among others, John Behler, the Bronx Zoo's curator of reptiles. Behler's passion was the Chinese alligator, a creature of the Lower Yangtze River Valley, where it builds intricate dens with as many as 20 chambers and passageways. But Yangtze farmers weren't impressed; the alligators ate their fish and ducks. Behler was desperate to focus attention on the reptile's plight, but how? There were only two pairs in the U.S., one at the Bronx Zoo, one at the National Zoo, and neither couple was showing any interest in making babies.

> *"Zoos are being reinvented, revolutionized."*

Behler persuaded the zoos to send the foursome on a group honeymoon. He figured that four alligators living in an environment similar to their natural habitat were more likely to breed than two separate pairs living in tanks. So in March 1976 he loaded the six-foot-long beasts into the back of his station wagon and drove 23-and-a-half hours straight, to the Rockefeller Wildlife Refuge in Louisiana. "I could hear truckers shouting over the CB," Behler recalls. "'Hey, lookee there! That wagon's got a bunch o' gators in the back!'"

The lucky couples were shown to adjoining half-acre pens, complete with wading pools and earthen mounds in which to practice their subterranean architecture. Alas, a harsh winter killed one male, but the survivor happily took his place and within three years was procreating enthusiastically with both females. Behler's experiment worked so well that Chinese alligators are now found in dozens of North American zoos. Back in the Bronx, Behler stands above a tank full of babies and contemplates a new problem: success. "We have to be careful not to overbreed them," he says, "or we'll have more than we can house."

The Cheetah Sperm That Had Three Heads

Zoos had long wallowed in jealous rivalry, but by the 1970s some had begun pulling together to save from extinction species like the Arabian oryx, a beautiful antelope. Such efforts became prototypes for the Species Survival Plan program, launched in 1981. Here's how SSP works: Zoo experts decide which endangered species should get the lion's share of zoo resources. For each one chosen (there are currently 134 species in the program), an SSP is designed, complete with a detailed list of goals. For instance, the SSP for the ring-tailed lemur aims to keep the nationwide zoo population at no more or less than 350 animals and to promote the conservation of its habitat in southern Madagascar.

> *"Conservationists warn that within a generation, one out of five species living on earth today may be gone forever. For all too many animals, zoos may be the last hope."*

A studbook, which JoGayle Howard, an infertility specialist at the National Zoo, describes as "a computer dating service for animals," is kept for each SSP. Planned parenthood works: Ninety percent of mammals in zoos today were born in zoos. As gruesome reminders of why careful breeding is essential, Howard keeps on hand photographs of cheetah sperm mutated by incest—some with three heads; some rolled up like balls, as if they are trying to catch their tails.

The Tamarin Who Got His Head Stuck in a Tree

Some species need more than a dating service. In 1985, only 18 black-footed ferrets were left in the world. Years of subsequent breeding attempts met with mixed results. (One problem: A few of the males had vampirish sexual tastes, biting females in the neck during intercourse with such force that they nearly killed them.) So Howard devised artificial insemination for ferrets, helping to raise the captive population to more than 600. In addition, more than 400 of the animals have been reintroduced into the wild, in the southwestern U.S.

Though the ferrets are flourishing, reintroduction is expensive and risky. It requires not only a protected natural habitat—a rarity in an increasingly polluted and populated world—but also a plentiful supply of animals with the skills to fend for themselves in an unforgiving wilderness. Golden lion tamarins, quick-moving monkeys with magnificent manes, have long been bred in zoos with great success. But early attempts to reintroduce them to the Brazilian rain forest faltered. The National Zoo's Benjamin Beck, who directs the species' reintroduction program, tells of a tamarin that died because its head got caught in a tree trunk while the animal was eating insects. How, Beck wondered, could tamarins raised in a zoo learn to survive in the wild?

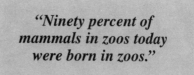

"Ninety percent of mammals in zoos today were born in zoos."

"We decided to release them on zoo grounds," he says. "That way, their environment would be constantly changing and they'd learn to make some of the same kinds of cognitive decisions they need to make in the forest. It worked like a charm." Beck's tamarins now boast a 60 percent survival rate in the forest. And their wild-born offspring do even better.

But despite these and other reintroduction successes, including the red wolf and the California condor, such programs are practical for saving no more than a handful of species. Some conservationists question whether the benefits of reintroduction are worth its costs—and also whether SSP plays fair with all of God's creatures.

The Rattlesnake Who Won an Island's Love

"Honestly, these are butt-ugly animals," says David Grow with a laugh as he introduces some of the cold-blooded creepy-crawlers at the Oklahoma City Zoological Park, where he is curator of herpetology. First, a Dumeril's boa, lifting its head from its fat coils to rudely flick its forked tongue. Next, a Galapagos tortoise named Debbie, with a face like Mr. Magoo's. Both have SSPs; in general, however, it's more difficult for such animals to find inclusion in the program. "We just can't compete with cute furry animals with big black eyelashes," says Grow.

Some experts fear SSP ignores the vast diversity of animal life in nature: Mammals make up two-thirds of SSPs, versus less than 1 percent of the wild. "Ninety-five percent of all creatures on earth are smaller than a chicken's egg," David Hancocks of the Arizona-Sonora Desert Museum has written. "Emphasis on the bigger, the cuter and the more spectacular result[s] in a skewed and narrow view of the animal kingdom."

But Grow is pragmatic about his beloved, neglected reptiles. "The important thing is to preserve the ecosystems where these animals live," he says. "The best way to do that is by showing people an animal that appeals to them, like, say, a rhino. And if you can inspire them to save the habitat of the Sumatran rhino, you'll be saving ten species of snakes."

On the other hand, who really wants to protect a snake—especially a venomous one that might sink its fangs into a tourist? Certainly nobody in Aruba until Toledo Zoo curator of herpetology Andrew Odum arrived there in 1986 and began telling anyone who would listen that Aruba was home to a creature that existed nowhere else: the Aruba Island rattlesnake. Arubans responded so enthusiastically that the snake's picture now appears on their money. And they want to make the rattler's 12-square-mile habitat a nature preserve. "We're pleased," says Odum, "but conservation is a long war. You can win every battle, then someone brings out the bulldozers and you're finished."

The Gorilla Who Took a Bite of the Big Apple

It's a long war, and often a confusing one. Consider Tiny Tim, a 38-year-old western lowland gorilla born in the jungles of Cameroon. Six years ago a nationwide campaign was waged to save him from the clutches of his SSP.

It all started after the gorilla SSP announced it wanted to move Timmy (as he is better known) from the Cleveland Metroparks Zoo to the Bronx Zoo. To many animal lovers, the plan seemed bureaucratic, cruel. The local paper ran stories about Timmy's amorous relationship with a female gorilla named Kribi Kate. Wouldn't it break his heart to leave her? A petition was circulated, rallies were held, and, finally, a lawsuit was heard in federal court to keep Timmy in Cleveland. The SSP prevailed.

Who was right? In Cleveland, Timmy lived in the kind of cage zookeepers now call bathrooms, because that was the only animal need they accommodated. (The zoo has since expanded and improved its gorilla exhibit.) He never felt the sun on his fur or the wind against his face. He spent most of his days sitting in his cage, doing nothing. And he had sired no young.

Today, Timmy lives in a spacious indoor-outdoor enclosure with five females. And his home will be about $30 million better when a six-and-a-half-acre residence opens in two years. Meanwhile, Timmy forages through hay for vegetables and sunflower seeds . . . that is, until one of his four babies (he has fathered six in the past four years) hops onto his back and wraps its arms around his neck.

Timmy's sons and daughters may never walk in the wild; they may never be truly free. But without them, their species might not survive. Like so many other animals in zoos today, they are ambassadors for their kind and, in a very real sense, ambassadors for nature itself.

Circus Animals Are Well Treated

by Matthew Carolan and Raymond J. Keating

About the authors: *Matthew Carolan is executive director of* National Review. *Raymond J. Keating is the chief economist for the Small Business Survival Committee.*

No more lions, tigers and bears? Oh my! The animal rights movement wants to ban animals from that great tradition—the circus.

This issue drew our attention recently when the 110-year-old Clyde Beatty-Cole Bros. Circus came to town. This year's (1995) Long Island, New York, stops were Bay Shore, Oceanside, Southampton and the Smith Haven Mall.

Clowns, "an array of aerial artists" and a human cannonball brought smiles to faces of all ages, as did the circus animals, including tigers, lions, elephants, horses and dogs.

Even though these animals are well cared for and seem quite happy, the animal rights movement says otherwise. They say circus animals are exploited, and suffer from disorientation, boredom, and "psychotic behavior." The activists want to end all animal acts in circuses.

Prior to the Smith Haven Mall show, the circus barker announced that activists were circulating petitions to get the government to ban animals from the circus. In contrast, he urged those in attendance to sign a petition declaring support "for having healthy and happy animals travel with the American Circus."

Circuses, of course, possess every incentive to take care of their animals. Abuse would not only risk one's livelihood but one's life as well. Mistreatment also remains unlikely, as most trainers form ties to animals, just as the rest of us do with the family dog. As the wife of a Cole Bros. elephant trainer once told *Newsday*, "They can't hurt something they love so much."

Common sense would dictate that anyone concerned about animals would work with circuses, not against them.

A new report by Daniel Oliver, author of *Animal Rights: The Inhumane Cru-*

Reprinted from Matthew Carolan and Raymond J. Keating, "Leave the Circus Out of PC Debate," *Newsday*, August 10, 1997, by permission of Matthew Carolan.

sade, estimates that 10 million people contribute to animal rights groups to the tune of $200 million.

Many of these donors confuse animal rights groups with animal welfare organizations. "Animal welfare . . . organizations have existed for decades and seek to improve the treatment and well-being of animals," while animal rights groups "seek to end the use and ownership of animals," Oliver observes.

Animal rights groups not only argue against animals performing in circuses, they want to abolish hunting, fishing, zoos, aquariums and marine parks, dog and horse racing, rodeos and horse-drawn carriages, even tropical fish tanks or other breeding and owning of pets. Eating meat, fish, poultry or dairy also make the animal rights lengthy list of no-no's.

Most disturbing is opposition by some activists to animals being used for medical research. Over the years, animal research has played a critical role in advancing treatments and cures for many diseases, including Alzheimer's, polio, cancer, AIDS, cholera, diabetes, leprosy and smallpox, and increasing knowledge of organ-transplant and other surgical techniques.

The bottom line philosophically is that animal rights groups see no moral difference between a human being and an animal. The movement is an odd mix of moral righteousness and moral relativism. In 1991, People for the Ethical Treatment of Animals (PETA) took out an advertisement comparing meat packers to mass-murderer Jeffrey Dahmer.

> *"Circuses, of course, possess every incentive to take care of their animals. Abuse would not only risk one's livelihood but one's life as well."*

At the time, PETA's lifestyles campaign director declared: "Abuse is abuse regardless of the species. We hope it will jolt a few people into realizing that what happened to those people is no different than what happens to animals."

Animals do not have rights (which would mean they could understand and carry out moral responsibilities), but humans do have a responsibility to be humane to all living creatures. That does not mean, however, that we must abandon modern advances in favor of the nature-worshipping vegetarianism of animal rights groups. (And, hey, what about plant rights?)

In such a confused age, we'll stick with the biblical injunction to man: "Rule over the fish of the sea and the birds of the air and over every living creature that moves on the ground."

When the circus comes back to Long Island, we want current and future generations to hear the roar of a lion and see the happy mayhem of the dog show. We also want our fellow man to benefit from medical research that must involve animals. Obviously, the animal rights movement has different priorities.

Rodeos Are More Dangerous for Humans Than for Animals

by Richard Sine

About the author: *Richard Sine is a former staff writer for the weekly San Jose, California–area* Metro *newspaper.*

Early Friday morning the big trucks roll into the enormous aluminum takeout box that is the San Jose (Calif.) Arena, carrying 1,770,000 pounds of dirt which will transform the place from fantasy frozen pond to fantasy dusty corral. More workers tape down plastic tarp to cover every inch of the carpeted hallways where cowboys will mill about and warm up. In the afternoon the enormous steel trailers pull up to the back, with the bulls' huge round eyes glinting through the narrow slots.

Met by Protesters

As the first group of rodeo fans arrive, the animal rights protesters are there to meet them. They are handing out fliers and carrying signs that read "Rodeo is no fun for animals" and "Violence to animals isn't a sport." They are a familiar sight to many of the fans, who reject the fliers, scan their clothing for signs of leather, and make the occasional sneering remark.

One of the protesters, a young woman from Santa Cruz dressed in a peasant-style poncho, confides her knee-jerk impressions to a reporter. "Most of them don't look literate," she says, "so I'm trying to save the pamphlets." Her friend, the one who's actually seen a rodeo while the girl was traveling in Guatemala, looks around derisively, as if this blue-collar crowd is nothing but a bunch of junkyard dogs. "These are scary-looking guys," he says. "With their tight jeans and boots, they look like they're ready to kick you."

It would not be too inaccurate to say these fans, this wave of denim and Stetson and pointy boots, are out for blood. But it's not necessarily animal blood.

Reprinted from Richard Sine, "Pain on the Range," *Metro*, March 28–April 3, 1996, by permission.

The Dodge Truck World's Toughest Rodeo, like an increasing number of rodeos, has dropped the roping and steer-wrestling events from its lineup. Those events, while closest to simulating the duties of real working cowboys, are the most highly criticized by animal activists—especially the calf roping, for its tendency to snap calves' necks and backs. Instead, this rodeo is mostly roughstock: cowboys riding bucking bulls and broncs, with a few women racing horses around barrels.

> *"When you compare the lives of the animals with that of their cowboys—it becomes a pretty tough call who really gets the sharp end of the spur."*

It's these hazardous events, especially the harrowing bull riding, which have increased rodeo's popularity in recent years. And when you're watching a cowboy get tossed around by these enormous animals, and you see the broken bones and the piddly payoffs and the shit-tough nomadic life these cowboys lead—that is, when you compare the lives of the animals with that of their cowboys—it becomes a pretty tough call who really gets the sharp end of the spur.

Just inside the stadium, a promotional video spells out the story: "Sports Pages KILLER RODEO," reads the blurb. "Rodeo action has never been like this. The raging bulls! The elusive calves! The stubborn steers! Killer Rodeo is cowboys crashing to earth from a hostile horse. It's bulls tossing their cowboys like rag dolls—and then stomping them. It's just plain pain on the range!"

A 50-Percent Buckoff Rate

John Growney, the stock contractor, wears a beige suede cowboy hat, a blue denim shirt and blue Wranglers a couple of shades darker than his ice-blue eyes. He is sauntering past his trailer toward his shiny white pickup. "The animals have had the whole winter off, they haven't competed since October. So they should be good and ready to buck," he says. "And my job is to buck cowboys." He climbs onto the cab and starts dropping fur-lined flank straps and saddles to the ground. "People go to a stock car race, they want to see a wreck. They go to a boxing match, they want to see someone get knocked out. We aim for over a 50-percent buckoff rate."

Growney is one of the top stockmen in the nation. He raised Red Rock, the red brindle bull who went unridden 309 times until the famous Lane Frost finally hung on for longer than the mandatory eight seconds. (Shortly thereafter, another bull punctured Frost's heart with its horn, killing the cowboy.) Growney still owns Wolfman, Red Rock's grandson, but Wolfman is back home in Red Bluff tonight. Instead, Growney has lined up a different, but equally scary-looking, bull as the star attraction. Actually, every bull looks pretty scary, once you see what it can do to a rider.

The stock enter the corral and the chutes through the back entrance. The cowboys use a side portal. In the tunnel behind the portal, cowboys are getting their hamstrings stretched and backs adjusted by two local chiropractors, who offer their services for free. Pauline Anderson, a slim, sweet-smelling woman with pale blue eyes and an all-black outfit, says more and more cowboys use her services every year. "Many cowboys are uninsured," she says. "They're afraid to use the ambulance, because they can't afford the ride. So, many come to us at every rodeo. We see a dislocated shoulder just about every night. And lots of broken thumbs and hands."

The cowboys are as "flexible as ballet dancers," Anderson says, but they also are prone to stiffness. "They get bumped around real bad by the broncs and bulls. Then they just sit in the car and drive for hours to get to the next rodeo."

Down the tunnel, maybe 20 cowboys are warming up in the dressing room, which smells powerfully of Flexal, a heat ointment. Casey Vollin of Salinas, Calif., a bareback rider with a passing resemblance to Mel Gibson, rubs the ointment all over his left arm, the one that hangs on. (Roughstock riders are not allowed to touch the animal with their other arm.) Then he tapes up every inch of his arm. He rubs rosin, a sandy yellowish pine distillate, on his hand and rigging handle to aid his all-important grip.

Vollin has not been able to stretch his arm out straight since his elbow surgery, which became necessary when the pain came all day, every day, and he couldn't brush his teeth and could hardly write his name. His left hand and thumb are lumpy with calcium and cartilage deposits from

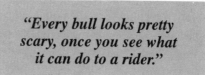

"Every bull looks pretty scary, once you see what it can do to a rider."

being broken innumerable times. Since his elbow surgery he's slowed his rodeo career down—checking in at only 80 rodeos a year instead of 110—and supplemented his income with auto detailing.

Vollin comes from a rodeo family. In 1990, his brother Rhett was kicked in the head by a bull on the day before his 30th birthday. The blow knocked the carpenter unconscious, and within 20 minutes he was dead.

Tonight, Casey Vollin jokes with his buddies, his fellow cowboys, to ease the tension. They all compete against each other for money, but they talk like they're all on the same team. They travel together, party together, help each other out in the chutes, and trade inside information on which are the toughest bulls and broncs.

Meanwhile, in the arena, announcer Zoop Dove is telling everyone in the half-full stands to shake hands with the nearest stranger.

The arena darkens, and the face of John Wayne appears on the telescreen. With "America" playing in the background, Wayne recites a poem describing why he rides: the mighty Tetons, the snow-flanked Rockies, the great Mississippi. Then, as women in sequined-denim blouses and gold-tasseled chaps ride around the arena carrying American flags, the national anthem is played. The telescreen shows idealized footage of small-town America, mixed in with idealized footage of U.S. soldiers jumping out of helicopters and trudging through swamps.

Surviving the Ride

Within a couple of minutes, the bareback riders are bursting out of their chutes. The telescreen captures the ugly grimace the cowboys assume, the look of utter concentration, just before the chute opens. Then the horses start to buck, and the grimaces are replaced by a sort of blank, puffy-cheeked mask, as if the cowboys' conscious minds have left them to sit out the ride. To get a high score, the cowboy's legs must kick out and spur the horse's shoulders every time it bucks.

Vollin is tossed off in less than eight seconds, and so gets no score. Another local cowboy, Wes Hoskins of Hollister, Calif., doesn't make it out of the chute as the horse falls on its side, kicking. Hoskins has to struggle to pull his hand out of his rigging. On his second try, he appears to narrowly escape being stepped on by his horse.

After the riders dismount, the horses dash around the arena, their hooves kicking dirt into the first couple of rows. On the dismount, the bronc riders at least have it better than the bull riders, because the bulls actually *chase* their riders. The bullfighter, dressed in clown garb, runs interference.

The animal rights activists outside the arena believe that these terrifying duels between man and beast are more staged than real. "Animals used in rodeos are not aggressive by nature," reads their flier. "They are physically provoked into displaying wild behavior. Electric prods, sharp sticks, and other devices are used on them. The tight flank strap, illegal in Ohio, is cruel, driving them into a frenzy by tricking them into trying to escape from an imagined encumbrance, and tissue is damaged by repeated blunt injury caused by spurs that are blunt or have rowels that roll."

There are no electric prods visible tonight, only the flank straps, always cinched around the broncs and bulls. Growney tells me the straps simply give horses and bulls that are naturally unbreakable a bigger incentive to kick and twist, rather than simply pogo up and down. San Jose horse

> *"The [flank] straps simply give horses and bulls that are naturally unbreakable a bigger incentive to kick and twist, rather than simply pogo up and down."*

veterinarian Robert Novick, who was hired by the rodeo producer to stand by along with the paramedics, dismissed the effect of the straps.

"In the great scheme of things, this is pretty innocuous," Novick said. "The animals are valuable to the rodeo operators. They buck about once a week, and for eight seconds of work they experience mild discomfort." (Most humane societies have a different view of the straps: "If the animals buck naturally, then let them," says Maia Carroll of the Monterey County SPCA.)

196

Chapter 5

Healthy Animals Are Necessary

The value of having healthy animals, or at least animals that will buck vigorously, is evident to anyone with a grasp of the rodeo food chain. Half a roughstock cowboy's score depends on how tough a ride his animal provides. If a cowboy draws an animal with a tame reputation, he may not travel to the show at all. If the stock contractor's animals don't put on a good show, he or she won't be hired by the rodeo producer. As a result, a particularly tough bull or bronc will fetch $10,000 or more on the open market.

The animals' high-profile role in the rodeo becomes clear at the beginning of the rodeo's most glamorous event, the bull riding. The arena goes dark and yellow spotlights swirl around the center gate. As the stirring theme from *Rocky* is played, the gates open to reveal Boomtown Gambler, a rust-colored bull with huge horns and jowls. The announcer works the boxing theme by announcing Boomtown's weight (1,700 pounds) and record (unridden in almost 100 tries). Boomtown trots gamely around the arena, as if he expects fans to shower him with rose bouquets.

> *"The animals are valuable to the rodeo operators. They buck about once a week, and for eight seconds of work they experience mild discomfort."*

When the bull is finished, a spotlight shines on the other side of the arena, where Buddy Gulden of Browns Valley, Calif., has raised his arms. The announcer heralds Gulden's state championships and National Finals performance. He also plays up his comparatively pathetic 165-pound weigh-in—okay for a man, but less than a tenth the weight of the bull.

Gulden is one of the few performers who manages to hang onto his bull for more than the requisite eight seconds. (The original cowboys on the range, by the way, did have to ride wild horses to break them. But none of them ever needed to break a bull.) When it is all over, I find Gulden sitting in the tunnel with his right foot bandaged and elevated, his left shin bandaged and padded. A paramedic with a clipboard crouches at his side. What happened to his foot? "Bull poked a hole in it," Gulden says laconically. It also kicked his shin.

According to Growney, the stock contractor, tonight was the first time Boomtown Gambler had been ridden in 95 tries. When I compliment Gulden for his accomplishment, however, the cowboy tells me the bull had been ridden fairly recently and fairly often. Perhaps Gulden was being modest or mistaken, but I never went back to Growney to straighten out the discrepancy. I preferred to let it drift into the realm of minor mythology, of tall tales and traveling shows.

Within a half hour, Gulden, his bandaged foot squeezed into his boot, has returned to the arena for the "short go," or head-to-head finals. For one horrifying moment, it looks as if the new bull, Ultimate Warrior, has stepped on the very same foot Boomtown Gambler had punctured earlier. But Gulden had merely gotten his spur stuck in a strap. The ride completed, the cowboy limped off the arena and into the arms of victory.

When the night's competition is over, Gulden and the other cowboys relax and joke back in the dressing room. This time, however, they've been joined by two young rodeo groupies, dressed almost identically in black hats and blazers, bolo ties and boots. The cowboys undress in front of them—known in the business as buckle bunnies—with no sign of embarrassment. As the blonde chats with Gulden and his companions in one corner, her brunette friend opens her blouse to a cowboy standing near the entrance to the bathroom. Soon a crowd gathers, and several cowboys sign the girl's breast. Tit signing, the cowboys later inform me, is a long-standing rodeo tradition.

Gulden removes his Wranglers to reveal a taped-up leg and knee braces. His sock is still blood-soaked. He'll skip the emergency room tonight, however, unwilling to put up with the endless wait. He'll go tomorrow morning instead.

A Small Payoff

Within a few minutes, a cowboy friend walks in and hands Gulden his check. For winning both rounds of the event that night, Gulden has won $1,200. Subtract from that his $100 entry fee. The second-place winner got $700; everyone else came out less than broke.

The rodeo veteran looks at the check and looks at me, a flicker of anger in his eyes. "Not a very good payoff, is it," he asks rhetorically, "for all they made it out to be."

Gulden puts his lifetime earnings at about $500,000, which sounds rich until you realize he's been risking his life in this sport for more than 15 years, longer than most bull riders compete before retirement. It was the 1980s before a rodeo cowboy ever made a million dollars in a lifetime, an accomplishment few have rated since. "Barry Bonds gets $7 million this year even if he plays or not," Vollin tells me. "We only get paid if we win. So you *have* to ride with injuries."

Gulden, however, is at least smart enough to take a pass on Saturday night. Saturday night's bull riding is cursed, even by rodeo standards. Frank Jackson is thrown off the bull and kicked in the head. He lies face down in the arena, still as a stone, as I experience a sickening flashback to an incident I had never seen—the death of Rhett Vollin. The crowd goes quiet. Paramedics descend upon Jackson, tape every part of his body to a stretcher, stick an oxygen mask on him, and carry him toward the portal. By that time, Jackson has regained consciousness.

> *"Twelve professional cowboys died in pro North American rodeo in 1994. . . . It is not surprising that so many have died. It is surprising how many have escaped with their lives."*

The downed cowboy gives a thumbs-up to the cheers of the crowd. Queen's "We Will Rock You" blares from the speakers. The fans begin to clap in time. And, within two minutes, another cowboy is out the chute.

Chapter 5

That cowboy, an Australian named Chris Lethbridge, gets his hand hung up in the rigging as he attempts to dismount. He is dragged in circles by the bucking and twisting bull, but escapes the arena with only the nip of a horn to the chin. The next rider, Mark Cibalski, is thrown off almost immediately. The bull runs him over, but miraculously does not touch him. KCee Bonick of Lake City, Calif., appears to get grazed in both shoulders by his bull's legs. He runs out of the arena and drops to one knee, a gesture of recovery or genuflection or perhaps both. Spike Sprague narrowly escapes a horn to the groin.

Twelve professional cowboys died in pro North American rodeo in 1994. After watching this show, it is not surprising that so many have died. It is surprising how many have escaped with their lives.

Lethbridge has made it to the finals round. He tilts his head to show his chin scrape and suggests amicably that when the show is over we head out to the Saddle Rack, chase some girls, maybe sign a tit or two. I climb up the stands to discuss this option with my friend, who has accompanied me to see his first rodeo. But my friend, shaken by the violence, looks a little pale. It's time to go.

Animals in the Entertainment Industry Are Abused

by Animal Alliance of Canada

About the author: *The Animal Alliance of Canada is an animal rights organization based in Toronto, Ontario, that fights animal cruelty through investigation, education, advocacy, and legislation.*

Attitudes about our treatment of animals and the environment are changing; we are beginning to realize that we do not have the right to exploit animals or nature. Animals used in entertainment are exploited for profit. This is both unnecessary and unacceptable. Children and adults alike must learn an appreciation and a respect for animals. The tricks performed in anthropomorphic animal shows do nothing to achieve this goal, but instead reinforce the idea of human dominion over animals. Quite simply, confinement, cruelty and abuse are not entertaining.

Circuses

Circuses with animal acts are suffering from an increasingly poor image as the public realizes that they are outdated spectacles. Critically endangered animals such as chimpanzees, elephants and tigers are forced to perform degrading and often fear-provoking acts. Many circuses are guilty of not providing the most basic of necessities, such as adequate care and housing for the animals.

Many methods used to train animals to perform tricks involve physical punishment. Animals may be beaten into submission with whips, metal hooks, wooden bats and clubs. Some are muzzled, choked with tight collars, shocked with electric prods or have their teeth or claws removed to make them more manageable.

Most circus animals are wild, not domesticated. They resist training because it is unnatural and may be painful or frightening for them. The discomfort they

Reprinted from "Animals in Entertainment," an Animal Alliance of Canada publication at www.animalalliance.ca/entertai.html, December 1997. Reprinted by permission.

endure may incite the animals to behave violently, and even de-clawed, trained animals may be a potential danger to their trainers and to the public.

Circus animals are often housed inadequately, spending the majority of their lives in small transportation cages called "Beast wagons." Regulations for cage sizes, where they exist, are often outdated and ignored. Canada has no laws specifically dealing with circus animal care and housing. The animals are denied basic freedom of movement and may not have enough room to stand up, or even turn around. The animals must eat, sleep and defecate in these cages. Their brief moments of illusory freedom only come when they perform. Some animals are kept in the same small cage for the weeks that they are not performing because few circuses invest in adequate off-season housing. Animals such as elephants and horses who are not caged may be permanently shackled. Such unrelieved confinement affects the animals both physically and psychologically.

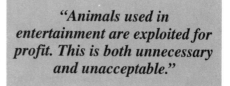

"Animals used in entertainment are exploited for profit. This is both unnecessary and unacceptable."

It is virtually impossible to provide an acceptable quality of life in circuses for animals that are wild by nature. Their physical, psychological and behavioral needs are so complex that the living conditions will always be inadequate. This situation is especially hard on animals such as elephants, who enjoy complex social lives in the wild. Veterinarians qualified to treat exotic animals are not common.

This suffering can easily end. Eliminating animal acts will simply mean increasing human performances. Circuses with all-human performances are both popular and successful. Animal acts have already been banned in several Canadian cities, as well as some European countries.

Rodeos

The rodeo is marketed as entertainment and sport for humans, but the treatment of the animals in rodeos may be barbaric. Ironically, human participants are considered brave and strong for facing these ferocious and unpredictable bulls and steers. "Cowboys" gain points in the competition by staying on a bucking horse the longest, or roping a steer the fastest. These people can be seriously injured or killed, but unlike the animals, they have a choice to participate.

Ear and tail twisting, spurring or striking incite the animals to buck violently. Horses may have "bucking straps" tightly fastened around their abdomens, putting pressure on their kidneys and lower backs. This pain, combined with fear, causes the animals to buck wildly. When the strap is removed, the animal calms down.

Marine Parks and Aquaria

No matter how spacious an aquarium tank may be, to wide-ranging, social animals such as dolphins and whales, it is a prison. Captured from the wild and removed from their natural family groups, most end up being displayed in barren, concrete pools filled with chlorinated water.

The artificial physical and distorted social environment experienced by most captive whales and dolphins has resulted in stress-related illnesses and high levels of mortality.

We simply cannot duplicate ocean conditions for whales and dolphins. For example, in the wild, beluga whales and orcas may travel long distances (20–100 miles) each day and dive hundreds of feet below the water's surface. These normal activities, and most others, cannot be performed in captivity. Lack of physical and behavioral stimulation may be an important factor in the decreased lifespan of most captive whales and dolphins. It is estimated that bottlenose dolphins live for 25–30 years in the wild, and that orcas live from 45–90 years. In captivity, most live less than 10 years.

Almost all captive beluga whales have come from the Churchill River estuary in Churchill, Manitoba. Because the population of belugas in captivity is not self-sustaining, they continue to be hunted for aquarium displays. Beluga whales originating in Canadian waters can no longer be captured for foreign aquaria. However, Canadian aquariums can still apply for, and obtain, beluga capture permits from the federal agency responsible for beluga management—the Department of Fisheries and Oceans. Once the whales have been in captivity for a period of time, there is a very real possibility of export to foreign aquaria.

What You Can Do

- Write to your City Council asking for an exotic animal ban.
- Write your City or Town Council requesting a by-law to stop the use of animals in rodeos and stampedes.
- Do not visit circuses, rodeos, aquaria, marine parks or other exhibits or performances where animals are exploited.
- Write letters to the editor expressing your feelings about animals in entertainment. . . .

Consumers Can Make a Difference

Animals continue to suffer in the name of entertainment to satisfy the whims of a minority and to generate profit. If spectacles such as circuses, marine shows and rodeos become even less and less popular with the general public, they will not make money. Without a financial incentive, these brutalities would end. It is up to us to become informed about these issues, and to act to end the exploitation of animals.

Zoos Are Prisons

by People for the Ethical Treatment of Animals

About the author: *People for the Ethical Treatment of Animals, headquartered in Norfolk, Virginia, is the world's largest animal rights organization.*

Despite their professed concern for animals, zoos remain more "collections" of interesting "items" than actual havens or simulated habitats. Zoos teach people that it is acceptable to keep animals in captivity, bored, cramped, lonely, and far from their natural homes.

Says Virginia McKenna, star of the classic movie *Born Free* and now an active campaigner in behalf of captive animals: "It is the sadness of zoos which haunts me. The purposeless existence of the animals. For the four hours we spend in a zoo, the animals spend four years, or fourteen, perhaps even longer—if not in the same zoo then in others—day and night; summer and winter. . . . This is not conservation and surely it is not education. No, it is 'entertainment.' Not comedy, however, but tragedy."

Life Sentence, No Parole

Zoos range in size and quality from cageless parks to small roadside menageries with concrete slabs and iron bars. The larger the zoo and the greater the number and variety of the animals it contains, the more it costs to provide quality care for the animals. Although more than 112 million people visit zoos in the United States and Canada every year, most zoos operate at a loss and must find ways to cut costs (which sometimes means selling animals) or add gimmicks that will attract visitors. Zoo officials often consider profits ahead of the animals' well-being. A former director of the Atlanta Zoo once remarked that he was "too far removed from the animals; they're the last thing I worry about with all the other problems."

Animals suffer from more than neglect in some zoos. When Dunda, an African elephant, was transferred from the San Diego Zoo to the San Diego Wild Animal Park, she was chained, pulled to the ground, and beaten with ax handles for two days. One witness described the blows as "home run swings."

Reprinted from "Zoos: Pitiful Prisons," a People for the Ethical Treatment of Animals publication at www.peta-online.org/facts/ent/fsent03.htm, May 15, 1997. Reprinted by permission.

Such abuse may be the norm. "You have to motivate them," says San Francisco zookeeper Paul Hunter of elephants, "and the way you do that is by beating the hell out of them."

Propagation, Not Education

Zoos claim to educate people and preserve species, but they frequently fall short on both counts. Most zoo enclosures are quite small, and labels provide little more information than the species' name, diet, and natural range. The animals' normal behavior is seldom discussed, much less observed, because their natural needs are seldom met. Birds' wings may be clipped so they cannot fly, aquatic animals often have little water, and the many animals who naturally live in large herds or family groups are often kept alone or, at most, in pairs. Natural hunting and mating behaviors are virtually eliminated by regulated feeding and breeding regimens. The animals are closely confined, lack privacy, and have little opportunity for mental stimulation or physical exercise, resulting in abnormal and self-destructive behavior, called zoochosis.

A worldwide study of zoos conducted by the Born Free Foundation revealed that zoochosis is rampant in confined animals around the globe. Another study found that elephants spend 22 percent of their time engaging in abnormal behaviors, such as repeated head bobbing or biting cage bars, and bears spend about 30 percent of their time pacing, a sign of distress.

One sanctuary that is home to rescued zoo animals reports seeing frequent signs of zoochosis in animals brought to the sanctuary from zoos. Of chimpanzees, who bite their own limbs from captivity-induced stress, the manager says: "Their hands were unrecognizable from all the scar tissue."

More than half the world's zoos "are still in bad conditions" and treating chimpanzees poorly, according to renowned chimpanzee expert Jane Goodall.

> *"Zoos teach people that it is acceptable to keep animals in captivity, bored, cramped, lonely, and far from their natural homes."*

As for education, zoo visitors usually spend only a few minutes at each display, seeking entertainment rather than enlightenment. A study of the zoo in Buffalo, N.Y., found that most people passed cages quickly, and described animals in such terms as "funny-looking," "dirty," or "lazy."

The purpose of most zoos' research is to find ways to breed and maintain more animals in captivity. If zoos ceased to exist, so would the need for most of their research. Protecting species from extinction sounds like a noble goal, but zoo officials usually favor exotic or popular animals who draw crowds and publicity, and neglect less popular species. Most animals housed in zoos are not endangered, nor are they being prepared for release into natural habitats. It is nearly impossible to release captive-bred animals into the wild. A 1994 report by the World Society for the Protection of Animals showed that only 1,200 zoos out of 10,000 worldwide are registered for captive breeding and wildlife conservation. Only two percent of the world's threatened or endangered species are registered in breeding programs. Those that are endangered may have their plight made worse by zoos' focus on crowd appeal. In his book *The Last Panda*, George Schaller, the scientific director of the Bronx Zoo, says zoos are actually *contributing* to the near-extinction of giant pandas by constantly shuttling the animals from one zoo to another for display. In-breeding is also a problem among captive populations.

When Cute Little Babies Grow Up

Zoo babies are great crowd-pleasers, but what happens when babies grow up? Zoos often sell or kill animals who no longer attract visitors. Deer, tigers, lions, and other animals who breed often are sometimes sold to "game" farms where hunters pay for the "privilege" of killing them; some are killed for their meat and/or hides. Other "surplus" animals may be sold to smaller, more poorly run zoos or to laboratories for experiments.

Ultimately, we will only save endangered species if we save their habitats and combat the reasons people kill them. Instead of supporting zoos, we should support groups like the International Primate Protection League, the Born Free Foundation, the African Wildlife Foundation, and other groups that work to preserve habitats, not habits. We should help non-profit sanctuaries, like Primarily Primates and the Performing Animal Welfare Society, that rescue and care for exotic animals, but don't sell or breed them.

Zoos truly interested in raising awareness of wildlife and conservation should follow the example of the Worldlife Center in London. The Center plans to create a high-tech zoo with no animals. Visitors would observe animals in the wild via live satellite links with far-off places like the Amazon rain forest, the Great Barrier Reef, and Africa.

What You Can Do

Zoos are covered under the federal Animal Welfare Act (AWA), which sets minimal housing and maintenance standards for captive animals. The AWA requires that all animal displays be licensed with the U.S. Department of Agriculture, which must inspect zoos once a year. However, some zoos that have passed USDA inspections with flying colors have later been found by humane groups to have numerous violations. Educate yourself. Read *Beyond the Bars*, edited by Virginia McKenna, Will Travers, and Jonathan Wray. It is available from Thorson's Publishing Group in Rochester, Vt.

It is best not to patronize a zoo unless you are actively working to change its conditions. Avoid smaller, roadside zoos at all costs. If no one visits these substandard operations, they will be forced to close down.

Rodeos Are Cruel and Inhumane

by Rob Jobst

About the author: *Rob Jobst is a freelance writer.*

> Last night's ninth-heat crash cast a pall over the seventh night of the Range-land Derby. "The track was in great condition" said chuckwagon driver Mark Sutherland. "It was just one of those nights. The horses were going down."
>
> —*Calgary Sun,* July 12, 1996

Death and suffering are a big part of rodeo. A big part. It would be difficult to dispute that an event that involves the roping of calves, the "busting" of bulls and the "breaking" of broncs is inherently violent toward animals.

A Picture of Abuse and Cruelty

But rodeo types don't like to dwell on that aspect of their sport. They prefer to drawl on about tradition, heritage and simpler times when one could beat up on animals without tofu-eatin' do-gooders giving them a hard time for it. Rodeo, they say, is about the cowboy way of life, the American frontier ethic and the kind of values that built a nation. It's about myths and legends. It's about salt-of-the-earth people, cold beers and dependable pickup trucks. To focus on the abuse suffered by animals is to miss the big picture.

Interestingly, for the animals, that is the only picture.

The allure of rodeo is, I suspect, lost on the thousands of cows and horses that are pushed, kicked, shocked, roped, spurred, wrestled and otherwise abused to entertain crowds of slack-jawed spectators. For them the rodeo experience is one of fear, confusion and pain. This is not rocket science, you don't have to be the brightest yokel on the farm to see that calf roping is an act of shocking brutality. Not even the good ol' boys that assure you that broncs absolutely love to buck—"They're born to it. Back on the ranch they buck for the pure joy of it"—will dare tell you that calves delight in the thrill of trachea-crushing deceleration. Or that steers love having someone jump on their backs, twist their necks and throw them to the ground.

Sadly, the animals are unable to explain to us exactly how frightening and painful the rodeo experience is for them. Luckily, we have the cowboys like T.K. Hardy to shed a little light on this sadistic pastime.

Hardy, a Texas steer roper, commented to *Newsweek*, "I keep 30 head of cattle around for practice at $200 a head. You can cripple 3 or 4 in an afternoon . . . so it gets to be a pretty expensive hobby."

Dr. C.G. Haber, a veterinarian who spent 30 years as a federal meat inspector, recalls that "the rodeo folks send their animals to the packing houses for slaughter. I have seen cattle so extensively bruised that the only areas in which the skin was attached was the head, neck, legs and belly. I have seen animals with six to eight ribs broken from the spine and at times puncturing the lungs. I have seen as much as two and three gallons of free blood accumulated under the detached skin."

Nice, huh?

Needless Deaths

Animals die in rodeos. They die needlessly and often. While preparing to write this story I was informed that a horse was killed just days earlier in the High River, Alberta, chuckwagon races. During the 1996 Calgary Stampede four horses were killed in three separate chuckwagon accidents. A witness told the *Calgary Herald*, "All of a sudden there was a gasp, and silence. The woman beside me started crying and I sure did. They put a blue tarp over everything . . . but the evening's proceedings continued. Right then I became an animal rights activist."

In 1995 three horses were killed in the Stampede rodeo: two during chuckwagon races and one after slamming its head against a metal gate. In 1986 a horrific chuckwagon crash resulted in the deaths of nine horses and made headlines around the world. In the intervening years other animals have died—crushed beneath chuckwagons, euthanized after having their legs broken, and even suffering heart attacks—all of them raw materials exploited for profit and tossed away like trash.

And let us not forget that the Calgary Stampede is the world's largest and richest rodeo, subject to higher standards and greater scrutiny than the thousands of two-bit rodeos that take place in North America every year. It's not hard to imagine the cruelties

"Animals die in rodeos. They die needlessly and often."

suffered by animals in these unregulated hickfests or in the countless corrals where cowboys and wannabes practice on living props.

Rodeo proponents will argue that the animals must be treated well, as the success of their sport relies on healthy animals to buck and run and all those other things that frightened, frustrated creatures do. They'll even tell you with a straight face that cowboys genuinely respect and even love their animals. So who, we might ask, would subject someone they respect to highly dangerous situations such as chuckwagon races? Who would allow someone they cared for to be subjected to cinch straps, electric prods, ear biting, lassoing, wrestling and spurring?

For a lesson in compassion it would be best not to confer with chuckwagon driver Kelly Sutherland who, after a training accident injured four of the horses on his team, told the *Calgary Herald,* "It just hurt my pride. That's about it."

A Brutal Business

After the day's events are finished and the cowboys are counting their prize money and picking Skoal from their teeth, the animals' suffering continues: bleeding wounds, torn muscles and ligaments, internal bleeding, broken bones, shock and terror. Kept in cramped pens or trailers, they often lie in mud and excrement, frightened and unloved. If their wounds are not deemed serious they can look forward to further deprivation and abuse. Otherwise, they will be sent to the slaughterhouse.

Rodeo is a brutal, immoral business that owes as much to the Roman practice of mass sacrifice as to the American ranching tradition. It has no place in a civilized society.

Bibliography

Books

Carol J. Adams and Josephine Donovan, eds.	*Beyond Animal Rights: A Feminist Caring Ethic for the Treatment of Animals*. New York: Continuum, 1996.
Lynda Birke and Ruth Hubbard, eds.	*Reinventing Biology: Respect for Life and the Creation of Knowledge*. Bloomington: Indiana University Press, 1995.
Matt Cartmill	*A View to Death in the Morning: Hunting and Nature Through History*. Cambridge, MA: Harvard University Press, 1996.
Paola Cavalieri and Peter Singer, eds.	*The Great Ape Project: Equality Beyond Humanity*. New York: St. Martin's Press, 1993.
Stephen R.L. Clark	*Animals and Their Moral Standing*. New York: Routledge, 1997.
Sue Coe	*Dead Meat*. New York: Four Walls Eight Windows, 1996.
Gail A. Eisnitz	*Slaughterhouse: The Shocking Story of Greed, Neglect, and Inhumane Treatment Inside the U.S. Meat Industry*. New York: Prometheus, 1997.
Alix Fano	*Lethal Laws: Animal Testing, Human Health, and Environmental Policy*. New York: Zed Books, 1997.
Gary L. Francione	*Animals, Property, and the Law*. Philadelphia: Temple University Press, 1995.
Gary L. Francione	*Rain Without Thunder: The Ideology of the Animal Rights Movement*. Philadelphia: Temple University Press, 1996.
Julian McAllister Groves	*Hearts and Minds: The Controversy over Laboratory Animals*. Philadelphia: Temple University Press, 1997.
Howard F. Lyman	*Mad Cowboy: Plain Truth from the Cattle Rancher Who Won't Eat Meat*. New York: Scribner, 1998.
Erik Marcus	*Vegan: The New Ethics of Eating*. Ithaca, NY: McBooks Press, 1997.
Jeffrey Moussaieff Masson and Susan McCarthy	*When Elephants Weep: The Emotional Lives of Animals*. New York: Delacorte, 1995.

F. Barbara Orlans et al.   *The Human Use of Animals: Case Studies in Ethical Choice.* New York: Oxford University Press, 1998.

David Petersen, ed.   *A Hunter's Heart: Honest Essays on Blood Sport.* New York: Henry Holt, 1996.

Evelyn B. Pluhar   *Beyond Prejudice: The Moral Significance of Human and Nonhuman Animals.* Durham, NC: Duke University Press, 1995.

Bernard E. Rollin   *The Frankenstein Syndrome: Ethical and Social Issues in the Genetic Engineering of Animals.* New York: Cambridge University Press, 1995.

Clifford J. Sherry   *Animal Rights: A Reference Handbook.* Santa Barbara, CA: ABC-CLIO, 1994.

Helena Silverstein   *Unleashing Rights: Law, Meaning, and the Animal Rights Movement.* Ann Arbor: University of Michigan Press, 1996.

Mary Zeiss Stange   *Woman the Hunter.* New York: Ballantine, 1998.

Donald D. Stull, Michael J. Broadway, and David Griffith, eds.   *Any Way You Cut It: Meat Processing and Small-Town America.* Lawrence: University Press of Kansas, 1995.

James A. Swan   *In Defense of Hunting.* San Francisco: HarperSanFrancisco, 1995.

Periodicals

Brian Alexander   "It's an Alaska Thing. You Wouldn't Understand," *Outside*, March 1995. Available from 400 Market St., Santa Fe, NM 87501.

Mark Bekoff   "Deep Ethology," *AV Magazine*, Winter 1998. Available from 801 Old York Rd., Jenkintown, PA 19046-1685.

Phil Berardelli   "Is Dr. Moreau Fable or Fact?" *Insight*, November 25, 1996. Available from 3600 New York Ave. NE, Washington, DC 20002.

Susan Brink   "Clashing Passions," *U.S. News & World Report*, May 4, 1998.

James Brooke   "Anti-Fur Groups Wage War on Mink Farms," *New York Times*, November 30, 1996.

David Jay Brown and Rebecca McClen Novick   "Nature of the Beast," *Sun*, October 1998. Available from PO Box 3000, Denville, NJ 07834-3000.

Stephen Budiansky   "Killing with Kindness," *U.S. News & World Report*, November 25, 1996.

Jill Howard Church   "The Elephants' Graveyard: Life in Captivity," *Animals' Agenda*, July/August 1995.

Bibliography

Jill Howard Church — "The Politics of Animal Research," *Animals' Agenda*, January/February 1997.

Stephen R.L. Clark — "Conservation and Animal Welfare," *Chronicles*, June 1996. Available from 928 N. Main St., Rockford, IL 61103.

Marjorie Cramer — "Vegetarianism: Myths and Realities, A Doctor's Viewpoint," *Animals' Agenda*, July/August 1996.

Michael E. DeBakey — "Hype and Hypocrisy on Animal Rights," *Wall Street Journal*, December 12, 1996.

Pat Derby — "The Abuse of Animal 'Actors,'" *Animals' Agenda*, July/August 1996.

Jared Diamond — "Playing God at the Zoo," *Discover*, March 1995.

Steven Alan Edwards — "Pork Liver, Anyone?" *Technology Review*, July 1996.

Frederick Forsyth — "The Kindness of the Hunt," *New York Times*, July 18, 1997.

Michael W. Fox — "The Second Creation," *AV Magazine*, Summer 1997.

Futurist — "Animal-to-Human Transplants," January/February 1997.

Jeff Getty — "The Tragic Hypocrisy of 'Animal Rights,'" *Wall Street Journal*, June 13, 1996.

Christine Gorman — "What's It Worth to Find a Cure?" *Time*, July 8, 1996.

Curtis L. Hancock — "Philosophers in the Mist," *Crisis*, March 1996. Available from PO Box 10559, Riverton, NJ 08076-0559.

Harold Herzog — "Ethics, Animals, Common Sense," *Forum for Applied Research and Public Policy*, Spring 1996.

Karl Hess Jr. — "Wild Success," *Reason*, October 1997.

Merle Hoffman — "Transspecies Transplants: Home-Grown Atrocities," *On the Issues*, Fall 1995.

Leslie Alan Horvitz — "Are Animal Advocates Biting the Hand of Dedicated Docs?" *Insight*, May 19, 1997.

William T. Jarvis — "Why I Am Not a Vegetarian," *Priorities*, vol. 9, no. 2, 1997. Available from 1995 Broadway, 2nd Floor, New York, NY 10023-5860.

Gina Kolata — "Tough Tactics in One Battle over Animals in the Lab," *New York Times*, March 24, 1998.

Jeffrey Marsh — "Concept of Animals Thinking Isn't Really So Birdbrained," *Insight*, January 18, 1993.

David Masci — "Fighting over Animal Rights," *CQ Researcher*, August 2, 1996. Available from 1414 22nd St. NW, Washington, DC 20037.

John McArdle — "The Age of Alternatives to Animal Experiments Has Arrived," *AV Magazine*, Winter 1997.

The Rights of Animals

John McArdle — "Xenotransplantation and Primates: Threats Masquerading as Cures," *AV Magazine*, Fall 1996.

James C. McKinley Jr. — "It's Kenya's Farmers vs. Wildlife, and the Animals Are Losing," *New York Times*, August 29, 1998.

Jim Motavalli — "Our Agony over Animals," *E: The Environmental Magazine*, October 1995.

Robert Pool — "Saviors," *Discover*, May 1998.

Bretigne Shaffer — "It's All Happening at the Zoo," *Wall Street Journal*, September 1, 1998.

Peggy Slasman — "Transplantation's Next Frontier: The Promise of the Pig," *Saturday Evening Post*, September/October 1997.

Henry Spira — "Less Meat, Less Misery: Reforming Factory Farms," *Forum for Applied Research and Public Policy*, Spring 1996.

Ike C. Sugg — "Getty's Fortune," *American Spectator*, October 1996.

Jessica Szymczyk — "Animals, Vegetables and Minerals," *Newsweek*, August 14, 1995.

Wendeline L. Wagner — "They Shoot Monkeys, Don't They?" *Harper's*, August 1997.

Kelly A. Waples and Clifford S. Stagoll — "Ethical Issues in the Release of Animals from Captivity," *BioScience*, February 1997.

T.H. Watkins — "The Wild and the Unwild," *Audubon*, March/April 1997.

Nancy Weber — "Wearing Fur and Proud of It," *New York Times*, December 18, 1996.

Todd Wilkinson — "Rodeos Sweep American West, but Raise Concern of Cruelty," *Christian Science Monitor*, April 30, 1997.

Joy Williams — "The Inhumanity of the Animal People," *Harper's*, August 1997.

Organizations to Contact

The editors have compiled the following list of organizations concerned with the issues debated in this book. The descriptions are derived from materials provided by the organizations. All have publications or information available for interested readers. The list was compiled on the date of publication of the present volume; the information provided here may change. Be aware that many organizations take several weeks or longer to respond to inquiries, so allow as much time as possible.

Americans for Medical Progress
421 King St., Suite 401, Alexandria, VA 22314
(703) 836-9595 • fax: (703) 836-9594
e-mail: AMP@AMProgress.org • website: http://www.amprogress.org

Americans for Medical Progress is a nonprofit organization that works to educate the public about medical research using animals and its importance to curing today's most devastating diseases. Its website lists current media articles regarding the use of animals in research as well as the fact sheets *Animal Research Saves Human and Animal Lives* and *Animal Research Is Critical to Finding a Cure for AIDS*.

The American Anti-Vivisection Society (AAVS)
Noble Plaza, Suite 204, 801 Old York Rd., Jenkintown, PA 19046-1685
(215) 887-0816 • fax: (215) 887-2088
website: http://www.aavs.org

AAVA advocates the abolition of vivisection, opposes all types of experiments on living animals, and sponsors research on alternatives to these methods. The society produces videos and publishes numerous brochures, including *Vivisection and Dissection and the Classroom: A Guide to Conscientious Objection*. AAVS also publishes the bimonthly *AV Magazine*.

The American Society for the Prevention of Cruelty to Animals (ASPCA)
424 E. 92nd St., New York, NY 10128
(212) 876-7700 • (212) 348-3031
website: http://www.aspca.org

The ASPCA promotes appreciation for and humane treatment of animals, encourages enforcement of anticruelty laws, and works for the passage of legislation that strengthens existing laws to further protect animals. In addition to making available books, brochures, and videos on animal issues, the ASPCA publishes *Animal Watch*, a quarterly magazine.

Farm Sanctuary
PO Box 150, Watkins Glen, NY 14891
fax: (607) 583-2041
website: http://www.farmsanctuary.com

Farm Sanctuary is a nonprofit organization dedicated to ending the use of animals for food production. It works through grassroots campaigns and operates rescue and rehabilitation shelters for farm animals. Its website offers information on veganism and current campaigns against animal cruelty. The organization publishes the quarterly *Farm Sanctuary Newsletter*.

Foundation for Biomedical Research (FBR)

818 Connecticut Ave. NW, Suite 303, Washington, DC 20006
(202) 457-0654
website: http://www.bresearch.org

FBR provides information and educational programs about what it sees as the necessary and important role of laboratory animals in biomedical research and testing. Its videos include *Caring for Laboratory Animals, The New Research Environment*, and *Caring for Life*. It also publishes a bimonthly newsletter, *Foundation for Biomedical Research*.

Fur Commission USA

826 Orange Ave. #506, Coronado, CA 92118
(619) 575-0319 • fax: (619) 575-5578
e-mail: furfarmets@aol.com • website: http://www.furcommission.com

Fur Commission USA is a nonprofit national association representing U.S. mink and fox farmers. Its goal is to educate the public about responsible fur farming. The commission offers several educational tools for all ages on fur farming, including the educational kit *Animals and Our Clothing* and the simulation game *People, Animals and the Environment*.

The Humane Society of the United States (HSUS)

2100 L St. NW, Washington, DC 20037
(202) 452-1100 • fax: (202) 778-6132
website: http://www.hsus.org

HSUS works to foster respect, understanding, and compassion for all creatures. It maintains programs supporting responsible pet ownership, elimination of cruelty in hunting and trapping, exposing painful uses of animals in research and testing, and abusive treatment of animals in movies, circuses, pulling contests, and racing. It campaigns for and against legislation affecting animal protection and monitors enforcement of existing animal protection statutes. HSUS publishes the quarterlies *Animal Activist Alert, HSUS Close-up Reports*, and *HSUS News*.

National Association for Biomedical Research (NABR)

818 Connecticut Ave. NW, Suite 303, Washington, DC 20006
(202) 857-0540 • fax: (202) 659-1902
website: http://www.nabr.org

NABR supports the responsible use and humane care and treatment of laboratory animals in research, education, and product safety testing. Further, the membership believes that only as many animals as necessary should be used; that any pain or distress animals may experience should be minimized; and that alternatives to the use of live animals should be developed and employed, wherever feasible. The association publishes the newsletter *NABR Update*, as well as an annual report.

Organizations to Contact

People for the Ethical Treatment of Animals (PETA)
501 Front St., Norfolk, VA 23510
(757) 622-PETA • fax: (757) 622-0457
e-mail: peta@norfolk.infi.net • website: http://www.peta-online.org

An international animal rights organization, PETA is dedicated to establishing and protecting the rights of all animals. It focuses on four areas: factory farms, research laboratories, the fur trade, and the entertainment industry. PETA promotes public education, cruelty investigations, animal rescue, celebrity involvement, and legislative and direct action. It produces numerous videos and publishes the quarterly magazine *Animal Times*, as well as various fact sheets, brochures, and fliers.

Performing Animals Welfare Society (PAWS)
PO Box 849, Galt, CA 95632
(209) 745-2606 • fax: (209) 745-1809
e-mail: paws@capaccess.org

Founded in 1985, PAWS provides sanctuary to abandoned and abused performing animals and victims of the exotic pet trade. The society also works to protect animals by educating the public about inhumane animal training and treatment. It publishes the books *The Circus: A New Perspective* and *Surplus Animals: The Cycle of Hell.*

Physicians Committee for Responsible Medicine (PCRM)
5100 Wisconsin Ave., Suite 404, Washington, DC 20016
(202) 686-2210 • fax: (202) 686-2216
e-mail: pcrm@pcrm.org • website: http://www.pcrm.org

PCRM is a nonprofit organization supported by both physicians and laypersons to encourage higher ethical standards and effectiveness in research. It promotes using computer programs and models in place of animals in both research and education. The committee publishes the quarterly magazine *Good Medicine* and numerous fact sheets on animal experimentation issues.

Psychologists for the Ethical Treatment of Animals (PSYETA)
403 McCauley St., PO Box 1297, Washington Grove, MD 20880
phone and fax: (301) 963-4751
website: http://www.psyeta.org

PSYETA seeks to ensure proper treatment of animals used in psychological research and education. Thus, it urges such projects to revise their curricula to include ethical issues in the treatment of animals. It works to reduce the number of animals needed for experiments and has developed a tool to measure the level of invasiveness or severity of animal experiments. Its publications include the book *Animal Models of Human Psychology* and the journals *Society and Animals* and the *Journal of Applied Animal Welfare Science.*

Index

Index